COLLECTING EVALUATION DATA

COLLECTING EVALUATION DATA

Problems and Solutions

Leigh Burstein
Howard E. Freeman
Peter H. Rossi

 SAGE PUBLICATIONS Beverly Hills London New Delhi

Copyright © 1985 by Sage Publications, Inc.

For information address:

SAGE Publications, Inc.
275 South Beverly Drive
Beverly Hills, California 90212

SAGE Publications India Pvt. Ltd.
M-32 Market
Greater Kailash I
New Delhi 110 048 India

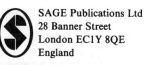

SAGE Publications Ltd
28 Banner Street
London EC1Y 8QE
England

Printed in the United States of America

Library of Congress Cataloging in Publication Data

Main entry under title:

Collecting evaluation data.

Includes bibliographies.
1. Evaluation research (Social action programs)—
Addresses, essays, lectures. 2. Social sciences—Method-
ology—Addresses, essays, lectures. 3. Evaluation
research (Social action programs)—United States—
Addresses, essays, lectures. I. Burstein, Leigh.
II. Freeman, Howard E. III. Rossi, Peter Henry,
1921-
H62.C567 1985   361.6′1′072   85-1848
ISBN 0-8039-2449-6

FIRST PRINTING

CONTENTS

Acknowledgment 7

Contributors 9

1 Perspectives on Data Collection in Evaluations
   LEIGH BURSTEIN and HOWARD E. FREEMAN 15

PART I
DATA SENSITIVITIES

2 Data Collection Strategies in the Minneapolis
   Domestic Assault Experiment
   RICHARD A. BERK and LAWRENCE W. SHERMAN 35

3 Observer Studies: Data Collection by Remote Control
   LEE SECHREST 49

4 Data Collection Issues in the Evaluation of the Effect
   of Television Violence on Elementary School Children
   RONALD C. KESSLER, J. RONALD MILAVSKY,
   HORST STIPP, and WILLIAM S. RUBENS 67

PART II
MOUNTING LARGE-SCALE FIELD STUDIES

5 A Tale of Two Surveys: Lessons from the Best and Worst
   of Times in Program Evaluation
   RONALD M. ANDERSEN, LU ANN ADAY,
   and GRETCHEN VOORHIS FLEMING 89

6 Field Sampling Problems in Data Collection for
   Evaluation Research
   SANDRA H. BERRY 107

7 Measuring Unfiled Claims in the Health Insurance Experiment
   WILLIAM H. ROGERS and JOSEPH P. NEWHOUSE 121

8 Issues of Data Collection in Assessing Programs Involving
   Crime Reduction: The Job Corps and Supported
   Work Evaluations
   CHARLES MALLAR and IRVING PILIAVIN 134

9 Some Failures in Designing Data Collection That Distort Results
   ALBERT J. REISS, Jr.   161

PART III
USE OF RECORD INFORMATION

10 Program Evaluation and the Use of Extant Data
   ELEANOR CHELIMSKY   181

11 Identification of Treatment Conditions Using Standard
   Record-Keeping Systems
   J. WARD KEESLING   207

12 Using Longitudinal Earnings Data from Social Security Records
   to Evaluate Job-Training Programs
   HOWARD S. BLOOM   220

13 An Information System for Planning and Evaluating Geriatric Care:
   The Duke Older Americans Resources and Services Program
   GEORGE L. MADDOX   247

14 From Science to Technology: Reducing Problems in
   Mental Health Evaluation by Paradigm Shift
   WILLIAM D. NEIGHER and DANIEL B. FISHMAN   263

REPRISE

15 Data Quality Issues in Evaluation Research:
   Summary Comments
   PETER H. ROSSI   300

Subject Index   313

Name Index   315

ACKNOWLEDGMENT

The conference and this publication were supported by Grant SES-8300712 from the National Science Foundation. This grant was administered by UCLA's Institute for Social Science Research. Earlier work on data collection in health evaluations was supported by a grant to the editors of this work from the National Center for Health Services Research (1-RO3-HS04676). Madalyn De Maria, Rita Williams, Victoria Gouveia, and Lorraine Cheng provided administrative and support services at UCLA; Jeanne Reinle of the Social and Demographic Research Institute, University of Massachusetts, managed the conference arrangements. Julie Lam, Joann Miller, and Quinton Thurman, University of Massachusetts graduate students, served as note takers at the conference; Margaret Beemer and Penny Wilkins provided editorial assistance. We are most appreciative of the support from NSF and NCHSR, and most grateful for the collaboration of our associates during the planning and conduct of the conference and the preparation of this volume.

CONTRIBUTORS

LU ANN ADAY is a Research Associate (Associate Professor and Associate Director for Research, Center for Health Administration Studies, University of Chicago. She has been Study Director or Principal Investigator for national surveys of access to medical care and community survey-based evaluations of innovative public and private primary care delivery programs. Dr. Aday is principal author of *The Utilization of Health Services: Indices and Correlates—A Research Bibliography; Development of Indices of Access to Medical Care; Health Care in the U.S.: Equitable for Whom?; Access to Medical Care in the U.S.: Who Has It, Who Doesn't;* and *Hospital-Physician Sponsored Primary Care: Marketing and Impact.* She received her Ph.D. in Sociology from Purdue University in 1973.

RONALD ANDERSEN is Professor of Sociology in the Graduate School of Business and Director of the Center for Health Administration Studies and the Graduate Program in Health Administration at the University of Chicago. His research interests include evaluation of health programs, social survey methods, use of health services, and international comparisons of health care systems.

RICHARD A. BERK is Professor of Sociology and Director of the Social Process Research Institute at the University of California, Santa Barbara. He has coauthored *Money Work and Crime: Experimental Evidence* and *Water Shortage: Lesson in Conservation from the Great California Drought, 1976-77,* both of which are evaluation studies.

SANDRA H. BERRY is a sociologist at the Rand Corporation, where she specializes in experimental design and methodology, including techniques for carrying out research in field settings. She supervised data collection for studies in health, criminal justice, energy, and housing. She designed and supervised data collection for Rand's Prescription Drug Information Study.

HOWARD S. BLOOM is Associate Professor at the Kennedy School of Government, Harvard University. He has published a number of articles on program evaluation methodology and has done applied evaluation work in the areas of employment and training, criminal justice, and housing. His current research activities focus on the use of experimental design and longitudinal data for evaluating employment and training programs.

LEIGH BURSTEIN is an Associate Professor in the Research Methods and Evaluation Specialization of the Graduate School of Education and Faculty Associate in the Center for the Study of Evaluation, University of California, Los Angeles. His primary research interests are in methodology for analyzing multilevel problems in program evaluation, secondary data issues, information systems in local school improvement, and educational quality indicators. He coedited *Issues in Aggregation* (Jossey-Bass, 1980).

ELEANOR CHELIMSKY is the Director of the U.S. General Accounting Office's Program Evaluation and Methodology Division. The division serves the Congress through evaluations of government programs, the development and demonstration of methods for evaluating programs, and the provision of design and measurement assistance to other GAO divisions. Mrs. Chelimsky came to the GAO from the MITRE Corporation. She is a former Fulbright Scholar, past president of the Evaluation Research Society, and a member of the Editorial Review Board for the Sage Research Series in Evaluation. She serves on the Editorial Board of Policy Studies Review and was the recipient of the 1982 Myrdal Award for Government.

DANIEL B. FISHMAN is Professor and Director of Psychological Services at the Graduate School of Applied and Professional Psychology of Rutgers University and current president of the Eastern Evaluation Research Society. Dr. Fishman has published numerous articles and book chapters in the areas of program evaluation and behavior therapy and is the author of *A Cost-Effectiveness Methodology for Community Mental Health Centers: Development and Pilot-Test*. Dr. Fishman is currently coediting two additional books: *Assessment for Decision: Psychology in Action*, with Donald Peterson; and *Paradigms in Behavior Therapy: Present and Promise*, with Frederick Rotgers and Cyril Franks.

GRETCHEN V. FLEMING is Director of the Department of Research at the American Academy of Pediatrics. Before coming to the Academy, she was a Senior Research Associate at the Center for Health Administration Studies, University of Chicago. She coauthored the books *Health Care in the U.S.: Equitable for Whom?* and *Access to Medical Care in the U.S.: Who Has It, Who Doesn't*. She was the study director for the Evaluation of the Municipal Health Services Program, funded by the Health Care Financing Administration and the Robert Wood Johnson Foundation.

HOWARD E. FREEMAN is Professor of Sociology, University of California, Los Angeles. He currently is engaged in several health care evaluations. Professor Freeman coedits *Evaluation Review*. The third edition of *Evaluation: A Systematic Approach* (coauthored with Peter H. Rossi) will appear in 1985.

J. WARD KEESLING is Technical Director for the Program Evaluation Operations Center of Advanced Technology, Inc. He received his Ph.D. in Education from the University of Chicago, specializing in measurement, evaluation, and statistical analysis. He has conducted nationwide evaluations of compensatory education programs for institutionalized juveniles, parental involvement in federally supported educational programs, and the administration of education programs. He has published papers on psychological measurement and research methodology and has consulted for local, state, national, and international educational organizations.

RONALD C. KESSLER is Associate Professor of Sociology at the University of Michigan. He has coauthored *Linear Panel Analysis: Models of Quantitative Change* and *Television and Aggression: The Results of a Panel Study*. He is the recipient of a Research Scientist Development Award from the National Institute of Mental Health and, under the auspices of this award, does research on the structural determinants of psychopatholgy.

GEORGE L. MADDOX is Professor of Medical Sociology, Departments of Sociology and Psychiatry, and Chairman of the University Council on Aging and Human Development, Duke University. He recently coauthored *Inflation and the Economic Well-being of the Elderly* and coedited *Aging and Alcohol Abuse*. The Duke Longitudinal Studies, which he directed from 1972 to 1982, received the 1983 Sandoz International Prize for Multidisciplinary Research in Aging.

CHARLES D. MALLAR is a Senior Fellow at Mathematica Policy Research and owner/operator of the 1975 Inn. He received his Ph.D. in econometrics from the University of Wisconsin at Madison in 1975. He has taught at Johns Hopkins University and was the principle investigator of the Evaluation of the Job Corps Program and several other projects for Mathematica Policy Research.

J. RONALD MILAVSKY received his Ph.D. from Columbia University and is now Vice President for News and Social Research at the National Broadcasting Company in New York. He is coauthor of *Television and Aggression: A Panel Study* (Academic Press, 1982) and of "TV Drug Advertising and Proprietary and Illicit Drug Use Among Teenage Boys" (*Public Opinion Quarterly*, 1976) and other articles. He is a member of the American Sociological Association and of the American Association for Public Opinion Research (AAPOR). He currently is president of its New York Chapter.

WILLIAM D. NEIGHER is Divisional Director, Research and Development for St. Clare's Hospital in New Jersey, and is Visiting Associate Professor of Psychology at Rugers University Graduate School of Applied and Professional Psychology. He is a past president of the Eastern Evaluation Research Society, and has been a frequent consultant and Chair of a Special Grant Review Committee for NIMH. As social/community psychologist, Dr. Neigher is an editor of *Evaluation in Practice* in addition to other books and articles in evaluation research and program management.

JOSEPH P. NEWHOUSE is Head of the Economics Department at the Rand Corporation. He received Bachelor of Arts and Doctorate degrees in economics from Harvard University. He currently is a faculty member of the Rand Graduate Institute and an adjunct professor in the UCLA Department of Medicine. He is the founding editor of *The Journal of Health Economics* and has been elected to the Institute of Medicine of The National Academy of Sciences. His biography appears in *Who's Who in America, Who's Who in Health Care* and *Who's Who in Economics*. Dr. Newhouse was the first recipient of the David N. Kershaw Award and Prize of the Association for Public Policy and Management. The award honors persons who, at under the age of 40, made a distinguished contribution to the field of public policy analysis and management.

IRVING PILIAVIN is Professor of Social Work at the University of Wisconsin, Madison and a senior fellow at Matematica Policy Research. Before coming to the University of Wisconsin he was a faculty member at the University of California and the University of Pennsylvania. His evaluation research interests have focused primarily on crime control and income maintenance programs. In addition, he has studied the conditions leading to criminal behavior and good samaritanism.

ALBERT J. REISS, Jr. is William Graham Sumner Professor of Sociology and in the Institution for Social and Policy Studies at Yale University and Lecturer in Law, Yale Law School. He is a member of the American Academy of Arts and Sciences and a past president of the Society for the Study of Social Problems and of the American Society of Criminology. He has done pioneering work in systematic social observation in field settings and was one of the developers of the National Crime Survey. His recent work is on compliance and deterrence systems of law enforcement.

WILLIAM H. ROGERS is a statistician at the Rand Corporation. He analyzes data and designs experiments in the health and demographics programs at Rand and has worked on many projects, including the Rand Health Insurance Experiment, a clinical cancer trial conducted in conjunction with local physicians, the Prescription-Package Insert Study, and the HIH Consensus Evaluation Study. Dr. Rogers also is active in software design for mainframes and microcomputers.

PETER H. ROSSI is Stuart A. Rice Professor of Sociology, University of Massachusetts at Amherst. He is the editor of *Handbook of Survey Research*. His interests include evaluations in the areas of criminal justice and natural disasters.

WILLIAM S. RUBENS is Vice President, Research, at NBC. He also is coauthor of *Television and Aggression*. In addition, Rubens has authored a number of articles on communications research, including "High-Tech Measurement for the New-Tech Audience" (*Journal of Critical Studies in Mass Communications*, 1984). He is past chairman of the Advertising Research Foundation (ARF), and a former president of the Radio and Television Research Council. He is a member of the Research Advisory Board of the National Association of Broadcasters (NAB); on the Board of Directors of the Electronic Media Rating Council (EMRC); a member of the Conference Board Research Council, the International Radio and Television Society, and the National Academy of Television Arts and Sciences.

LEE SECHREST is Professor and Head of the Department of Psychology at the University of Arizona. He was, until recently, Director of the Center for Research on the Utilization of Scientific Knowledge in the Institute for Social Research at the University of Michigan. He also was Professor of Psychology and of Medical Care Organization, having taught earlier at Florida State University, Northwestern University, and Pennsylvania State University. He was trained in clinical psychology at Ohio State, receiving his Ph.D. in 1956. He has a strong current interest in improving the quality of scientific data and in methodology more generally.

LAWRENCE W. SHERMAN is Professor of Criminology at the University of Maryland at College Park and Director of Research of the Police Foundation. He is the author or coauthor of over 60 books and articles on crime and police issues, including *Scandal and Reform: Controlling Police Corruption, Police and Violence*, and *The Quality of Police Education*. He currently is directing several randomized field experiments on the punishment of crime.

HORST H. STIPP is Director, Social Research, at NBC. He received his M.A. in Sociology from the Free University in West Berlin and his Ph.D. from Columbia University. Stipp is coauthor of *Television and Aggression: A Panel Study* and of "The Impact of Fictional Television Suicide Stories on U.S. Fatalities: A Replication" (*American Journal of Sociology*, 1984). He is a member of the American Sociological Association, and of the American Association for Public Opinion Research (AAPOR).

CHAPTER

1

PERSPECTIVES ON DATA COLLECTION IN EVALUATIONS

Leigh Burstein
Howard E. Freeman

The rubrics "evaluation" and "evaluation research" describe a remarkably diverse and heterogeneous set of activities. They include small, laboratory-like "true" experiments, large-scale regional and national quasi-experiments, time-series analyses of differing complexity and sophistication, monitoring studies that may involve massive and elaborate management information systems or data recorded by one or two observers, and assessments that depend on the collection of unobtrusive measures. Likewise, the interests, training, and intellectual perspectives of persons who identify themselves as "evaluators" and "evaluation researchers" are equally varied. Some are research specialists in such fields as education, health, and criminal justice; others are statisticians and data analysts whose work cuts across a range of substantive areas; and still others are program managers, planners, and policy makers who do evaluations as an adjunct to these work roles.

Given the diverse array of activities and actors, it is not surprising that there is serious disagreement about whether experimental designs are essential to measuring the effectiveness of programs, whether one or another analytical procedure is the most appropriate means of reaching correct inferences, whether insider or outsider evaluations are most useful—indeed, about the entire range of evaluation procedures except the importance of data collection. If there is a single common thread throughout the field of evaluation research and one consistent concern among evaluators, it is with the nature and quality of the data with which they work. No amount of wisdom and substantive knowledge, no amount of statistical data massaging, and no degree of persuasiveness in reporting results can compensate fully for faulty, defective, incomplete, invalid, or unreliable data.

The importance of data in evaluation research is the *raison d'etre* of this book. Its chapters were first presented as papers at a small working conference held with support from the National Science Foundation. The chapters range widely in their foci, emphases, methodological orientations, and substantive examples. The glue that binds them together is that their authors, who have done and are doing evaluations, have had to think about and cope with data collection problems in their own work. Some of the chapters are more conceptual than others; some confront data collection issues across different substantive areas whereas others are focused on a narrower band of evaluations or even a single one; and some propose practical solutions to data collection problems whereas others simply alert us to the difficulties involved in the data collection process. But taken together, these chapters provide strong testimony about the critical need for thought and work on the art and technology of data collection.

THE IMPORTANCE OF DATA COLLECTION

The importance of data is not, of course, a "discovery." All empirical investigators, and certainly social researchers, are committed to continually improving data collection practices. To the extent that evaluation research is seen simply as the application of social research procedures, the issues that surround data collection are no different than those encountered in any investigation. Certainly those of us whose interest in evaluation was shaped and stimulated by Campbell's (1969) provocative ideas about an experimenting society, whose training is rooted in the early field studies of interpersonal influence, political behavior, and educational styles, and whose culture heroes included Lazarsfeld (Lazerfeld et al., 1948), Lewin (1951), and Stouffer (Stouffer et al., 1949) should feel comfortable with this outlook.

At the same time, however, there are persons in evaluation who argue that data collection in their field is qualitatively different than in ordinary research investigations. Evaluation research, at least according to Cronbach (1982) and others, differs in perspective and process from "science." Their position is that the purpose of evaluation is to provide guidance to program staffs and policy makers rather than to contribute to theory development.

Accordingly, the intent of evaluation studies is to document the utility and implementation of purposeful actions rather than to temporarily find "truth" by rejecting a null hypothesis. Furthermore, the evaluator is always engaged in a political process that detracts from taking an "objective" posture (Cronbach et al., 1980).

Fortunately, it is not essential to decide conclusively whether or not data collection is qualitatively different in the evaluation enterprise than in "ordinary" social research. However, raising the issue is not done simply to demonstrate our erudition. Rather, it is to alert the reader that, explicitly and implicitly, the contributors to this volume have different outlooks on the issue.

There is much more consensus among chapter authors, however, that the special circumstances that surround data collection activities in evaluations often make it difficult to obtain clear and unequivocal research results. Indeed, our motivation for initiating the conference stemmed from earlier consideration of the problems of data collection in evaluation research, based primarily on a review of health care evaluations (Burstein et al., forthcoming). Our review of studies of interventions in medical care suggested an extensive range of data collection problems that obscure the findings of the evaluations undertaken. The list is long, and our observations are necessarily incomplete.

The Stakes and Stakeholders in the Evaluation Arena Differ from Those in "Conventional" Social Research.

Without belittling work primarily undertaken for an audience composed of investigators' peer groups of social researchers, being proved "wrong" by subsequent studies of colleagues usually provokes only embarrassment and perhaps some notoriety. But conventional social research rarely results either in misplaced resource investments, which may occur as a consequence of program and policy decisions based on evaluations rooted in defective data, or in the withdrawal of resources because of criticisms of the data used.

Moreover, the audience of stakeholders for evaluation findings frequently demands different validity standards. In evaluation research, outcome measures need to be reassuringly close to the changes that are presumed to eventuate because of the intervention; proxy measures used to control and adjust for differences between intervention and comparison groups must have clear relationships to the actual phenomena that may be interfering, confounding, or concealing findings.

The difference in stakes and stakeholders is readily apparent in the frequently cited controversy about Head Start. Antagonists of findings about the limited efficacy of this national program were able to argue forcefully both about the validity and reliability of the educational skill tests used as outcome variables and about whether preprogram school performance and measures of educational competence are sufficient measures on which to adjust the postprogram measures of performance (Smith and Bissell, 1970). Similar issues have been raised about the use of self-perceptions and self-reports of health status in evaluations of medical care delivery interventions, about data obtained on supplementary income in guaranteed annual wage evaluations, and about arrest information in criminal justice evaluations.

The Conditions Under Which Evaluations Are Undertaken Pose Particular Problems in the Design of Instruments and in the Actual Collection of Data.

There are exceptions, but most evaluations must be bid, planned, implemented, and completed in relatively short time frames. A frequently heard criticism of the utility of evaluations is their lack of timeliness. The evaluator is confronted often with the impossible need to try to meet anticipated delivery dates and at the same time produce results based on measures with high reliability and evidence of construct validity.

The reliability issue, alone, raises special problems. Conventional researchers generally stress statistical significance and are primarily concerned with rejecting false hypotheses. The reduced magnitudes of relationships that result from using measures with low reliability are undesirable in conventional studies. But as the acceptance of false hypotheses is the cardinal sin, reduction in the "true" magnitude of relationships because of low reliability is not necessarily regarded as disastrous to the research enterprise. In evaluations, however, where perceptible impact or benefits to costs typically are the judgmental criteria of program worth—not simply significant differences—low reliabilities of measures have severe consequences for the appropriate utilization of evaluation results.

The Emphasis on Studying "Special" Populations Is More Pronounced in Evaluation Research.

Social programs more often than not are directed at "problem" persons, families, and groups. Whether the targets are the least able educationally, the aged and chronically ill, released convicts, the homeless, welfare clients, or other groups, the special features of the data sources in many evaluations require extraordinary data collection approaches and procedures. For example, in these times there is a major interest in the problems and outcomes of patients with chronic illness whose posthospital settings are organized in different ways with varying skill levels of health practitioners. Yet obtaining information by interview and observation from elderly persons living in only partially cooperating settings is clearly a challenge. Although much of social research is confronted with similar circumstances, to a much greater extent conventional investigators compared with evaluators can tailor their research interests to minimize or avoid data collection problems.

Likewise, data collection in evaluations needs to take into account the delivery system and intervention site characteristics. Clients, patients, or whatever term is used to describe the targets of interventions, see themselves and are seen by the providers of the intervention as primarily being there for service and not as the subjects of an evaluation. Interviews, tests, and observations that impinge on treatment activities often must be forsaken or restricted if the evaluation is going to proceed at all.

Other issues that either came up in our review of health evaluations or that were raised at the conference included a wide range of problems that either were not anticipated in the original designs of the evaluations or were not possible to fully rectify during their implementation. They included the consequences of eliminating and modifying items and collection procedures in longitudinal evaluations; the unique concerns associated with using measures obtained by participant and nonparticipant observers; and the quality of data when administrative records are the major data source.

CONFRONTING DATA COLLECTION PROBLEMS

In our earlier work in the health area, we became concerned with whether or not the data collection problems faced by each evaluation were unique, or whether there were solutions that were applicable to at least a range of evaluations. The question of generic solutions to data collection problems was a recurring subject of discussion at the conference. Clearly, general solutions applicable to all evaluations are optimal. Realistically, however, in many cases only experientially derived guidelines are possible, and their application may need "tailoring" when utilized in subsequent evaluations.

The "cleanest" way of minimizing data collection problems is to anticipate them in the design of the evaluation. In an ideal design, not only should the various standard practices be attended to (such as item reliability, interviewer training procedures, and the like) but provisions should be made to obtain supplemental information in order to statistically adjust estimates during data analysis (such as having available data collector characteristics to assess interviewer bias).

Such an ideal approach is not always possible, given the resource and time constraints that plague investigations, for example, insufficient time for piloting measures. Moreover, as conference participants frankly acknowledged, many problems cannot be anticipated during the design phase of an evaluation. Much of the discussion at the conference consequently focused on methods of "damage control" through creative design modification, revisions in data collection, and innovative analytical procedures.

It is the unique problems that arise in implementing specific evaluations that limits opportunities to apply "canned" solutions to data collection problems. Many of the specific data collection problems and the ways they were handled that are discussed in the chapters that follow are anecdotes, although the experiences reported may prove useful to evaluators confronted with similar situations. Both recurring problems and solutions are documented across chapters, however, suggesting that there are opportunities for generalizable strategies for improving data collection and reducing the consequences of faulty data in evaluation research.

THE CONFERENCE

As we observed in our review of health evaluations (Burstein et al., forthcoming), evaluators almost never provide either candid assessments of the data collection problems or their efforts to resolve the problems they encounter. This is the case in both published papers and the more lengthy project reports provided funding agencies. Yet both our own experiences and interviews with project directors as part of the foray into health evaluations document a myriad of data collection faults that often seriously impinge on results. At the same time, we found that many evaluators are acutely aware of the limitations resulting from their data collection procedures, and they frequently take steps to mitigate their impact. A conference seemed to be a sensible and economical way to surface the range of problems evaluators face and to learn how they attempt to solve them.

We were encouraged by Murry Aborn of the National Science Foundation to develop such a conference on improving data collection in evaluation. There was agreement that the meeting should be limited to a small number of participants in order to maximize interaction and to encourage open and frank disclosure of the problems in data collection in evaluating social programs. In selecting participants, we chose persons who held key roles in the conduct of evaluations; we also made an effort to obtain diversity in substantive and methodological expertise.

We acknowledge that the group is unrepresentative. We drew on persons from our own "networks," and the persons invited, more often than not, had undertaken large-scale or national evaluations. As a consequence, the participants' interests tend to focus on the external generality of their results rather than on the immediate and program-specific applicability of their work.

Participants were provided a list of topics to cover in the papers they were asked to prepare in advance of the conference. They were encouraged to report on one or more evaluations that they had conducted, to identify the data collection problems encountered and the solutions they developed to deal with these problems, and to estimate the effects of unsolved and unanticipated data collection faults on their results. In addition, we urged them to consider the generality of their problems and the applicability of the ways they resolved their problems to other evaluations. The final product is a purposive admixture of vivid vignettes of data collection experiences, the routine and creative ways participants sought to cope with data collection limitations, and insightful analyses of the implications of their work for improved data collection in the field.

AN OVERVIEW OF THE BOOK

The papers included in this volume cover the waterfront in substantive focus, evaluation design, and methodology, as well as the range of data collection problems addressed. Any effort to categorize them is arbitrary. One dominant theme is data sensitivity—the ways program implementation, technical knowledge required of data collection, and the reactivity of targets impinge on evaluations. A second is the ways that the complexities of mounting evaluations—the nuts and bolts of carrying out field work—affect the quantity and quality of the data collected. A third is the limitations imposed on evaluations by the need to rely on record information in various phases of conducting evaluations. This seems to be a viable classification for discussing the individual chapters.

DATA SENSITIVITY

Data collection invariably is bounded by the purposes of the program, the character of the intervention, the context in which the intervention and evaluation occur, and the choice of outcome criteria of the evaluation. Berk and Sherman's attempt to evaluate the utility of different strategies for reducing domestic violence illustrates the interdependencies of the design and implementation aspects of evaluations and their consequences for data collection. Their assessment of the results of arresting spouses for domestic violence (compared with ordering the offender from the home or mediation) required police to follow a prescribed pattern in whom they arrested and whom they did not. But the very nature of domestic violence suggests that the treatment protocol might be compromised. In fact, the police were reluctant to follow the design in selecting persons to be arrested and, hence, the study became a quasi-experiment rather than a true one. Berk and Sherman anticipated the possibility of treatment degradation in planning their study, and their data collection included measures to adjust for nonintervention differences between the three treatment groups.

In Sechrest's evaluation of emergency medical technicians, complications arose because of the demands placed on the data collectors. Sechrest's field observers collected their data under difficult field conditions; emergency medical problems do not occur only during banker's hours, nor with predictable periodicity. Consequently, there is substantial down-time interrupted by brief periods of frantic activity during which the observer is expected to faithfully complete the observation protocol. Berk and Sherman also had a scheduling problem because of the irregularity with which spouse abuse occurs.

The observation of emergency medical practices, however, was distinctive because of the special technical knowledge necessary to validly undertake data collection. It simply was not enough to be able to monitor response time, the kinds of treatments administered, and the personal sensitivity of the technicians to the patient's plight. Quality of treatment in rendering emergency care is critical: Issues such as the accuracy of diagnosis and appropriateness of treatment needed to be examined as well. In order to obtain data about these dimensions, medical expertise is required. Sechrest's study points to a common data collection dilemma. On one hand, there is the option of either employing data collectors who already have special training or devoting resources and time to high-level training in order to insure the necessary expertise. On the other hand, there is the option of confining data collection only to measures obtainable by minimally trained data collectors with consequences for the validity of the evaluation information.

The panel study of television viewing and aggression conducted by Kessler, Milavsky, and their associates highlights method of choice complications in measuring the impacts of social programs and activities. In large-scale panel studies the only cost-effective way to collect data is to survey targets (in this case, elementary school children) and other relevant actors (in their study, peers, teachers, parents). Yet the method of choice limits the ways to control for "social desirability biased" data. In their case, normative beliefs about aggression and television viewing among respondents may have affected the validity of their reports. Moreover, the youthfulness of the targets may be related to the problematic reliability estimates obtained.

Kessler and the NBC evaluation group were sensitive to these potential problems from the outset; they built validity checks into their survey instruments, used multiple respondents in order to triangulate on key variables, and continually revised and adapted their methodology to reduce threats to their conclusions. We have clear documentation from their study that, as social expectations and norms influence survey responses in many evaluation studies, investigators must incorporate procedures to verify data quality and, in many cases, need to carry out auxiliary validity studies in order to rule out competing explanations of results.

In each of the three studies discussed there were unavoidable data collection complications. Only police could implement the spousal arrest treatment; reports of emergency medical practices by persons without expertise are problematic for judging the quality of care; and nonsurvey (i.e., experimental observational) studies of television viewing and aggression would lack external validity and be prohibitively expensive and impractical to conduct. Thus, the only realistic option is to anticipate data collection complications during the planning of an evaluation and to minimize them through a combination of design and analysis procedures, as well as through the ways data collection is undertaken.

MOUNTING LARGE-SCALE FIELD STUDIES

Another issue that was discussed in several of the conference papers was the consequences for data collection resulting from the complexities of undertaking large-scale field studies. These discussions focused on the nuts and bolts of data collection. In Andersen, Aday, and Fleming's paper on evaluations of the Community Hospital and Municipal Health Services programs, several tradeoffs faced in undertaking large-scale surveys are examined. One critical tradeoff was related to specifying the boundaries of the survey area. In both of these evaluations the target populations are the users of hospital-linked community health centers. But for economy of data collection, the option of confining the study group to catchment areas that contain the majority of the relevant population was appealing, although using this procedure underestimated the users who lived outside such areas (and in a sense provided a biased sample).

Berry's paper describes strategies for managing field efforts and provides specific techniques for maintaining data quality she and her Rand associates employed in evaluations undertaken in different fields. In a prescription information field experiment, for example, there was no way to avoid the use of third parties (in this instance, pharmacists) to carry out the intervention (varying the degrees of detail about prescriptions targets received). As Berry's paper illustrates, the data collection task in this case was one of providing sufficient incentives for the pharmacists so that they followed the experimental protocol and continued to participate during the life of the program.

In the paper on the Rand Health Insurance Experiment, Rogers and Newhouse are concerned with the accuracy of the measures of use of health services obtained by surveying patients. Again, any other means of collecting the information from the large group of participants would have been prohibitively expensive and probably viewed as intrusive. Rogers and Newhouse describe the auxiliary studies they conducted to assess the magnitude of underreporting of claims and false reporting and the ways their results were used to adjust analyses of program impact.

The contaminating influences that occurred in two large field studies to assess program impact (the Job Corps and the Supported Work initiatives) are the core of Mallar and Piliavin's paper. In the Job Corps Study the difficulty of collecting needed data on preexisting differences between experimental and nonrandom comparison groups in quasi-experiments introduces contaminations. In the Supported Work Experiment the consequences of enrolling participants with potential social background differences at various times during the study are the main deterrents to appropriate inference. Although Mallar and Piliavin are able to model the kinds of analytical efforts that tend to reduce the impact of these contaminations when examining program effects, they are candid in their judgments that more ambitious efforts are needed to fully mitigate the problems they have identified.

Reiss focuses on two data collection complexities in the measurement of crime rates that plague assessments of program impact in the criminal justice area. One problem addressed is the differences in rates that occur when alternative data collection procedures are used. He illustrates this point by contrasting the results of using police records and self-report victimization surveys, for there is only partial overlap between criminal encounters included in the two data sets. Neither source, he documents, reflects the true incidence of crime. Reiss suggests the use of capture-recapture procedures, widely used to measure wildlife populations, as a means of overcoming the biased results obtained by conventional approaches.

The second problem Reiss considers is the effects of dynamic changes in the composition of populations on the estimates of program impact obtained from survey data. He provides examples of both routine dynamic processes (such as changes in the status of household respondents) and program-induced changes (for example, the possible reduction in domestic violence incidents because of the breakup of the relationship between the victim and the offender). More complex data collection designs are required, Reiss argues, in order to deal with the types of dynamic shifts discussed by Reiss (including the Berk-Sherman study reviewed at the conference).

The papers focusing on implementing data collection in evaluations clearly do not exhaust the range of problems that impinge on assessments of impact. At the same time, they are sufficient in number to alert evaluators to the extent to which evaluation results are dependent on the sampling strategies employed and the opportunities available to remove data collection problems by analytical procedures.

QUALITY OF RECORDS INFORMATION

In our own work on data collection we paid insufficient attention to the importance of record information in program evaluation. Existing records, whether they be "administrative" (i.e., for documenting service delivery), routine citizen reports (e.g., Social Security records), or long-term indicator information (e.g., FBI Crime Reports), are used in evaluations in a variety of ways. They may serve to identify the target population for programs, define the sampling universe, describe program participants and the contexts in which programs are implemented, and measure both the interventions delivered and outcomes of the initiatives.

The criteria often are different for judging the quality of record information in terms of their original purpose for being and their utility in evaluation research. In many cases record information is sufficiently accurate for routine administrative functioning but not for treatment specifications and program monitoring purposes. For example, although a five-choice structured question on annual earnings may provide sufficient accuracy for monitoring trends in the proportion of persons in various income groups who are clients of an agency, it may not be precise enough for use in either sample selection or outcome measurement.

The papers that consider data collection problems associated with record information reflect the range of ways in which such information contributes to evaluation activities. Chelimsky examines the role of existing administrative and statistical data systems maintained by the federal government and identifies the likely effects on data quality of recent funding cutbacks for maintaining such systems. She draws on the experiences of the U.S. Government Accounting Office to identify the specific ways in which evaluation studies draw support from data systems and problems resulting from inadequacies in these data.

The use of record information to measure program impact is illustrated in two papers. Keesling discusses three educational evaluations (California Early Childhood Education Program, Title I, and a local school district's evaluation of its federal compensatory education program) in which existing program records were used to measure treatment exposure. In all three cases, the failure to build in auditing procedures to insure record accuracy weakened the quality of the information as measures of actual (as opposed to intended) treatments.

The strengths and weaknesses of longitudinal Social Security data for estimating program-induced income gains are examined by Bloom. Bloom uses Social Security earnings in his analysis of the outcome of CETA training programs. Inherent weaknesses of these data are due to truncation in reporting of earnings. Bloom discusses his attempts to combine Social Security data and information from Current Population Manpower Survey in order to decompose earnings gains into components associated with participation in the labor force, types of employment, hours worked, and wage rates. This effort reveals other sources of reporting errors in routine data collections, ones that potentially limit their value for impact assessments.

The papers by Maddox and by Neigher and Fishman highlight issues and problems in the development and use of information systems. Information systems may use both routine treatment records and special surveys to monitor program implementation and to provide baseline data for judging the impact of an intervention. Maddox describes the development of the Duke Older American Resources and Services (OARS) Program, which was designed to aid in planning and evaluating geriatric care. Difficulties in maintaining records over time are discussed. The complications arise due to the age-related impairments of the elderly. On one hand, these impairments make them likely candidates for exposure to multiple interventions; on the other, the quality of information they might provide in self-reports or interview is adversely affected.

Neigher and Fishman clearly view the information systems they have developed as management tools. Their discussions of mental health information systems in Colorado and New Jersey identify the barriers to effective data collection for documenting the effectiveness and efficiency of services.

They argue for building in stronger incentives against bias in administrative record-keeping and suggest that a technological paradigm may be better suited than a scientific one for developing information systems suitable for managerial evaluations.

As a set, these papers point to the importance of records information in virtually all forms and phases of program evaluation. Lack of concern about data quality verification as part of routine data collection efforts is highlighted. Data collection and monitoring practices that might lead to criminal culpability in financial records go on virtually unabated with respect to other records and survey data, although they are central to program evaluation efforts.

CROSS-CUTTING ISSUES

Across the papers, there are several recurring data collection issues that merit further discussion. These issues are the consequence of decisions made about target selection and sampling procedures, including the choices of the observation units (for example, sampling individuals or groups) and the periodicity of data collection; treatment implementation, in particular, the components of the intervention to which clients are exposed; and the measurement of program outcomes, especially the need for reliable and valid means of capturing potentially diverse effects.

TARGET SELECTION AND SAMPLING PROCEDURES

In general, the data collection complications stemming from target selection are least when a carefully circumscribed treatment is directed at a well-defined clientele for a specific period of time. In studies originally designed to be randomized field experiments (e.g., the health insurance experiment described by Rogers and Newhouse, the spousal arrest experiment discussed by Berk and Sherman, and the prescription drug information experiment discussed by Berry) the likelihood of not fully realizing randomization could be estimated and potential reasons for only partial randomization anticipated. Thus, data collection activities could be augmented so that analytical adjustments of treatment impact could be made.

When either the intervention or the delivery system employed are relatively amorphous, the data collection complications associated with target selection mount. For example, Maddox needed to adopt a dual sampling frame of clients and services provided in order to develop an information system for evaluating geriatric care. Each of the sampling frames introduced problems that increased the difficulties of developing and carrying out an adequate data collection plan. At the same time, the availability of two "data sets" (clients and services) enhanced the possibility of uncovering program impact.

The choice between sampling events compared with time periods is another issue that has consequences for data collection. In Sechrest's study of emergency medical technicians and the Berk-Sherman study of domestic violence incidents, the choice was to focus on incidents (occurrence of emergencies or of acts of domestic violence). This choice affected the number of observations that could occur during the course of the study. Time sampling might have resulted in either a larger or smaller sample size in both cases. In one of the studies (Sechrest), incident sampling was a wise decision as the frequency of incidents was greater than that estimated, thus shortening the period of field work. At the same time, incidence sampling may minimize the proportion of cases occurring during low incident periods. In such a case, a nonrepresentative sample of the types of incidents may result.

In longitudinal designs, target selection decisions introduce other data collection problems. For example, in their panel study of television viewing and aggression, Kessler and his colleagues were constrained by their methods of measuring aggression, as well as by economic considerations, to keep the same sample of schools and classrooms throughout the study. Data necessary to examine the effects of sample attrition, because they maintained the same sample of classrooms and schools but not of students, were collected and analyzed. In Mallar and Piliavin's evaluation of the Supported Work Experiment, program participant vacancies were replaced by a randomly selected program applicant. Thus, additional information to adjust for differences due to point of entry into and exit from the program was necessary.

As indicated above, the nature of social programs and their targets virtually assure that complications due to sampling constraints will occur, even in cases in which there is randomization of targets. Many of the evaluations discussed at the conference point to the value of collecting auxiliary information on the characteristics of targets so that sources of nonequivalence among comparison groups may be taken into account. Techniques for analytically modeling systematic selection biases (the term used to characterize a variety of sources of nonequivalence) have matured. The papers by Bloom and by Mallar and Piliavin illustrate how such analytical adjustments are done, and several other authors (Berk and Sherman, Andersen et al., Kessler et al., Rogers and Newhouse) allude to the employment of this analytical technology in their evaluation efforts as well.

TREATMENT IMPLEMENTATION

A common explanation for the failure to detect the impact of social programs is the investigators' failure to adequately address the study of treatment implementation. Obviously, in order to determine the impact of a program, it is necessary to know that participants actually received the intended treatment. The increased concern with measuring actual treatment features and program implementation in current studies places increased demands on data collection.

Participants at the conference repeatedly highlighted the importance of monitoring interventions and studying program implementation. The need to anticipate treatment variation and deterioration during the design of data collection was emphasized. Several investigators built in incentives (both positive and negative) for the deliverers of services. For example, Berry's description of the treatment monitoring on the prescription drug information experiment identifies a number of effective means for both controlling the quality of data collection and monitoring the effectiveness of the delivery system conditions. Neigher and Fishman describe some of the incentives built into their information system in order to enhance data quality in community mental health programs.

Other means of assessing program exposure entail multiple methods of measurement in order to enhance validity and reliability. For example, in their efforts to measure television viewing (their "treatment condition"), Kessler et al. used several different methods of collecting data on TV shows that the targets watched. For example, to authenticate one measure, they included both "dummy" and time-competing TV programs on the list of possible choices a subject might have watched. Kessler and his colleagues then were able to use this information to see if there were any systematic differences in accuracy of reporting due to characteristics of the targets (e.g., age, ethnicity), and whether differences in reporting accuracy affected the estimation of the relationship between viewing and aggression.

The collection of systematic data about the existence and quality of treatment conditions is essential. Failure to do so has consequences for reaching appropriate estimates of program impact, as Keesling's recounting of experiences in characterizing compensatory education treatments clearly illustrates. Possible avenues for improvements in this area are readily identifiable, although the likelihood of establishing the necessary incentives for better data quality and covering its attendant costs are less obvious.

OUTCOME MEASUREMENT

Over the years, investigators have learned about the consequences of focusing on too limited a set of indicators of program impact. A particular indicator introduces both its own definition of the valued benefits of social programs and its own set of limitations as a measure of these benefits. In other words, different outcome measures carry their own sets of excess baggage (in terms of invalidity and unreliability) that corrode their fidelity in estimating program impact.

For example, difficulties with crime measurement and arrest records are considered by Reiss, Berk and Sherman, and Mallar and Piliavin. Self-reports of criminal behavior and police records on arrests introduce different constructs. Whether observed differences in program impact on reported crime versus arrests are substantive (due to aspects of the program) or spurious (the residue of differences in data collection practices and quality) warrants careful thought. The Rogers-Newhouse and Kessler et al. papers point to similar issues arising in the measurement of utilization of health services and of the aggressive behavior of children.

The reduction of the consequences of faulty data collection on measuring program outcomes again points to the value of multiple methods of measurement. Multiple methods can clarify the possible sources of bias (and their effects) in primary outcome measures. Alternatively, outcome measures with different sources of data collection problems can be used in the hopes that the analyses of these different indicators converge on similar estimates of program impact.

THE QUEST FOR GENERALIZATIONS

The basis for the conference was more than the consideration of specific data collection problems in individual evaluations. An important outcome, we hope, was to identify transferable solutions to these problems. Obviously, the emphases in specific papers reflect to varying degrees the social program fields in which the studies were conducted, the outcome foci of the evaluations, the designs employed, and the types of data collected. But do field, study design, and data types matter when it comes to data collection problems and their solutions?

To the degree that our contributors' studies and the data collection issues considered are representative of the broader domain of program evaluation, the answer appears to be "only in a synergistic way." In other words, it is impossible to order individual dimensions of evaluations such as substantive field, type of design, and source of data, or permutations and combinations of them, in their influence on the nature of the data collection problems encountered in a specific evaluation.

At the same time, there does seem to be a common set of strategies employed by the conference participants to minimize the consequences of data collection problems. First, they maintained skepticism from the outset that their data collection plans would work exactly as they intended. This outlook stimulates efforts to document the relevant characteristics of targets, sites, and data collectors. It also leads to careful description of treatment conditions.

Second, the authors point to the value of collecting multiple measures of key variables. Finally, there was general consensus that data quality is dependent on the investigator's commitment—of time, resources, and effort. Targets, service deliverers, and data collectors do not inherently value the information they are expected to provide or gather. Thus, the investigator must provide the motivation and incentives required to obtain accurate and useable data.

The message of this book's chapters is that one cannot escape problems in collecting evaluation data. To minimize these problems, the investigator relies on applied problem-solving that includes both anticipating conditions and situations likely to affect program functioning and reasoning about the array of design, measurement, implementation, and analysis issues that might obscure the assessment of program impact. We hope that the chapters will enlighten the reader because they provide experience-based insights on data collection problems in evaluations and guidance on ways to reduce these problems, or at least the ways an experienced group of evaluators sought to responsibly engage themselves in such an effort.

REFERENCES

BURSTEIN, L., H. E. FREEMAN, K. A. SIROTNIK, G. DELANDSHERE, and M. HOLLIS (forthcoming) "Data collection: the Achilles heel of evaluation research." Sociological Methods and Research.

CAMPBELL, D. T. (1969) "Reforms as experiments." American Psychologist 24 (April): 409-429.

CRONBACH, L. J. (1982) Designing Evaluations of Educational and Social Programs. San Francisco: Jossey-Bass.
———and Associates (1980) Toward Reform of Program Evaluation: Aims, Methods, and Institutional Arrangements. San Francisco: Jossey-Bass.
LAZARSFELD, P. F., B. BERELSON, and H. GAUDET (1948) The People's Choice. New York: Columbia University Press.
LEWIN, K. (1951) Field Theory in Social Science. New York: Harper & Row.
SMITH, M. S. and J. S. BISSELL (1970) "Report analysis: the impact of Head Start." Harvard Educational Review 40: (January): 41-104.
STOUFFER, S. A. et al. (1949) The American Soldier: Combat and Its Aftermath. Manhattan, KS: Military Affairs/Aerospace Historian.

PART I

Data Sensitivities

DATA COLLECTION STRATEGIES IN THE MINNEAPOLIS DOMESTIC ASSAULT EXPERIMENT

Richard A. Berk
Lawrence W. Sherman

Incidents of spousal violence have long been troublesome for police offi-cers. The many reasons need not concern us here (see Parnas, 1967; Black, 1980; Berk and Loseke, 1981), but they derive from a hesitance to intervene in disputes between family members, unsubstantiated beliefs that such inci-dents are particularly dangerous for police officers (Margarita, 1980), and an accurate perception that offenders are rarely sanctioned. In addition, po-

AUTHORS' NOTE: This article draws on a study made possible by team effort involving many people. Nancy Wester was in charge of on-site data collection. Coding, data entry, and file con-struction were supervised by Phyllis Newton. We received helpful suggestions and insights from Sarah Fenstermaker Berk, Peter H. Rossi, Albert J. Reiss, James Q. Wilson, Richard O. Lempert, and Charles Tittle. But most important was the cooperation we received from 42 pa-trol officers of the Minneapolis Police Department and Chief Anthony Bouza. Finally, although the study was conducted by the Police Foundation under funding from the National Institute of Justice (grant 80-IJ-CX-0042), the data collection instruments were developed at the University of California, Santa Barbara for another research project on spousal assault funded by the NIMH Center for Studies in Crime and Antisocial Behavior (grant RO1 MH34616-01). Views expressed in this article are those of the authors and do not necessarily reflect the official posi-tion of the U.S. Department of Justice.

lice officers have been whipsawed between clinical psychologists recom-
mending mediation as the best police response (Bard, 1970) and, more
recently, feminists claiming that offenders are criminals who should be
treated as such (Langley and Levy, 1977: 218). In short, "domestics" constitute a substantial portion of police business and yet police practice has been
mired in confusion and ambivalence.

The policing of spousal violence is surely a major social problem but, at
the same time, it presents a rare opportunity for applied researchers. In
1980, The National Institute of Justice funded a randomized experiment in
Minneapolis intended to test three kinds of police interventions. The details
of the experiment can be found elsewhere (Sherman and Berk, 1984; Berk
and Sherman, 1984); for our purposes, only a few points need be discussed.
First, the three randomly assigned treatments included arresting the offender, ordering the offender from the premises (a common practice), and
some form of advice, which could involve mediation. Second, for legal and
ethical reasons, the treatments were only to be applied to misdemeanor assaults for which in Minnesota police are empowered but not required to make
arrests if there is probable cause to believe that a cohabitant or spouse had
committed an assault against the other party within the preceding four hours.
Third, the major outcome of policy interest was whether or not a new incident occured in which the original offender assaulted the original victim.
"Recidivism" measures were obtained from official police data (e.g., arrest
reports) and a panel of 12 follow-up interviews with victims. Fourth, a sample of approximately 300 cases was obtained with approximately 100 cases
in each treatment group. Finally, a series of statistical analyses revealed that
the arrest intervention was most effective in deterring new incidents of
spousal assault.

This chapter addresses methodological questions that arise from issues
surrounding data collection. This is a side of the Minneapolis experiment
that we have not emphasized previously. More than data collection will be
considered, as it can only be understood within the context of a research design and the statistical analyses that follow.

MEASURING TREATMENT AND ASSIGNMENT PROCESSES

The Minneapolis experiment was implemented by patrol officers who
volunteered for the study. These volunteers were recruited through a process
that unfolded over many meetings with police administrators and line officers, and culminated in a three day retreat during which the volunteers and

researchers were able to consider at length the myriad details of the experiment. Some time also was allocated to role-playing how the officers would determine which types of family violence were to be included in the experiment and how the treatments would be implemented.

Once the experiment began, police officers were required to carry a special pad of report forms, each color coded for one of the three treatments. Upon encountering a situation falling within the experimental guidelines, the officers were to apply the treatment indicated by the color of the form on the top of the pad. As the forms were stapled together in random order, all treatments, in principle, could be randomly assigned.

However, police also had to be given the option to "upgrade" the separation and advice treatments to an arrest if (1) the offender would not leave the premises when ordered to do so, (2) if the officers were assaulted, (3) if a restraining order was violated, or (4) if the victim persistently demanded that the offender be arrested. In other words, the random assignment was compromised by design when serious legal or practical obstacles intervened; loopholes had to be provided, although police officers were given strict guidelines on when random assignment could be violated.

The provision of loopholes meant that it was necessary to collect data on both the *designated* treatment (indicated by color-coded form) and the treatment actually *delivered*. Anticipating the need to correct statistically for the violations to random assignment (for the technical details see Berk and Sherman, 1984), information was collected concerning the circumstances under which the randomized treatment was voided. Information on designated and delivered treatments were elicited by the color-coded forms, which were brief, self-administered questionnaires to be filled out by police officers and delivered to our research staff. The forms asked, for example, whether a gun was involved, whether the offender appeared to have been drinking, and whether the offender assaulted a police officer. Using this and other information, we were later able to model effectively the full assignment process (including both the role of the randomly designated treatment and factors leading to treatments that were not randomly assigned). The result was consistent estimates (in a statistical sense) of the treatments' impacts, which revealed larger effects than would have been obtained had we been unable to adjust for the degradation of the randomization.[1]

The information available from the color-coded forms, however, provided only measures of the *nominal* treatment, with a general notion of treatment *content*. Subtle aspects of police intervention were more difficult to measure. For example, the manner in which an arrest is made can affect the rate of repeat incidents. To measure such content, the initial interview with victims included over a dozen questions asking how they perceived the police intervention. For instance, questions dealt with whether victims thought an arrest had been made, whether the police officers tried to calm people down, and whether the officers listened to the victim's side of the story. From an analysis of these variables in interaction with the delivered treatments, the arrest treatment appeared to be most effective when the police officers established an alliance with the victim (in the eyes of the victim). We interpreted this effect partly in terms of the victim's empowerment; when a perceived alliance with the police was established, he or she could threaten the offender more credibly in the future with a call to the police.

Unfortunately, all statistical analyses relying on data from the initial interviews with victims were complicated by somewhat disappointing response rates. Our interview staff was composed of local women with a mix of ethnic backgrounds who were recruited and trained specifically for the study. The mix of ethnic backgrounds was thought desirable because respondents probably would feel more comfortable talking to people like themselves. Local connections were thought to be important in keeping track of respondents who were likely to move during the course of the study. We also arranged to pay respondents $10, and later $20 for the initial interview and to undertake up to 20 callbacks, many of which were in-person because the victim had no phone. Nevertheless, our response rate for the initial interview was a modest 63 percent, easily low enough to introduce sample selection bias (Heckman, 1979; Berk, 1983).[2]

The color-coded forms were filled out on the full sample of respondents, providing a partial data set with no missing cases. This allowed us to model the nonresponse and then make the recommended statistical adjustments (Heckman, 1979) in analyzing data from the nonrandom subset of respondents interviewed. There was little evidence of systematic patterns of nonresponse, and the adjustments left the original story virtually unchanged.

It would have been useful to also interview offenders. As previous research on spouse abuse has noted, however, it was extremely difficult to obtain the requisite cooperation. Wife batterers are known to rely heavily on denial when asked to consider their actions; plausible accounts were hard to acquire. Many offenders were naturally reluctant to cooperate when facing the prospect of further criminal justice sanction. For these and other reasons, too few interviews with offenders were obtained to use their responses in our data analyses.

It is perhaps worth stressing that both the main effects of the treatments and their interaction effects with treatment content were only credible insofar as the police volunteers followed the random assignment of intervention.

This was not always the case. For example, some police officers may have developed a strong preference for a particular kind of intervention based on a dispatch call and previous contact with the household. In this situation, should an unsatisfactory treatment have surfaced in the random assignment, the officer may have tried to circumvent the experimental design (with the best of intentions).

In designing the study, a number of situations were anticipated in which such temptations might materialize; these were discussed thoroughly in the initial training sessions. We also met once a month with the experimental officers to reinforce previous lessons and discuss any new problems. Participating police officers were volunteers who had committed themselves to the study for over a year, so it is unlikely that any officers consciously would have tried to sabotage the study.

It still was necessary to implement five strategies to determine whether officers were "cheating." All five involved the collection of additional data. First, each of the color-coded forms was numbered sequentially. Had the officers applied the treatments in nonrandom order, the dates and times on the forms would have arrayed the interventions differently from the sequence number. This happened in four cases, and the officers responsible were reprimanded gently. After that, no such anomalies surfaced. In principle, a clever and highly motivated officer could have changed the times and dates on his color-coded form to correspond to the times and dates on his offense (and perhaps arrest) reports. But why such an individual would volunteer to participate in the experiment is difficult to understand. Unlike the experience with some earlier police experiments (e.g., Kelling et al., 1974), there apparently was no conflict over the experiment sufficient to promote sabotage.

Second, it was recorded which officers applied which treatments. This made it possible to determine whether certain officers were systematically more likely to apply certain treatments; no such patterns emerged.

Third, the police officers indicated on the color-coded forms several features of the incident along with a few essential characteristics of the parties (e.g., ethnicity). This made it possible to explore whether the treatments received were a function of the incident or the background of the victim and/or offender. There was some speculation, for example, that arrests would be made disproportionately when the offender was black, hispanic, or native American. Again, no such pattern appeared.

Fourth, a police computer printout was obtained for each month, which detailed all arrests made, tabulated by the name of the arresting officer. If any domestic violence arrests made by officers involved in the study had been recorded without our receiving the color-coded form, it was discussed at the monthly meeting. After four or five incidents of this kind, the problem stopped; 100 percent reporting of arrests followed. There were, unfortunately, no comparable means to check on the other two interventions.

Fifth, we attempted to observe the officers applying the treatments as they encountered domestic assault situations. This strategy failed, primarily because incidents falling within the experimental guidelines were rare, relative to the total time on patrol. For this study, there had to be evidence of a misdemeanor spouse assault *and* the suspect had to be present when the police arrived. Hence, the ride-along strategy turned out to be far too costly in terms of research staff time. As a result, we switched to a "chase-along" strategy in which observers rode in their own cars with police radios and tried to respond to *all* domestic calls within their precinct. But this, too, proved inefficient. Finally, we asked that one police car in a precinct receive all domestic calls and that our observers ride only in that car. Unfortunately, this was vetoed by the department.

Additional data were collected to address three contingencies: (1) planned violations of the random assignment, (2) the need to address treatment content, and (3) the possibility of officers altering the random assignment of interventions. All three efforts proved so useful that were we to do the experiment again, we would invest even more heavily in measures of treatment implementation and content. There is a need to document still more thoroughly when treatments were applied nonrandomly and to understand better how arrests may empower victims.

MEASURING POLICY-RELEVANT OUTCOMES

The central outcome of interest was whether there was a new incident in which the original offender assaulted the original victim. Perhaps the most direct indicator from a policy point of view was whether the Minneapolis police recorded a "failure." The interventions were, after all, designed around incidents coming to the attention of criminal justice authorities.

In theory, failures could be reflected in three kinds of official records: offense reports, arrest reports, and the on-line dispatch system. First, in Minneapolis whenever police on the scene believe that a crime has been committed, departmental policy requires them to fill out offense reports describing what occurred. In fact, at least during the experiment, they sometimes did not do this unless an arrest was made. Second, when an arrest is made, an arrest report is required; this was always done during the experiment. (Officers failing to file arrest reports ordinarily face lawsuits and disciplinary action.) Third, the dispatch system automatically registers the nature of every incident as initially reported by the caller and the location to which the police car is dispatched. Offense reports and arrest reports provide a great deal of information, including the names of all people involved, the time of the incident, and the exact address. Information from the dispatch system is far more sketchy. When a patrol car is sent to an apartment building, for example, it often is impossible to determine which apartment unit was entered.

From all three data sources it was possible to define two kinds of failure variables. The first kind was a dummy variable coded 1 for a posttreatment failure and 0 for an absence of a posttreatment failure. It was not always easy to determine, however, whether a failure occurred after the treatment. Each intervention was by design linked to a violent incident so, in principle, an offense report should have been filed. For about a third of the cases, there also was an arrest report. If the date and time listed on these documents accidentally differed from the date and time listed in the color-coded form (which characterized the intervention), the offense and arrest reports could erroneously appear to be products of totally different incidents. If this artifactual incident was dated after the intervention, it might appear to be a failure. There also was the possibility that the reverse could occur, and offense and arrest reports genuinely documenting new violence shortly after the intervention might be incorrectly seen as duplicates of the reports associated with the intervention. In short, it took a lot of thought and computer coding to properly tag the offense and arrest reports reflecting true failures.

Material copied manually from the dispatch system was far more difficult to handle. The major problem was our inability to determine if a call to a given location really involved one of our experimental households. The result was a very uncertain measure of failure. Indeed, there were nine cases in which we knew for certain that a failure had occurred because a second (and, in one case, a third) intervention was applied to the same household. Yet in only a single instance did our failure measure, which was derived from the dispatch system, correctly detect one of these failures. The dispatch measure of failure had a correlation of virtually zero (and slightly negative) with the other two measures of failure.[3]

The study ultimately produced only a single official measure of a repeat incident, that is, whether there was a postintervention failure indicated on offense or arrest reports. When this was regressed on measures of the treatments delivered (via logistic regression), a substantively and statistically significant effect was found. Compared to the advise and separation treatments, arrest reduced the rate of repeat violence.

Because this study was designed to rely on a follow-up during which not all cases failed, it was, unfortunately, prey to a now widely recognized problem of built-in "right-hand censoring." Simply put, this distortion arises because some cases that ultimately fail are treated as successes because the follow-up period is not long enough. The statistical result is a form of sample selection bias. Our follow-up period was at least six months for all cases; no doubt some would have failed after the data collection ceased. Consequently our estimated treatment effect for arrests was suspect.

In response, we developed another measure of recidivism: the amount of time between the intervention and a failure, if a failure occurred. For cases that did not fail, the elapsed time was taken as the interval between the intervention and the end of the follow-up period. Then it was possible to apply a proportional hazard rate regression (Lawless, 1982: chapter 7), which adjusts for right-hand censoring. All this was possible because we anticipated the need to apply a proportional hazard rate regression model and, hence, to collect data on when interventions were applied, when failures occurred, and when the follow-up period ended. These findings corroborated our prior understanding that arrests were clearly most effective in reducing repeat violence.

One criticism of the use of failure measures based on police data is that many spouse abuse incidents are not reported. But if the underreporting is unrelated to the treatments received (i.e., if the underreporting is the same across treatment groups), unbiased estimates of treatment effects may be obtained (although estimates of the intercept are biased). For police policy, reported assaults are of most immediate concern.

A more telling concern with the official failure measures is that arrests may deter reporting of new violations and not the violations themselves. For example, an arrested offender may threaten the victim with still more serious violence if he or she ever calls the police again. Then one may find a reduction in reported abuse that is clearly artifactual.

Anticipating these concerns, victimization data were collected through 12 follow-up interviews spaced about two weeks apart. There were many reasons for so many waves over so short a period, but perhaps the most important was the need to respond to right-hand censoring. In addition to the biases that might be produced by the finite (and short) follow-up period, significant attrition was expected over time. Thus, the effective length of the follow-up period would vary across respondents and different cases would be subject to different degrees of right-hand censoring. Proportional hazard technique will handle such complications, but only if the timing of failures and attrition is known.

Attrition over the 12 follow-up interviews was substantial, so that by the final wave, only about 50 percent of the original sample remained. Nevertheless, we were able to obtain consistent estimates of any treatment effects, thanks to the proportional hazard approach. Once again, the arrest treatment was clearly more effective in eliminating abuse than were the other two interventions.

One still might have objected that the treatment could differentially affect the measurement of repeat violence in victim interviews. If arrested offenders made more serious and credible threats to their victims than did other offenders, victims might be discouraged from cooperating properly in the interview process. Were this the case, we should have found differential interview completion rates by treatment category. None materialized. There was still the possibility, however, that victims under the arrest condition were reluctant to report new violence for fear of retaliation. But this seems unlikely as such victims were less likely to grant interviews to begin with. Moreover, this possibility was contradicted by the parallel findings from the official and self-report data.

Even with the parallel findings from the official and self-report data, there remained the possibility that our findings did not demonstrate that arrest deterred the offender from committing additional acts of violence, except insofar as jailing physically removed him from the home. From a theoretical and policy point of view, then, it was important to determine what role incapacitation might have. To determine this, during our interviews the victims were asked (1) how much time (if any) the offender had spent in jail after being arrested and (2) how long it was before he or she returned home. When a variable based on these items was added to the statistical analysis of the experiment, no incapacitation effect was found. Moreover, the effectiveness of arrest was not diluted. In retrospect, these findings were not surprising, as the majority of arrested offenders returned home within 24 hours and virtually all had returned home within a week.

To summarize, failure measures were derived from two distinct sources: official police records and interviews with the victims. In addition, we formulated the outcome in two complementary ways: the presence or absence of a failure and the elapsed time between the intervention and either a failure or the end of the follow-up period. These options were made possible by anticipating the kinds of data that would be required. The result was a series of mutually reinforcing findings, all revealing arrest to be the most effective treatment.

MEASURING OTHER TREATMENT
EFFECTS AND INTERACTIONS

For policy reasons, the experimental effect on new violence was of greatest interest, but it has been anticipated that there might be other outcomes of interest. Of particular concern in some circles was that an arrest might affect the offender's employment. Consequently, a great deal of information was obtained from the victim on the offender's employment situation, both in the initial interview and each of the 12 follow-up interviews. This information was, unfortunately, inadequate to determine what impact an arrest might have on employment. Approximately half of the offenders were unemployed at the time the treatments were applied; given only a 63 percent response rate for the initial interviews, the high rate of unemployment meant that there was a very small sample from which to determine whether an arrest cost offenders their jobs.

Another outcome was marital stability. In particular, some commentators were concerned that arrests might break up marriages. Without worrying here about whether marriages in which one member assaults another are worth saving, information was collected at each wave concerning the victim's current living arrangements. From this it was possible to determine if any of the police interventions had an impact on subsequent relations with the offender; no effects were found.

Finally, there was interest in whether any of the treatments were more effective for some kinds of offenders than others. Thus, "rap sheets" were obtained for all abusers with previous arrests in Minnesota and the victim was questioned at length about the offender's background. In brief, no evidence was discovered that would suggest interaction effects between any of the treatments and the offender's biography. For example, it had been anticipated that offenders who had been arrested previously would be less deterred by an arrest for spouse assault. For them, there was already evidence that an arrest was not an especially powerful deterrent. We attributed the failure to find such interaction effects to the fact that even offenders with long histories of wife battery (according to their victims) rarely had prior arrests for spousal assault. Hence, the arrest treatment was a genuine novelty for virtually all offenders we studied.

GENERAL PROBLEMS OF DATA COLLECTION

The Minneapolis experiment can be viewed more broadly as raising a number of more general data collection problems identified by Burstein, et al.(forthcoming). One of the most important is distortions produced in the treatments by the process of data collection when inherent construct and external validity problems are built into the experimental design.

In the case of the present study, such problems revolved around the efforts by our interviewers to call and meet with victims over a six month period. As all three treatment groups were exposed equally to the data collection procedures, estimates of the treatment effects are, in principle, unbiased (although estimate of the intercept may not be). However, the interviews themselves could be understood instead as treatments, a possibility that complicates the policy implications of the findings of the study.

Using this interpretation, the interviews involved in the study could be functioning as a form of surveillance. This principal tool of police work may be defined as a process by which people are deterred from committing crimes because they know that their actions are being routinely monitored. Surveillance can be undertaken in many ways: from patrol cars, on foot, or even through home visits (as in alleged child abuse cases) and telephone calls (as in community corrections programs). In the Minneapolis experiment, the interviews may have been experienced by victims (and, indirectly, offenders) as a kind of surveillance that, in turn, could affect in two ways the generalizability of our findings.

First, as suggested above, our overall failure rate (across all three treatment groups) may have been influenced. Indeed, there is some evidence that the overall failure rate during the sixth month of the follow-up period was lower than the overall failure rate in the preceding six months, although estimates of the pre- and postintervention failure rates were elicited by very different means. Fortunately, estimates of the overall failure rate were not an important feature of our experiment.

Second, it is conceivable that one or more of our treatments would have had different effects under some other sort of data collection strategy (e.g., relying totally on official records). For example, perhaps arrests would have been relatively less effective without the "surveillance" provided by the interviews. Clearly, any replications of the Minneapolis experiment would benefit from conceptualizing the interviews much like another treatment, within a factorial design. For example, a random half of the subjects might be interviewed every two weeks as in the Minneapolis study, while a random half might be interviewed only at the end of the six month follow-up period. It would then be possible to test for interactions between the police interventions and the interviewing procedures.

The experiment also is an example of how the conditions under which data are collected can vary over time. First, early disappointments with the response rate for the initial victim interviews led us, after about 50 interviews, to increase payments to respondents from $10 to $20. (There were no payments for the follow-up interviews because of budget constraints.) Unfortunately, the response rate did not subsequently improve.

Second, it was difficult to control the settings in which the interviews with victims took place. Some victims had no phone, so every contact had to be by personal visit or, failing that, by letter. Regardless of how the contact was made, victims preferred extremely varied places in which to be interviewed: at home, in a local coffee shop, in our research office, and others. In addition, several interviews in the victim's home were interrupted by the offender's arrival and completed with him or her at home (but presumably out of earshot).

Third, in response to victim attrition and interviewers' impressions that some victims were failing in the biweekly telephone follow-ups to report new incidents of violence, we began, after about the 75th case, to make every fourth follow-up a face-to-face interview. Interviewers reported that this improved matters, but no confirmation has yet been found in our data.

Although it always is preferable to maintain one's data collection procedures over the full course of an experiment, it does not appear that the findings were seriously jeopardized. The decisions to increase payments to respondents and conduct every fourth follow-up interview in person are uncorrelated with the treatments assigned and, hence, cannot bias treatment effect estimates. Variation in the conditions under which the interviews were conducted could be associated with the treatments and the outcome, but there is no particular reason to believe that this is so. Unfortunately, as data on where the interviews were conducted were not collected, it is impossible to determine what effect, if any, the interview environment had.

CONCLUSIONS

Although the Minneapolis experiment was hardly flawless, it represents at least a solid effort in program evaluation. Perhaps the project's greatest strength was the use of random assignment. We are increasingly convinced that until there is a compelling body of social science theory with which to properly specify causal models, true experimental or strong quasi-experimental designs are essential for sound impact assessments. The study benefitted enormously from the fact that two treatments (i.e., arrest and separate), having clear definitions, were relatively easy to deliver and were subject to credible verification. In our view, far too many program evaluations are doomed from inception by interventions that cannot be properly and consistently delivered. Finally, the study benefitted from having the resources to collect a wide variety of data from many different sources. It cannot be overemphasized, however, that the data collection was undertaken in the context of a particular research design and in anticipation of the kinds of statistical analyses that would be necessary. More generally, we believe that the role of data collection in evaluation research cannot be effectively addressed in the abstract, but must be linked to the other major components of any evaluation enterprise. This is not to say that better data collection procedures cannot be developed or that data collection must remain more of a craft than a science. It is to say that whatever the advances, data collection procedures must be integrated into the anticipated research design and statistical analyses.

NOTES

1. As a result of the upgrading of some separation and advise treatments to arrest, there was a nonrandom migration of cases away from the randomly assigned interventions. We hypothesized that the upgrading would involve troublesome offenders who also would be more likely to commit new assaults in the future. Hence, the separation and advise treatments were losing high risk cases, whereas the arrest treatment was gaining high risk cases. Without proper adjustments, therefore, the migration would tend to make the arrest treatment look less effective relative to separation and advise.

2. There were a host of practical and ethical problems associated with the victim interviews. For example, we had to be very careful not to incite another assault. This meant that all phone calls and visits to the household had to have a "cover" in case the offender was nearby. Sometimes our interviewers pretended that they were a representative from a well-known department store. It also was often necessary to conduct the interviews away from the victim's home (e.g., at a local McDonald's). It was equally important to protect our interviewers from the offenders; one interviewer narrowly escaped serious assault when the offender arrived home unexpectedly. We made it clear to victims that the face-to-face interviews needed to be done in private and, when possible, interviews were conducted away from the victim's residence. This was all made more difficult because the incident of domestic violence brought many of our respondents to move while the study was in progress. This meant that a great deal of time was invested in difficult detective work. The fact that our interviewers were local people with good connections in the community helped enormously.

3. The unit of analysis was the intervention. When a household was exposed to a second (or third) treatment, the "clock" was reset; we essentially began the sequence of interviews from the beginning. The original intervention, however, was not discarded. Thus, there are (a few) more cases than households.

REFERENCES

BARD, M. (1970) Training Police as Specialists in Family Crisis Intervention. Washington, DC: U.S. Department of Justice.
BERK, R. A. (1983) "An introduction to sample selection bias in sociological data." American Sociological Review 48: 386-398.

— — — and L. W. SHERMAN (1984) Police Responses to Family Violence Incidents: An Analysis of an Experimental Design with Incomplete Randomizing. Santa Barbara: University of California, Department of Sociology.

BERK, S. F. and D. R. LOSEKE (1981) "Handling family violence: situational determinants of police arrest in domestic disturbances." Law and Society Review 15: 315-346.

BLACK, D. (1980) The Manners and Customs of the Police. New York: Academic Press.

BURSTEIN, L., H. E. FREEMAN, K. A. SIROTNIK, G. DELANDSHERE, and N. HOLLIS (forthcoming) "Data collection: the Achilles heel of program evaluation." Sociological Methods and Research.

HECKMAN, J. J. (1979) "Sample selection bias as a specification error." Econometrica 45: 153-161.

KELLING, G. L., T. PATE, D. DIECKMAN, and C. BROWN (1974) The Kansas City Prevention Patrol Experiment. Washington, DC: Police Foundation.

LANGLEY, R. and R. R. LEVY (1977) Wife Beating: The Silent Crisis. New York: John Wiley.

LAWLESS, J. F. (1982) Statistical Models and Methods for Lifetime Data. New York: John Wiley.

MARGARITA, M. (1980) "Killing the police: myths and motives." Annals of the American Academy of Political and Social Science 452: 63-71.

PARNAS, R. I. (1967) "The police response to domestic disturbances." Wisconsin Law Review 12: 914-932.

SHERMAN, L. W. (forthcoming) "Experiments in police discretion: scientific boon or dangerous knowledge?" Journal of Law and Contemporary Problems.

— — — and R. A. BERK (1984) "The specific deterrent effects of arrest for domestic assault." American Sociological Review 49, 2: 201-271.

OBSERVER STUDIES:
DATA COLLECTION BY REMOTE CONTROL

Lee Sechrest

It often is the case that data collection must depend on the use of observers. For many reasons, it may be desirable to observe performances directly rather than to depend on self-reports, records, or other indirect information. The use of observers does entail special problems in collecting data and assuring its quality. In this chapter I will describe some of the more frequent and troublesome problems and point to ways of improving upon common situations even if solutions cannot be promised to the problems. Readers are urged to consult Weick (1968) for a more extensive and most useful discussion of observational methods.

RESEARCH CONDITIONS REQUIRING
REMOTELY CONTROLLED DATA COLLECTION

A number of conditions render remotely controlled data collection strategies attractive.

Obscured performance

The behaviors we want to know about may not occur under circumstances that permit direct observation by the investigator or his or her professionally trained staff. The only practicable way to obtain data may be to send out observers. The most evident reason for an obscured performance is that it occurs in remote settings. Emergency medical technicians and police, for examples, carry out their most critical performances in places and at times that make observation difficult at best. Moreover, the performances tend to be stochastic with respect to many variables so that one cannot predict, other than in a most general way, when and where they will occur; one cannot simply arrange to be on-site for a cardiac emergency or a burglary in progress. A second factor that may obscure behavior is that critical features of the behavior are private. Thus, one cannot be directly privy to a police patrolman's thoughts while considering whether to make an arrest; one must devise some means for getting access to those thoughts, for example, interrogations by an observer. Finally, some behaviors may involve technical complexities that make their nature or significance obscure except for a specially trained person. Technical complexity (e.g., as is involved in emergency medicine) may make the use of trained observers an attractive or even necessary strategy.

Ambiguous products

At art fairs the products of painters, potters, and weavers are judged on their own merits. To use a legal term, *res ipsa loquitur*, the thing speaks for itself. One does not think of having to go into the studio of the artist to see how the object was accomplished. In emergency medicine, on the other hand, one does not end up with a product that is readily interpretable without reference to the process by which it was produced. An accident victim may arrive at the emergency department of a hospital in very bad shape; the field emergency personnel may or may not have handled the case well.

Need to detect critical performances

If one is interested in the performance of a worker on an assembly line, the frequent and repetitive nature of the work involved may mean that relatively brief periods of direct observation may be all that is required in order to understand performance. In many instances, the nature and pace of the work may mean that workers are virtually interchangeable—if you've seen one, you've seen them all. For other purposes, however, routine performance may be of little interest; what one is interested in is the occasional critical situation. Most medical "emergency" runs are routine and easily handled. Interest is in those critical situations in which performance makes a difference in the way things turn out.

Since extraordinary, critical performances of any kind tend to be infrequent, it often is necessary to rely on observers who, expensive as they are, are cheaper than reporters who are research professionals.

Requirements for large numbers of data points

An investigator interested to know generally how emergency medical technicians spend their tours of duty could, in a very few days, get a good idea of what they do and how they do it by riding with them. A few days with an emergency squad working out of a firehouse are all that are required to learn what everyday EMT life is like. But if an investigator wanted to know how emergency medical personnel respond to true medical emergencies, the variability would be sufficiently great that data on more than a few such calls would be required. In our study of programming for mentally retarded persons, it was necessary to have data concerning multiple persons across several days, times of day, types of activity, and so on. These circumstances virtually necessitate the use of trained observers.

Reactivity of self-assessments

Self-recording of behavior may be an unreliable data source. Respondents may not be motivated to provide self-recordings or they may not be able or motivated to provide accurate data. Under such circumstances, the use of observers may be required. For example, as those responsible for programming for mentally retarded persons were being challenged in a federal court to substantiate the adequacy of that programming, on-site observation was virtually demanded. Moreover, as a large proportion of the training was being carried out by relatively low-level personnel, it was uncertain that they would be able to report accurately on the adequacy of their performances, even if they were motivated to do so.

OVERVIEW OF TWO PROJECTS
MAKING USE OF OBSERVERS

This study will draw on the experiences of other investigators and on my own vicarious experience obtained while serving on various advisory panels. In general, however, this study relies on personal experience with two projects involving the behavior of observers.

PERFORMANCE OF EMERGENCY
MEDICAL TECHNICIANS

Satisfactory methods for evaluating the performance of emergency medical technicians have been difficult to come by. Paper-and-pencil tests, supervisor ratings, and other inexpensive ways of assessing performance have been suspect. During the latter part of the short-lived enthusiasm for emergency medicine in this country, it appeared that the development of alternative methods at least could be used to validate what other methods would be desirable. Accordingly, I conducted a study, sponsored by the National Center for Health Services Research, to develop methods of assessment. The proposal focused on observations of actual performances of emergency medical technicians during actual emergency runs. A field staff was hired, including four observers, who were trained . A data collection instrument and protocol were developed and the observers gathered information on ambulances in a large city for one year.

IMPLEMENTATION OF A COURT-ORDERED
TRAINING PROGRAM FOR MENTALLY
RETARDED PERSONS

In a landmark case, Wyatt vs. Stickney, a federal judge ordered a state school for the retarded in Alabama to provide programming for residents that would increase their independence and prepare them for eventual release into the community. Such independence could be in group homes if no more independent circumstances could be achieved. A later case, Wyatt vs. Hardin, resulted from a complaint that the orders of the court were not being carried out. One issue was whether the programming to teach skills of independent living was actually being carried out and, if so, whether implementation met the spirit of the court's original order.

A legal action firm, acting on behalf of the plaintiffs, approached the author and a colleague to see how useful and valid information could be collected for a study of this issue. We proposed and were promised modest funding to carry out an observer study. We recruited and hired eight observers (one dropped out, leaving seven), developed an observer protocol, trained the observers, and deployed them in the institution for four days to obtain detailed information on actual staff behavior related to programming requirements.

POSSIBLE REACTIVITY OF OBSERVER METHODS

An obvious concern in using observers is that their presence may alter the nature of performances, making observer methods "reactive" (Webb et al., 1981). As obvious as that possibility may seem, research evidence suggests that behavior may often be little affected by observers. Behavior of physicians (Peterson et al., 1956) and police (Reiss, 1971; Skolnick, 1966; Van

Kirk, 1977), among others, appear not to have been noticeably affected by the presence of observers, unless one assumes that the undesirable behavior that was noted would have been even more frequent and worse had observers not been present.

Concern about reactive effects of observers may be exaggerated. Reactivity to observers may be limited for several reasons. First, although initially marked, reaction to observers may decline rapidly as they become simply part of the situation. Obviously, reactivity would be greatest in a study in which many people were observed for short periods of time and least in a study involving longer periods of observation of fewer persons. Second, an artificial or uncharacteristic performance is difficult to sustain over any substantial period of time. In our study of mental retardation programming for the courts, we found that the institution simply could not manage the arrangements required to "look good" over a period of several days. Police patrolmen may watch their language for a period of time with a new observer, but before long the accustomed words begin to pop out. Third, reactivity may be limited because people being observed do not know how to behave in any better way than they do under observation. Physicians may commit blunders in the presence of observers because they really do not know how to do any better. Certainly, the emergency medical technicians we observed sometimes performed poorly because they simply were unable to do better. Finally, it is likely that most people are relatively unresponsive to the presence of observers because most of the time they believe that most of what they do is the right thing to do. One of the trainers we observed with a mentally retarded person tried to employ caramels as an edible reinforcer, probably not knowing how poor a choice that was. Police often are quite unapologetic about "roughing up" a person they are arresting because they believe that behavior to be appropriate.

INITIATING AN OBSERVER STUDY

Before an observer study can begin, a number of arrangements and decisions must be made. Two sets that require attention and often are not mentioned in recommendations for fielding observers are described.

NEGOTIATING AN AGREEMENT FOR DATA COLLECTION

To collect data by remote control, it is of the greatest importance that negotiations for that data collection be done with care. Once in the field, observers are likely to have little clout with the persons they are observing, and cooperation of persons in self-recording of behavior is essential. In our study of emergency medical technicians, for example, it was necessary to negotiate an agreement with administrators and supervisory staff that under no circumstances short of the occurrence of a crime would information obtained by an observer be revealed. As it happened, that clause was important and later had to be invoked. We did not, on the other hand, anticipate the resistance to the use of tape recorders that was encountered. As their use had not been negotiated, that part of our plan had to be abandoned.

Resistance to data collection to be carried out by observers or by self-recording may reflect issues other than those inherent in the nature of the research. Researchers need to be fully aware of the social and political context within which the research is to be done. Some early resistance to our data collection on emergency medical technicians was clearly a manifestation of resistance to "top brass" in the department hierarchy rather than to the research itself. In studying programming for institutionalized retarded persons, we were fully aware that the administration of the institution, facing a suit in a federal court, was interested in creating no more than a superficial impression of cooperation. We also were aware that the institutional staff varied widely in their attitudes, but that many of them had been told that the institution would be closed and that they would lose their jobs if the court suit was lost.

There is an obvious advantage in negotiating in a hierarchical organization such as a police or a fire department. If the top-level administrators give their approval to a study, cooperation down the line is likely to be enhanced. But that does not guarantee cooperation. As intimated, lower level personnel who are to be observed or who are to provide data may resist data collection as a way of getting back at the administration for other problems. If there appears to be substantial hostility on the part of line personnel toward the administration, it may be better simply to abort the study.

DEPLOYMENT, DROSS, AND REPRESENTATIVE DATA

In order to develop a plan for data collection that will be affordable, efficient, and scientifically useful, it is necessary to have a reasonably good estimate of the yield that can be expected from particular efforts. Such estimates often are surprisingly difficult to obtain. Over the course of planning a good many studies, I have come to appreciate the powerful effects in the real world of the cognitive bias known as the *availability heuristic* (Kahneman and

Tversky, 1973). Estimates of the frequency of events will be strongly biased by the cognitive availability of instances of those events. For instance, in one study a cancer surgeon overestimated by 100 percent the number of breast cancer procedures he did per year—two per week estimated versus one per week actual. Rescue personnel also have substantially overestimated the number of emergency runs they make, the number of cardiac arrests they handle, the frequency of multiple trauma accidents, and so on. A realistic expectation is that any estimate of the frequency of a dramatic or otherwise highly salient event is likely to be quite high.

Other estimates are problematic simply because the persons involved may not segment their experiences in the way that a social scientist requires. In another study, police whom we asked to estimate the number of discrete incidents they handled per day found it difficult to think in such terms. Consequently, it was difficult to know the extent of the data collection effort that would be needed to satisfy our scientific requirements. It was expected that it would be necessary to collect data for a period of up to one year, but data collection actually stopped after only about six months.

In planning data collection for assessing the quality of programmed training and other activities for mentally retarded persons, it was necessary to guess that in four days of observation of up to around 30 residents, representative enough data could be gathered to arrive at a conclusion. That guess was informed only by a cursory inspection of the institution and its records; nothing more could be done. That this period of observation proved adequate was partly a function of good luck.

A major problem stems from the fact that performances of interest often are only stochastically predictable. Cardiac emergencies, accidents, and so on are not scheduled or regular events. They can occur any time and in any place. They are predictable in that weekend evenings are active times for medical emergencies, Tuesday mornings are quiet, and certain areas of cities tend to produce relatively large numbers of emergencies. But those expectations are true only in general. Our observers rode many Friday evening shifts when nothing happened; in police observer studies the same thing happens. Sometimes investigators as well as observers feel that the observers invariably are in the wrong place at the wrong time (the availability heuristic again). One of the advantages of self-reporting of behavior is that concern about the dross rate is markedly lower and relatively inexpensive (although data processing is not).

One is, therefore, tempted to try to deploy observers to take advantage of the stochastically predictable element of critcal performances. One wants to put observers into ambulances during the busiest times, on the busiest days, in the busiest places. There are two problems with that strategy, one practical and one scientific. The practical problem is that the times, days, and places that are most productive from a data standpoint often are the least desirable from the standpoint of the observer. How many observers can be recruited and kept on the job when they must work weekend evenings and all holidays and when they must regularly commute in from their suburban homes to center-city worksites?

The scientific problem is that there is a likely trade-off between rates of return from data collection efforts and the representativeness of the findings. One gets highest returns from observers of emergency personnel by deploying them in the center of the city on Friday and Saturday evenings. But the data collected there and then may not be especially representative of emergency events occuring in other areas of the city and at other times. The choice was made to maximize return rates, as to have done otherwise would have been far too expensive or would have resulted in trivial sample sizes. For example, emergency squads on the periphery of our city averaged fewer than two runs per day; those in the center of the city averaged six or seven. Nonetheless, it was necessary to temper our deployment strategy by practical concerns for the motivation and morale of our observers; they could not be expected to work every weekend and constantly in the center of the city.

The deployment plan followed unquestionably produced biases in our data. These biases are difficult to estimate in a quantitative way and can only be allowed for generally in interpreting findings. For example, the victims and bystanders involved in the emergency runs we studied were, on average, of lower socioeconomic status and probably were more likely to be black than the average for the city. The EMTs studied did, on occasion, display regrettably insensitive, and sometimes irresponsible, behavior. Whether that behavior would have occurred with equal frequency, or at all, in other areas of the city is unknown. It also is possible that EMTs in busy areas were overworked at times and were less sensive for that reason. The EMTs were, to some extent, self-selected for the areas in which they worked; and yet assignments to some units rather than others also were used for disciplinary reasons by the department. It is not known how much effect these differential assignments may have had on our data.

PREPARATION FOR THE FIELD

Once negotiations for the use of observers are complete and the times and places for observation have been settled, steps must be taken to acquire observers and prepare them for the field.

SELECTION OF OBSERVERS

Social science knows remarkably little about what it takes to be a good observer. In a fairly extensive study of the problem, Turner (1974) concluded that good observers "see more to see." That is not an easy capacity to assess. Others of his results suggested that extraversion-introversion, visual ability, and gender correlate with observer ability in such a way as to tempt Turner to conclude that the best observer would be an introverted, near-sighted, female.

Based on experiences of others in selecting police observers (Van Kirk, 1977; Bieck, 1978), we believed that the requirements for riding on ambulances, observing emergency incidents, and recording information correctly would include a relatively phlegmatic personality, a capacity (only bordering on cynicism) for distancing oneself from events, physical endurance, intelligence, and good handwriting. We also expected that good observers would have to be willing to take orders and to do things according to protocols provided them. These were, too, about the same things sought when selecting observers for the study of mental retardation programming.

One issue that arises regularly in observer studies is whether observers must have expertise in the kinds of performances they are observing. Experience in police observation studies suggested that expertise might not be of great importance. The observer's task is simply to note what happens and record it accurately. Later events suggested that this assumption was not entirely correct. The collection of good quality data of the kind required to answer questions should begin with a careful analysis of the kinds of questions to be answered and consideration of the kinds of data required. Then one is led to consideration of the kinds of observer skills that are required.

In selecting observers for the emergency medical technicians study, it was believed that if observers had basic training in emergency work, which meant about 80 hours of classroom training, they should be trainable as good observers. This was, however, assuming that the task was one of determining whether some "mandated" treatment for a particular condition did or did not occur. It was soon discovered that a second equally important question was whether a treatment given was well performed. It was one thing to note whether an attempt to administer oxygen was made, and quite another to determine whether the administration was made correctly (e.g., whether the mask used had a good seal against the face). To a great extent it was possible to compensate for our anticipatory failure by altering the training of the observers and providing a more explicit protocol for judging adequacy of and errors in treatments. In the end, however, it was discovered that a critical deficiency in our study was that we could not say whether treatments that had been administered were, if not mandated, appropriate, and treatments that had been omitted were, if mandated, justifiably omitted. Those judgments would have required observers with at least as much expertise in emergency medicine as the EMTs being observed. That is, observers would have to have been trained as paramedics, with up to six months of training, rather than simply 80 hours.

In the study of mental retardation programming, graduate students served as observers. They were relatively expert in the training procedures they were to look for. That was fortunate, for many of the deficiencies noted would simply not have been obvious otherwise. Graduate students were used in part because of time pressures that precluded training less expert persons to be observers.

The conclusion reached at this point is that there is no substitute for knowing ahead of time exactly what data will be needed and then ensuring that observers have the background necessary to collect those data. The more technical the performance, the greater the expertise required of observers. If judgments about the appropriateness of some action are to be required, expertise is necessary, both for making accurate judgments and for supporting their credibility once they are made.

TRAINING IN DATA COLLECTION

The most important step in training of data collectors is to define the task. The most important step in defining the task is to define carefully the data that are to be collected. The second most important task is to develop an instrument suitable for collecting those data. A properly prepared protocol will assist greatly in defining the task and in guiding the observer through it, including the accurate recording of observations.

Again, based on prior experience of investigators doing observations of police, we believed that the critical orientation of training should be toward how and what to observe in one's own or another's performance. Training should focus not on how to do some task, but on how to observe it, what to look for. In training observers of EMTs, we made no effort to bring them to any level of expertise in performing EMT tasks, although they were rehearsed in all such tasks. Training focused on watching the task being performed and looking carefully to see exactly how it was done. Similarly, in training observers of mental retardation programming, the emphasis was on watching. Observers were not, for example, necessarily familiar with the details of procedures for teaching retarded persons how to put on belts or eat with forks.

Simulation exercises are useful in training and validating observers. Such exercises were conducted, probably not enough, in the observer studies. Simulations may be virtually the only way of testing observers to determine how they are doing and to provide feedback. Putting an extra person, a trainer, on an ambulance was not practicable. On the other hand, good simulations often are expensive to mount. Considerable time was devoted to setting up simulations for our EMT observers, including training actor-victims, assembling materials, providing for recording, and so on.

In the case of the mental retardation programming study, we could not arrange for simulations because we really did not know what to observe until we were on the premises of the institution. Therefore, we had to use 20 percent of the total time available to us on the first day of observation to train and check out observers by sending them out in pairs so that they could check out each other.

Training data collectors may not be cheap; it probably should not be cheap. As indicated, we had to devote 20 percent of our allocated time for observing mental retardation programming to training observers. In the EMT study, we allowed and fully used two months of time for training observers, who then worked for one year. We never felt that the training could have been done adequately in less time. If the data are not worth the training costs, they are probably worth a great deal less than we would like to think.

PROTOCOLS FOR DATA COLLECTION

A complete data collection protocol will consist of the data collection instrument itself, instructions on how to use it, possible supportive or other backup materials, and instructions and procedures for overall conduct during data collection.

Development of protocols

One can develop data collection protocols based on prior experience and pretesting and then train data collectors to use them. In our EMT study, an evolutionary strategy was followed that permitted participation by observers but also gradual refinements as more was discovered about the requirements of the task. We began with a simple data form that required only limited effort and that left observers with plenty of time just to look around and absorb what was going on. The form was complicated gradually as the observers developed their skills and sensitivities. The complications were guided by discoveries about what was practical and helpful. For example, very soon it emerged that the two-sheet form that we thought we would use was better replaced by a single sheet printed on either side.

The participation in the design of the data collection instrument for the EMT study was of great value. A much better instrument was obtained than would otherwise have been possible, but also an instrument to which those using it had a commitment. Virtually no complaints were received about the data form.

Characteristics of a good data collection form

Collecting data nearly always requires a tradeoff between completeness and simplicity of the process. One wants as much data as possible, but a longer, larger, denser, more complicated form will produce problems. Multiple-page forms are cumbersome, large pieces of paper blow in the wind, type eventually gets too small to read, or spaces get too small to write in. Or there simply is more to keep track of and to record than time will permit.

A good observer form must be explicit about the data that are to be recorded and about the response options that are required. Initially, our EMT data instrument was nonspecific about the recording of times, and they were being variously recorded by a 12-hour and a 24-hour clock system. Problems discovered too late could have resulted in serious deficiencies.

Good data collection forms also should be efficient with respect to effort required for recording data, monitoring data collection, data entry, and file construction. Here, again, however, there are likely to be tradeoffs. Items that require only checkmarks, circles, or similar techniques of recording may reduce the richness of information. The seeming simplicity of such items may, on the other hand, tempt researchers to ask for more data than can readily be observed. Observers can be encouraged to add notes concerning unusual incidents or responses, but such notes require coding that may be difficult. Moreover, differences between observers in response to invitations to make notes may result in biases in terms of sources of data. To the extent that data forms are designed so that items are precoded, data entry will be facilitated and errors may be avoided.

SPECIFYING PROCEDURES AND RULES

A satisfactory protocol for data collection should consist of more than the data recording instrument itself. In nearly every instance in which data must be collected remotely, provision must be made for a variety of circumstances of varying likelihood that could impede data collection or threaten data quality. For example, in the EMT observer study we guessed that situations might arise in which EMTs being observed would ask to see the data form to determine what was recorded. The decision was that any such request would be acceded to; as it happened, very few requests were made. In the mental retardation study an important element in the plan for data collection was that it should not reveal which resident's programming was being observed at any one time. The institution staff responded with various tactics designed to try to discover which resident was the one for which data were being recorded (e.g., by removing residents from the room one by one). Our protocol instructed observers simply to shift their focus to another resident until the one of interest returned.

TESTING ADEQUACY OF OBSERVERS AND SELF-REPORTERS

An obvious and critical question in the use of observers is whether their reports are accurate. That is as true for those reporting on their own behavior as for those observing the behavior of others. Establishing accuracy is no simple matter.

A standard way of testing for accuracy is to determine whether two observers agree in their reports. Ordinarily, one would think of sending two observers into the field together and then determining the extent of their agreement. However, that is not always possible. There was not room on emergency vehicles for two observers, and it would have been very expensive to have deployed observers in that way for any length of time. It was possible to check observers against one another in the mental retardation programming study, but only at considerable cost in terms of a reduced data base.

The data recorded in the retardation programming study were mostly binary in form and simply indicated whether a particular activity did or did not take place during a brief time period. Not all the items to be recorded were of a completely objective nature (e.g., warmth, friendliness of interaction). As is well known, percentage agreement between observers is not an especially good measure of agreement as it depends heavily on the marginals. For a number of our data, marginals were highly skewed as, in most time intervals, the behavior of interest clearly did not occur. A simple percentage agreement capitalized on that fact and the estimates were very high. The preferred measure of agreement is kappa (Fleiss, 1973), which takes chance agreement into account. The kappas we obtained were sometimes disturbingly low. The problem, however, was that observers could not always agree when, for example, a positive verbal reinforcement did occur, although they agreed on when such reinforcements did not occur. Ultimately, the problem was resolvable in the particular instance because the whole issue centered on the low rates of occurrence of some critical responses, and even if one counted a positive occurrence observed by either observer, the rates were still low.

The EMT observer case was more difficult to resolve. Ultimately it was necessary to develop simulation exercises that could be observed by two or more observers, whose recordings then could be compared. Even then, we did not succeed in getting data on observer agreement as definitive as we would have liked. Part of the difficulty was the same problem with skewed marginals that afflicted the mental retardation programming study. Most performances were unexceptional and observers had no trouble agreeing on that. Too late, we realized that to get maximally informative observer agreement scores, we should have identified a set of reasonably critical tasks and arranged to have them performed repeatedly by experienced EMTs, with deliberate errors introduced on enough trials to obviate the problem of skewed marginals.

Thus, neither study succeeded in obtaining more than minimally satisfactory information on the accuracy of observers. Nonetheless, other grounds support the notion that data provided by the observers were of reasonably good quality, but the studies would have benefited from better assessments of observer accuracy.

THE DATA COLLECTION PHASE

Problems with observer studies and the work of conducting them by no means end once data collection has begun. No matter how good the arrangements up to the point of going into the field, one cannot assume that all will go well from that point on.

MONITORING DATA COLLECTION

Any study in which data collection is done by what is here called remote control must include mechanisms for immediate, continuous, and close monitoring of data collection. Even if observers have been carefully selected, thoroughly trained, and provided with an excellent protocol, it ought not be assumed that problems are unlikely or, if likely, minor.

Control

Observers need to be controlled carefully, beginning with monitoring of assignments to ensure that observations are actually made in the places and at the times specified and that the targets are the correct ones. For a variety of reasons, assignments may not be carried out as planned. Sometimes it is necessary to alter plans; a mechanism must be in place to make sure that alterations occur in a specified way and that any alterations are noted. For example, in our EMT study there were occasions on which observers could not ride on the unit to which they were assigned. A typical reason was that the unit was being used that day for training purposes. It was necessary to have a mechanism that did not permit the observer to make his or her own choice of unit to ride with and that ensured that the substitution was accurately and usefully recorded. During the course of the retardation programming study, one or both investigators circulated regularly among the observers to determine that they were where they were supposed to be and to help with any problems that might have arisen.

Control should also be exercised over data collection instruments. Police departments number traffic citation forms, summons, and so on, and officers are responsible for each and every form. That close control is employed to ensure that officers do not tear up forms in response to citizen pressures, that they do not use them for wrong purposes (e.g., intimidating citizens). In police observer studies and in our EMT studies, close control over forms has been desirable to ensure that observers do not destroy forms they have started to fill out during events that "turn bad." It also was important that forms be filled out in the field and not recopied in the station after events are over. Therefore, all forms should be numbered, assigned by number to particular observers, and logged out and in.

Nonadherence Problems

Despite the best efforts, observers may not adhere to procedures. We were aware of specific problems in our EMT observer project. To begin with, only close and continuous monitoring kept observers close to the deployment schedule we had devised. As indicated, it was fairly often necessary to abort an assignment, for example, because the unit to be observed was preempted for training for that day. Observers had their favorite units to ride with, perhaps because of the atmosphere around the particular fire station, because of liking for a particular EMT, or because of the area of the city involved. As it was relatively easy for an observer to create a reason not to accept any particular assignment, our supervisory staff had to be quite firm about procedures for changing assignments. Observers also did not particularly like to ride on weekend evenings, at least once the novelty had worn off, nor on holidays. Pressure had to be exerted to keep them to their assigned schedule of days and times as well as to particular units.

Observers also failed at times to follow prescribed procedures or drifted into nonprescribed ways of doing things. For example, observers were supposed to carry clipboards with data instruments attached to them and were to record observations directly on the form. The EMTs, however, carried small, inconspicuous note pads on which they made notes that were later transferred to run forms. Our observers thought themselves conspicuous and began to carry the same small note pads themselves, later filling out the data instruments. That behavior probably persisted for three or four days before it was detected and corrected by our staff. Only constant monitoring saved the project from serious procedural departures.

There were additional problems with inadequate recording of data, some also reflecting a drift from previously satisfactory behavior. Observers tended to lapse into nonstandard abbreviations, to use deviant methods of marking responses, and so on. They also had to be reminded regularly of the necessity of recording the positive nonoccurrence of certain critical responses. And despite our efforts at screening, illegible handwriting was a constant threat. No matter how well-trained observers are and how good everything looks at the beginning, protections against deterioration are essential.

Early Data Entry and Computer Checks

Our data were entered into computer files as soon after we received them as possible. That procedure is strongly recommended. Early data entry is likely to identify problems in recording of data, handwriting legibility, and so on. In addition, it may be possible to use computer checks on the data to identify problems. For example, one might use such checks to determine whether observers are reasonably consistent in their use of various response categories, in the means and variances of their observations, and the like. On the other hand, it is not necessarily simple to make such checks for they often require considerable effort directed toward the construction of computer files before one is quite ready for that task. Although we had hoped to do computer checks on data coming in from the field in the EMT observer study, our checks were at best rudimentary.

COMMON PROBLEMS WITH OBSERVERS

Earlier experiences reported to us by managers of police observer studies indicated that problems arise from the fact that observers tend to get coopted by those they are observing. Police observers, for example, sometimes tend to "get into" policing and come to identify too closely with the officers with whom they are working. That identification can be assumed to destroy objectivity. For many persons, there is considerable seductiveness in the excitement and at least superficial glamour of occupations that deal in crisis.

Aside from monitoring, we attempted to limit the likelihood of cooptation by constantly rotating our observers among units so that they did not ride for very long with the same personnel. We also developed very clear procedural rules prohibiting them from helping EMTs in any way unless specifically requested to do so and then only in purely incidental ways (e.g., by holding a piece of equipment or lifting a stretcher). Monitoring sessions with observers provided opportunities for them to talk through their feelings about working with EMTs and for staff to reinforce objectivity and noninvolvement.

Observers are likely to get overconfident after a period of time on the job. They develop expectations about what they are going to see that may lead them to record more on the basis of those expectations than on the basis of what actually happens. As indicated previously, they tend to drift into a variety of undesirable observational and data recording habits. It is by no means easy to keep observers alert and functioning as if they were naive.

Observers also tend to get bored. The redundancy in the task is great, so the task ceases to be interesting after a time. In the EMT study we had to struggle to keep up the morale of the observers over the last three or four months of data collection. They were inclined to find excuses to take days off, to become careless in work habits, to complain about small matters, and so on. We gave them unanticipated holidays, decreased weekend assignments, promised performance bonuses, and tried other stratagems. Without these efforts, data quality would have suffered greatly.

CONCLUSIONS

Use of observers often is an attractive, even necessary, way of collecting data. Observers may be able to provide data available by almost no other means. Observer studies are not, however, simple and inexpensive to mount. The task to be undertaken by observers must be carefully specified in advance so that the right kinds of observers can be selected and given the right kind of training. Very little is known about how to select good observers, and we try to pick people who are generally intelligent and competent rather than for any very specific skills. Training observers may be expensive, but if the cost of observers can be justified, the cost of their proper training can also be justified. Part of training, and a critical task in any case, is the development of a good observer protocol, including rules and procedures for conduct in the field. Special arrangements often are necessary in order to be able to demonstrate that observers are dependable research instruments. Once in the field, observers must be continuously and carefully monitored if the quality of data collected is to be maintained and documented. Despite our best efforts, many things can go wrong, and only diligent, committed researchers are likely to be able to make effective use of observers.

REFERENCES

BIECK, W. (1978) Personal communication.

FLEISS, J. L. (1973) Statistical Methods for Rates and Proportions. New York: John Wiley.

KAHNEMAN, D. and A. TVERSKY (1973) "On the psychology of prediction." Psychological Review 80: 237-251.

PETERSON, O. L., L. T. ANDREWS, R. S. SPAIN, and B. G. GREENBERG (1956) "An analytical study of North Carolina general practice, 1953-54." Journal of Medical Education 31: 1-165.

REISS, A. (1971) The Police and the Public. New Haven, CT: Yale University Press.

SKOLNICK, J. H. (1966) Justice Without Trial: Law Enforcement in a Democratic Society. New York: John Wiley.

TURNER, J. L. (1974) "Powers of observation: the measurement and correlates of observational ability." Dissertation Abstracts International 35 (2-B): 1031-1032.

VAN KIRK, M. L. (1977) Response Time Analysis. Kansas City, MO: Kansas City Police Department.

WEBB, E., D. T. CAMPBELL, R. D. SCHWARTZ, L. SECHREST, and J. GROVE (1981) Nonreactive Measures in the Social Sciences. Boston: Houghton-Mifflin.

WEICK, K. E. (1968) "Systematic observational methods," pp. 357-451 in G. Lindzey and E. Aronson (eds.) Handbook of Social Psychology. Reading, MA: Addison-Wesley..

DATA COLLECTION ISSUES
IN THE EVALUATION OF THE EFFECT
OF TELEVISION VIOLENCE
ON ELEMENTARY SCHOOL CHILDREN

Ronald C. Kessler
J. Ronald Milavsky
Horst Stipp
William S. Rubens

In this article we discuss the data collection problems that arose in a study of television violence and the aggression of children. The investigation was a six-wave panel study of some 3200 children in the second through sixth grades in two Midwestern cities. Data were collected over a three-year period in group administration sessions held in classrooms.

The main data collection tasks were to assess each child's level of aggressiveness and to obtain detailed information about the television programs he or she had viewed over the past month. We decided on a peer nomination

AUTHORS' NOTE: Correspondence should be sent to Ronald C. Kessler, Institute for Social Research, University of Michigan, Ann Arbor, MI 48109. Preparation for this chapter was partially supported by Research Scientist Development Award 1-K02-MHC0507 and Research Grant 1-R01-MH37706 from the National Institute of Mental Health.

method of assessing aggression and an aided recall method of asking about recent viewing based on a search of the literature as well as our own exploratory work.

This case study is of more than passing interest because its design and data collection methods are the procedures of choice in current research on the television-aggression relationship. Although an experimental design would yield less equivocal results if it could be implemented in the field, field experiments have been notoriously ineffective in this area. Television viewing is so central in the lives of most children in our society that experimental assignment to a low television viewing condition usually causes reactions that invalidate the experiment. In two classic studies of manipulated exposure to television, for example, the boys who were deprived of their favorite shows became more aggressive, even though they watched less television violence (Feshbach and Singer, 1971; Wells, 1973).

Because of this problem, the panel design has been adopted by most recent researchers. Indeed, there is general agreement that the most direct evidence on the influence of television violence currently available comes from panel studies such as the one discussed here (Cook et al., 1983). Furthermore, all three of the major panel studies that have played a prominent part in the current policy debate on the television-aggression relationship are based on the same classroom administration and peer nomination aggression procedures used in this study (Eron et al., 1972; Huesmann, 1982; Milavsky et al., 1982).

This chapter discusses data collection problems associated with the measurement of television exposure and then with aggression. Each section begins by discussing the problems envisioned before going into the field and the pretest work on which the decision to use certain measures was based. Data collection procedures are described that were developed to minimize faulty measurement. Problems encountered in the field are discussed next, along with the procedures developed to deal with these problems as they arose. Each section closes with a discussion of the way we dealt with these data collection problems in the data analysis.

Despite care in planning for a number of data collection problems in the pretest work, we found ourselves confronted with some unanticipated problems in the field. In one case, a problem was identified only after data analysis had begun and field work was over. The implications of these various problems for the validity of the results obtained are evaluated, and we speculate on ways in which future work might profit from our experience and guard against some of the problems we encountered.

DATA COLLECTION PROBLEMS
IN MEASURING TELEVISION VIEWING

The television exposure measure used in this study was developed on the basis of a comprehensive review of the available literature, including commercial research by the television rating services and a pretest in which alternative methods were compared. On the basis of this preliminary work, we discovered that although the method selected here was the best one available to us, there were still some children who had difficulty with it and gave inaccurate viewing reports. We therefore made a number of adjustments between the pretest and the actual study (a) to increase the likelihood that accurate answers would be obtained and (b) to devise a method for determining when a child gave inaccurate information. After the first wave of data was analyzed, we still found that a substantial number of children—especially those in the second grade with poor reading skills— had difficulties with the measure. In response to this, we launched auxiliary analyses in the course of the study to determine more precisely the nature of their responses. In the end, we documented that the measure yielded accurate data for most children and that some children overreported viewing behavior. We were able to use this knowledge in the data analysis phase by developing special estimation procedures that distinguished between children who gave accurate and inaccurate viewing reports.

SELECTION OF EXPOSURE MEASURE

For the purposes of this study, we needed an exposure measure that would provide accurate data on children's television viewing behavior over several weeks under normal, real-life conditions. As we wanted to assess the effects of different program contents, we needed information on viewing of specific programs, not a general measure of overall exposure. It was the purpose of the pretest to find a measure that would meet these objectives.

Before beginning this study, there had been a great deal of academic and commercial research on the methodology of assessing television viewing. A number of different data collection strategies had been developed and investigated for accuracy and ease of implementation. This legacy proved invaluable.

The most helpful findings that shaped our early thinking about data collection issues were the following (for a detailed review, see Stipp, 1975):

(1) Mechanical procedures of monitoring the use of television sets produce very precise data on the time a television set is turned on, but those methods are not capable of determining who is watching.

(2) Mechanical procedures could be augmented to provide individual viewing data by the use of a video camera that keeps a continuous log on the people who are sitting in front of the set. However, many refusals to have this type of equipment installed are likely.

(3) In the absence of mechanical procedures, repeated telephone interviews yield the most accurate data on current viewing. These are not feasible for measuring the viewing behavior of specific individuals, though, as they place a prohibitive burden on the respondent.

(4) Self-report data can be obtained by using either a television viewing diary or a recall procedure. In studies of young children, both approaches also have been used with mothers or older siblings as informants. Research on the accuracy of such methods indicates that mothers tend to underestimate children's viewing. At the same time, young children have difficulties giving accurate reports about their viewing.

With this information as background, a preliminary decision was made to use some form of informant report. Reasonably accurate data could be obtained by personal interviews using aided recall methods (probes for the names of programs) over a 24-hour recall period, but information on viewing over a longer time period was required for the desired substantive analyses. For the latter purpose, we sought a method that would yield good data on viewing patterns over a period of between two weeks and a month. Daily personal interviews for several weeks could sensitize respondents to the purpose of the study and thereby affect their reporting. Other methods were sought to meet the needs of the study: for instance, a diary, a retrospective questionnaire, or a personal interview.

Pretest

To adjudicate among the contending possibilities, a pretest was administered to 200 children in the first through fourth grades (about 50 in each grade). In this pilot work, an early version of the aided recall questionnaire eventually used in the study was administered to the children and a subsample was recruited to keep a diary at home for the next week. The diary was to be filled out by either an older sibling supervised by the mother or only by the mother. The children in this subsample were interviewed every morning of the week the diary was kept about the previous day's television viewing. Interviewers were trained to note and record any indications that the child was having difficulty recalling the previous day's viewing. At the end of the interview/diary week, group interviews were held with the focal respondent, the mother, and (when applicable) the older sibling to discuss inconsistencies among the different reports.

Several important results emerged from this pretest. First, diaries completed by mothers or siblings seriously underreport the viewing of children in this age range. In many cases in which the mother had agreed to keep the diary, it was actually the child who kept it. Such young children had difficulties making accurate entries or remembering to update the diaries. Furthermore, mothers had a tendency to underreport viewing to a considerable degree. Mothers seldom checked to find out if their child had watched television while at a friend's house. They tended to forget that their child was also watching when the parent watched an adult show. Mothers also often failed to record the fact that their child watched programs when the mother was away from home or in a different part of the house.

It is worth noting that a supervised diary method had previously been used by Schramm et al. (1961) in a study of middle-class children and their mothers. Our pilot work, in contrast, was conducted in a lower-class sample. Data quality control is problematic in a sample of this sort. Furthermore, we found that it was difficult to enlist the cooperation of the mothers of children in this sample, which meant that a large-scale application of this method would lead to substantial missing data problems. In short, the diary method was infeasible for the study.

At the same time, the pretest demonstrated that the aided recall questionnaire was a suitable instrument for studying children in the second through fourth grades. (First graders had great difficulty with the questionnaire.) There was generally high agreement between reports in the questionnaire and those subsequently elicited from daily interviews.

Despite these encouraging results, the aided recall questionnaire yielded inaccurate data for some respondents. Titles of four nonexistent programs were put in the questionnaire as "dummy" programs. An analysis of viewing reports for these dummies showed that 38 percent of the second graders and 33 percent of the third graders mentioned viewing at least one of them, with averages of 2.6 and 2.0 respectively. The fourth graders had a much lower rate of reported dummy viewing.

Children who reported viewing nonexistent programs also reported suspiciously high overall viewing patterns. Previous research on aided recall methods indicated that some respondents exaggerate past viewing considerably and we suspected that this might be the case with the children who checked the dummies. The fact that age was strongly related to these reports also suggested that difficulty in understanding the instrument and following instructions could have played a part.

Despite this difficulty, the pretest demonstrated that the aided recall questionnaire performed well for most children and that there appeared to be no reasonable alternative. Therefore, this method was chosen for the full study. The pretest experience suggested the continued use of dummy shows and convinced us that special efforts should be made to make the instrument as understandable as possible to young respondents. A protocol was developed that would be read aloud to the children to monitor the administration of the questionnaire in a group setting. It was concluded that first graders are too young to use this procedure and so the full study was based on a sample of children in the second grade or older.

DATA COLLECTION PROCEDURES

The questionnaire and its administration were devised in such a way that young children would have the least possible difficulty completing it. Television programs were listed on four pages. The first page listed about 15 prime time shows, the second about 11 weekend daytime programs, the third about 12 daily (weekday) programs, and the last page about eight movies—a total of about 45 shows. This number was cut down from 70 used in the pretest in order to reduce respondent burden. Response options also were simplified and the format changed to make the task easier.

Questionnaires were administered in classrooms by teams consisting of an administrator and one or two monitors, depending on class size. Administrators were trained by the project staff. The degree of training proved to be inadequate to prepare the teams for handling problems that arose during the first administration, particularly among the younger children. It became apparent that more direction was needed to insure uniformity of procedure. Therefore, beginning in Wave II each administrator worked from a written script that was read to the classes. This guaranteed that administration was constant from one classroom to the next. Monitors were given a "Monitor's Guide," which detailed their tasks and spelled out exactly what to do and say.

After the administrator and the monitor(s) had introduced themselves, the method of administration was explained to the children. Then the administrator read the questions, demonstrated the procedures, and clarified the concepts.

ADJUSTMENTS DURING DATA COLLECTION

Although careful administration procedures helped children give accurate responses, an analysis of the Wave I questionnaires showed that a full fourth of the children checked dummy programs. This is a high proportion and, although marking a dummy does not necessarily mean that the rest of the TV questions were answered inaccurately, it did suggest the possibility of a relatively large number of poor reports. When we examined other characteristics of the children who claimed viewing of dummy programs, it turned out that they were from low SES homes, scored low on IQ measures, and were high on peer nominated aggression.

To detect the importance of erroneous reports, ways of making invalid reports of viewing were increased. In subsequent waves, a number of program pairs that were aired exactly at the same time on different stations were included in the measure, until by Wave V there were five such program pairs. These provided a second check on inaccuracy by allowing us to identify respondents who told us that they regularly watched two shows aired simultaneously. Reports of this sort—claiming to regularly watch two programs aired at the same time—were strongly correlated with viewing dummy shows ($r = .40$). Although it is, of course, possible to switch back and forth between different programs (even before the advent of remote control), it is not easy to believe that this would be done with regularity between five program pairs. The strong correlation with marking dummy programs confirmed the suspicion that this was indeed an indicator of poor reporting.

The third indicator of poor reporting was a pattern of consistently marking programs as viewed either always or never that we discovered when we looked at the first wave's questionnaires. It seemed some children simply marked most programs they had seen as watched always (instead of 1, 2, or 3 times out of 4 telecasts) and only those they never watch as "zero." As a result, they claimed to watch a tremendous amount of TV—presumably an exaggeration. We suspected that these children had either misunderstood the instructions or simplified the task of answering the TV questions by turning our five-point scale (0, 1, 2, 3, 4 seen out of 4 weekly shows) into a simple no-yes dichotomy, a pattern of behavior already documented to exist among poorly educated adults when they are asked to fill out measuring instruments with scales (Stipp, 1975: 56-66).

In any case, commercial ratings data already showed that most people watch weekly programs once, twice, or three times a month, but rarely every time they are aired. Therefore, it was assumed that this response pattern would be related to the other indications of less valid reporting. Correlations of extreme responses with dummy viewing and with claiming to watch simultaneously aired programs were both found to be highly significant ($r = .34$ and $.80$).

On the basis of this evidence, a special study was conducted of this apparent pattern of poor reporting. Its main concern was whether children who exaggerated their viewing in this way were providing inaccurate reports or were actually very high viewers who thought that they might have seen the dummy programs or simultaneously aired pairs. The determination was important for our substantive analysis, as children who gave reports of this sort not only had high viewing scores but also high aggression scores. This meant that a decision about whether they were valid or invalid reporters and should or should not be included in the analyses would affect the television-aggression association.

Validity Studies

Two separate studies were conducted to deal with this question. The first was a "picture test" study added on to the Wave IV data collection. The study was prompted by the fact that most children who marked dummy programs in the early waves were second and third graders. This suggested to us that deficits in reading and writing skills might be involved in the inaccuracy. And so we wanted to use a method that minimized the need for these skills.

Pictures of a number of actors and some cartoon characters who had recently appeared in TV series at that time were put on separate pages, on each of which were six pictures. Respondents were asked to pick the one who was a character on the series. For example, one question instructed respondents to "draw a circle around the picture of the one who captures and studies animals in the TV show called Wild Kingdom." The character depicted was a relatively new addition to this show.

Our hope was that differences in recognition could be used to assess validity of viewing reports. However, this procedure did not work very well. The great majority of the children were able to pick the correct picture. In some classrooms, enthusiastic children called out the correct answer for all to hear, thus invalidating the data from the whole class. Not surprisingly, only a small association between self-reported viewing and the ability to pick the correct face was found ($r = .10$).

This failure prompted us to devise another study in conjunction with the Wave V data collection. On three consecutive weekdays shortly after the regularly scheduled data collection, 150 boys were interviewed about their activities, including television viewing on the previous day. These boys were fourth and fifth graders, half of whom marked dummies in Wave V.

On the days covered by the interviews, the boys were asked to describe the current story lines of the shows they reported viewing. A comparison of actual and reported story lines was used to check the validity of self-reports. It was discovered that many of the boys who reported incorrect story lines for a program aired on the previous day were actually describing programs that they had seen a day or two eariier.

The results of this study were illuminating. On the average, viewing reports of respondents who had marked dummy programs were about 30 percent higher than the viewing validated for a comparable time period. Validated viewing for other respondents was only about five percent lower than in the questionnaire. Furthermore, although boys who marked dummies and had other signs of validity claimed to be very heavy viewers in the questionnaire reports, their validated viewing was only about eight percent higher than that for other children. The conclusion is clear: Invalid reporters substantially overestimated their actual television viewing. This produced a considerable upward bias in the television-aggression correlation in the sample as a whole, as these children also had above average aggression scores. A number of investigations were also made to determine the accuracy of the reports by the other children and it was found that they, as a group, gave very accurate reports.

"Invalid" Reports and Data Analysis

From these validity studies, the conclusion was drawn that a group of respondents had given exaggerated or otherwise inaccurate television reports. We considered adjusting for their errors by deflating the score of each child who reported dummy program viewing or in some other way showed signs of invalidity, but eventually decided that there could be no decision rule for how much to deflate these children's viewing scores. The validity tests were aggregate tests and there is reason to believe that there was variation in the amount of exaggeration between children who were invalid.

To deal with this problem, all central analyses were estimated twice. The first time invalid reporters were removed entirely. They were included the second time, and their television viewing scores were treated as if they were accurate. This made it possible to investigate the influence of invalidity on substantive results and provide lower and upper bound estimates, respectively, of television effects.

DATA COLLECTION PROBLEMS
IN MEASURING AGGRESSION

Because this study included children between 7 and 12 years of age, we did not focus on serious, violent, or criminal aggression. Although these are of the utmost concern to society, they are rare among preteens. In addition, we chose not to focus on aggressive attitudes or self-image or hostile feelings, all of which had been used as outcomes in earlier studies (Comstock and Rubinstein, 1972). We tried to concentrate instead on aggressive behavior of a sort that exists among elementary school children.

As this work was motivated by a desire to go beyond the evidence available in laboratory studies, it was decided at the onset to measure aggression in the context of daily life. Surrogate measures of hitting bobo dolls, punching padded boards, or pressing buttons that supposedly inflict noxious stimuli were rejected as inadequate.

PRETEST RESULTS

There was no previously validated measure of aggression in the literature that could be used to design this study. Four ways of measuring aggression were experimented with before we decided on the one ultimately used: self-reports, mother-reports, peer rating, and teacher ratings. Asking children directly about their aggressive behavior produced low estimates compared to peer ratings or teacher reports. This finding corroborated other research that had found underreporting in the self-reports of children, so this method was rejected.

The second method was to ask mothers to rate the aggressive behaviors of their children. This method produced unrealistically low estimates, even lower than those found in self-reports. The method was further flawed by the fact that the mothers of children who were rated most aggressive by other methods were least likely to cooperate.

The third method was a peer nomination procedure that had been used in a panel study of the television-aggression relationship later published by Eron et al. (1972). They reported good reliability and some evidence of concurrent validity in their study of elementary school children with this approach.

The fourth method was a teacher rating. In a pretest, teachers also filled out peer nomination questionnaires. Their nominations were consistent with those of the children. This result was replicated in the larger study, in which correlations between peer and teacher ratings ranged from .55 to .58 across waves. At the same time, peer nominations were more highly correlated with both self-reports and mother-reports than were teacher nominations. For this reason, peer nominations were selected as the primary data collection method.

This decision was made without direct validation. We considered launching an unobtrusive observation study of aggression in the classroom and on the playground, but eventually rejected this because it was not possible to make observations truly unobtrusive. We also feared that this data gathering might affect the behavior we wanted to measure, especially serious forms of aggression. Reliable coding of the observed data—distinguishing playful and aggressive punching, for example—would also be difficult, especially as observations generally would have to be from a distance. Finally, we were dissuaded by the logistical problems that are associated with observing children long enough to obtain stable ratings of aggression.

The most serious issue of validation that arises in peer nomination comes from the necessity of obtaining data from an entire classroom in order to score any one child's aggression. This meant that children could not be retained in the panel once their parents had moved to a new school unless their entire new class was enrolled in the study. This was impossible, so the study suffered serious panel attrition. This had serious implications for the external validity of the results, which is discussed later.

DATA COLLECTION PROCEDURES

Data collection included obtaining information about each child's behavior from all children in the classroom. Children were asked to identify members of the class who fit descriptions of behavior or other characteristics, for example, "who tried to hurt others by pushing or shoving?" The names or nicknames of all members of the class were obtained from the teacher and listed for each question; children drew lines through as many names as applied. Questions about aggression were interspersed with questions about prosocial behaviors and several neutral topics to avoid response set.

To make the task easier, names of boys and girls were listed separately in alphabetical order by first name for every question. Nicknames were used to ensure that the children would recognize whom we were asking about. Names were alphabetized to help children find the person they wanted to nominate. A response option, "no boys" or "no girls," was included at the bottom of each column to remove the ambiguity for coding created by a blank page. Randomizing the order of names on successive pages was considered, but this approach was rejected. Eron and his associates had found that position of names did not affect nominations. Our young respondents might have become confused had the name order been changed for each question. A consistent order was used and its effects were examined during the data analysis.

Although Eron and his associates had obtained satisfactory results with third graders, our pretest showed that children in the second grade and some in the third grade had difficulty completing the task. Special data collection procedures therefore were devised.

To aid children who were not good readers, all questions were read aloud twice in the class. Each question was printed on a different colored sheet of paper so monitors could see which questions were being answered by children at a particular time. This gave the administrator a way of knowing when to go on to the next question and it helped the monitors determine who was having difficulty completing the questions.

ADJUSTMENTS DURING DATA COLLECTION

In negotiating access to the schools the school administration had been promised that total interview time would be kept to a manageable length (under 45 minutes). This made it necessary to reduce the number of aggression items used in the original Eron study from ten to four. Each aggression item was measured both with and without reference to a specific time period. Thus, for each item there were two questions, one asking, for example, "who pushes or shoves?" and the other "Who happened to push and shove yesterday?" These measures were included to make sure that the aggression items asked without reference to time (which was the format used by Eron and his associates) measured actual aggressive acts that occurred in the recent past rather than a reputation that is only loosely tied to behavior.

Analysis of the aggression scores obtained in the first three Waves showed that the items lacking a time reference were strongly associated with recent behavior. Although the means for the "yesterday" items were consistently only about half as large as those for the items without time reference, they had high loadings on the strong single factor that emerged in a factor analysis of all eight items. Factor loadings ranged from .72 to .91 for the "yesterday" items and from .86 to .93 for the items without a time reference. On the strength of this evidence, we dropped the "yesterday" items after Wave III.

At the beginning of the study, school administrators in one of the two cities expressed concern about delinquent behavior questions. Questions about illegal activities were therefore avoided in the initial data collection. The four aggression indicators asked about hitting/punching, pushing/shoving, saying mean things, and lying. However, after the first two waves we were able to demonstrate that the children were not being disturbed by the data collection and so were given permission to include questions about more serious aggressive behaviors. Two additional items were included about stealing and damaging property.

Along with these changes in the aggression measure, it was necessary to make an important adjustment in the data collection procedures used for sixth graders in one city. During the study, this city switched sixth graders into a middle school system in which they rotated among different classes in the same way as high schools. This created difficulties for the peer nomination procedure, for these children no longer spent an entire day with the same classmates.

Although no way to correct for this change was discovered, we continued to administer the questionnaire in the sixth grade in this city, using members of homeroom classes as raters. Separate analyses of reliability of the aggression index in this subsample showed it to be equally reliable to scores based on elementary type classrooms. Therefore, no adjustment was necessary in the estimation of television effects.

ADJUSTMENT DURING DATA ANALYSIS

It wasn't until the data collection phase was complete that the validity of the aggression items was investigated. The study concentrated on the possibility that some classroom context factors might have influenced the quality of data collected. This could have happened in any number of ways, but those examined most closely were class size, position of name on the class list, gender composition of raters, absenteeism, and type of class situation (either children remain in a single classroom or rotate through a number of different classes with a homeroom at the beginning of the day). The total effect of these variables was statistically significant but quite small, accounting for between three percent and six percent of the variance across waves. These errors did not appear to distort the estimated influence of television violence on viewer aggression, and as a result, they were ignored in the data analysis.

Additional analyses were recently performed that suggest that the classroom context problems were dismissed too quickly. Kenny (1984) suggested that the peer nomination method might produce an artificially high estimate of the stability of aggression by introducing a "nomination bias." If this is true, then the size of the television coefficient may have been underestimated in our through-time analysis.

The type of bias Kenny envisions would exist were there a between-class difference in the probability that children with the same objective behavior would be nominated as aggressive because of differences in the nomination behaviors of those who rate them. To determine whether ignoring this possibility affected the results of this study some of the central analyses were repeated with a revised aggression score that takes out between-class variance. If Kenny's reasoning is correct, the regression coefficients linking television violence to within-class variance should be larger than those associated with between-class variance.

Our analysis failed to support Kenny's speculation, but it turned up a surprising result: Far from yielding stronger evidence for a television-aggression association, the analysis of within-class aggression showed the association to be smaller than in the original analysis. To give a rough idea of how much smaller, the average value of the coefficient b_2 in the model for boys

$$AG_t = b_0 + b_1 \, AG_{t-t'} + b_2 \, TV_{t-t'}$$

is .093 when the regular peer nomination measure is used and .070 when the within-class measure is used. Among girls the difference is much more striking: .065 with the regular measure and -.023 with the within-class measure.

These results show that the relationship between mean levels of television viewing and mean values of aggression between classes is stronger than the relationship between viewing and aggression within a class. A substantive interpretation would suggest that putting a child in the company of classmates who watch a lot of television will be more influential in leading that child to become aggressive than exposing the child him- or herself to violent television shows. A methodological artifact interpretation would be that children who watch a lot of violence on television perceive (and rate) their peers as more violent than those who watch less television violence. There is no way in the aggregate data to provide a critical test between these contending interpretations.

This issue has not yet been resolved, although it is possible to get some insight into it by returning to the behavior of individual classroom raters and seeing if their perceptions of the amount of aggression among their peers is associated with their own television viewing. As all three major panel studies of the television-aggression relationship among elementary school children have measured aggression in this way, the outcome of this analysis may well lead to a reinterpretation of the accumulated evidence.

DISCUSSION
EFFECTS ON VALIDITY

In assessing the extent to which the problems encountered in this study affected internal and external validity, three problems will be considered: invalidity in the television viewing measure, classroom context effects in the peer nomination aggression measure, and attrition of geographically mobile children. The last of these problems was exacerbated by the fact that the peer nomination method of assessing aggression was used, rendering it impossible to launch an effort to maintain the original panel through personal follow-ups.

Although the invalidity of some children in their reported television viewing was documented clearly, this problem appears the least serious of the three in affecting the validity of our results. Careful analysis of invalid reporting allowed us to adjust for it in data analysis. Between 70 percent and 80 percent of respondents in each wave gave viewing reports that were free of any signs of invalidity. It was possible to conduct all central analyses in this subsample of valid reporters and thereby avoid contaminating the estimates.

There remains the possibility that invalid reporters constitute a special subgroup of children among whom television violence has a particularly strong effect. If this is so, our failure to obtain accurate reports from these children would affect the external validity of results. However, evidence within the study itself argues against this possibility. A rather extensive analysis of the correlates of invalid reporting yielded strong evidence of age, race, IQ, and socioeconomic differences between the children whose data were invalid and those whose data were valid. There is no evidence of subgroup specifications of the television-aggression relationship among valid reporters who differ on any of these dimensions. On the basis of this evidence, it is unlikely that this relationship is stronger among invalid reporters than other children. This interpretation is corroborated by another analysis that was possible because nearly all of those who gave invalid reports in one wave gave valid reports in other waves. An analysis among those respondents at times they gave valid reports showed no TV effects.

The impact of data collection problems associated with the peer nomination aggression measure is potentially more serious. The television-aggression relationship, as noted, is different when estimated on the between-class and within-class components of variance, particularly among girls. It is not yet clear if this is because peer nominations are associated with the nominator's television viewing. This raises the possibility that television viewing affects perceptions of the aggressiveness of one's classmates. An influence of this sort would distort the peer nomination aggression measure and bias upward the estimated effect of television on aggression. This and other interpretations are currently under investigation.

The attrition problem, in our view, does not affect the validity of estimates. A rather extensive analysis of the characteristics of children who moved to new schools shows that their television viewing and aggression differ only minimally from those who remained. Furthermore, distinctive demographic characteristics of children who moved are not implicated in specifications of the television-aggression relationship among children who remained in the study.

Attrition did seriously reduce the power of our analysis. At the time the study was designed, statistical power did not loom large in our thinking. Up to that time the main evidence available on the relationship between television and aggression had been experimental and in this literature the effects of television were substantial. We anticipated that we would be looking for associations that were sufficiently large that they could be detected in samples of moderate size. As it happened, though, nonexperimental research in natural settings has subsequently shown that the relationship between television violence and viewer aggression is more modest in the field than in the laboratory. As a result, this analysis was plagued by an inability to interpret a pattern of small positive associations that were not significant by normal statistical criteria.

Increasing attrition over time also hampered efforts to investigate the possibility that the relationship between television and aggression varies as the time lag between the two variables changes. In our data the changing sample composition made it impossible to interpret changing associations across different lags in substantive terms, although at least one group of reviewers has ventured to make such an interpretation (Cook et al., 1983). Furthermore, because so many cases were lost when the full six waves of data were analyzed simultaneously, it was necessary to work with partially overlapping wave-pairs in the analysis. This made it impossible to develop a precise method of assessing the simultaneous significance of all the effect coefficients in the six waves because the 15 wave-pairs under investigation contained redundant information.

SUGGESTIONS FOR CORRECTIVE PROCEDURES

In retrospect, a number of decisions would now be made differently. Those that touch on the issues raised in the preceding pages are discussed in this section.

Television Viewing

Although the approach we took to assessing television viewing was the best one available, it bears a recognizably serious invalidity problem. This is especially true among very young children and poor readers. At the time the study was designed, we were so concerned about this that we abandoned the initial plan to include first-graders. In retrospect, it might have been better yet to have begun with a sample of third-graders.

There are at least two issues here. First, how will it be possible to study the developmental influence of television viewing in samples of younger children? Second, how can the problem of invalidity in samples of elementary school children?

To study very young children, it is impossible to use a self-report approach that requires reading and writing skills, so parent reports are the most promising approach. Singer and Singer (1981) claimed good success with parent reports in a study of preschoolers. However, the burdens placed on parents led to a high level of refusal. In the Singer and Singer study, for example, only about half the families originally approached agreed to participate in the study. As noted earlier in the description of our pretest results, the evidence is clear that parents of highly aggressive children are particularly likely to refuse participation in a diary study. On the basis of this evidence, parent reports still do not appear to provide adequate data for making broad inferences about the television-aggression relationship. Given this conclusion, representative studies of television viewing among preschoolers may well be unfeasible at this time.

There are better prospects for developing valid data collection procedures for school-aged children. Our work has shown that accurate data can be obtained with aided recall methods and that invalidity can be detected by including dummy programs and simultaneously aired programs in program checklists. On the basis of these facts, it might be possible to develop correction rules to adjust for retrospective recall bias in aided recall methods of this sort.

A correction would require a validation study of the sort conducted after Wave V of this study, but with a much larger sample. It would be necessary to obtain independent data on validated viewing and self-reported viewing and to estimate a regression equation in which the ratio of the latter to the former was predicted from information about dummy program reporting, simultaneously aired program reporting, extreme response reporting, and perhaps other indicators of invalidity. This equation would yield a formula for deflating each respondent's self-reported viewing score to arrive at an estimate of actual viewing. It probably would be necessary to include a larger sample of dummy programs and simultaneously aired program pairs in the lists than those used in this study if stable adjustments are to be obtained.

Aggression

There are two important data collection problems associated with the peer nomination method of assessing aggression. The first is that a child's aggression score can be influenced by characteristics of nominators independent of the child's actual behavior. In particular, if nominating behavior is linked to the television viewing of nominators, the television-aggression association will be systematically distorted. Evidence has already been presented which is consistent with the possibility that bias of this sort exists in our data.

The second problem is that a peer nomination method makes it necessary to administer questionnaires to an entire class in order to obtain an aggression rating for any one child in that class. Because of this problem, no attempt was made to retain in the panel children who moved to a new school. Nearly 450 children were lost to panel attrition because of the geographic mobility of their families, nearly 29 percent of the number who were eligible to remain in the study for the full three years. (Some of the older cohorts graduated out of the study at the end of the first of second year when they moved into junior high school. These children are not included in the above count or percentage calculation.) This is a very high percentage, magnified in part by the fact that one school in the sample was in an area that underwent urban renewal in the middle of the study and so suffered very high attrition. A self-report measure or teacher nomination measure would have reduced this attrition by following geographically mobile children.

It is possible that with more careful efforts a teacher nomination method could have been developed that would have yielded data equal to that obtained in the peer nominations. Had such a method been developed, it would have been possible to follow attritors more easily and avoid the introduction of classroom context bias.

Our optimism about developing a reliable teacher nomination method comes from the fact that peer and teacher nominations correlated between .54 and .58 across the six waves of data collection. These are extremely high correlations given that teacher nominations yielded four-point indexes as compared to the 0-400 indexes obtained from peer nominations. It is likely that the coarse categorization accounts for the smaller correlations of the teacher nominations with self-report and mother-report aggression scores than that found for the peer nominations.

The aggression measures were not directly validated. If an attempt is made to develop a teacher nomination method as a replacement for the peer nomination procedure, it would be useful for the two methods to be validated against some more objective standard. We considered doing a study of this sort by coding videotaped observations of classroom and playground interactions. With the massive advances that have been made in video technology in the past few years, an approach of this sort now strikes us as possible.

Uncertainties in coding some observations would invariably crop up, but these could be reduced by interviewing the children involved. Danger exists that cameras would be intrusive. But the presence of video cameras in banks and grocery stores has become so common that this difficulty could be overcome after an initial novelty period has passed. Furthermore, by combining observational coding with peer and teacher nominations it would be possible to resolve many of the interpretational uncertainties by referring to the other data sources.

REFERENCES

COMSTOCK, G. A. and E. A. RUBINSTEIN [eds.] (1972) "Television and social behavior: a technical report to the surgeon general's advisory committee on television and social behavior," vol. III in Television and Adolescent Aggressiveness. Rockville, MD: U.S. Department of Health, Education and Welfare.

COOK, T. D., D. A. KENZIERSKI, and S. V. THOMAS (1983) "The implicit assumptions of television research: an analysis of the 1982 NIMH report on television and behavior." Public Opinion Quarterly 47: 161-210.

ERON L. D., L. R. HUESMANN, M. M. LEFKOWITZ, and L. O. WALDER (1972) "Does television violence cause aggression?" American Psychologist 27: 253-263.

FESHBACH, S. and R. D. SINGER (1971) Television and Aggression: An Experimental Field Study. San Francisco: Jossey-Bass.

HUESMANN, L. R. (1984) "Television: ally or enemy?" Contemporary Psychology 29, 4: 283-285.

— — — (1982) "Television violence and aggressive behavior," pp. 126-137 in D. Pearl et al. (eds.) Television and Behavior: Ten Years of Scientific Progress and Implications for the Eighties, Volume II: Technical Reports. Rockville, MD: U.S. Department of Health and Human Services.

KENNY, D.A. (1984) "Television violence, aggression and the NBC study." Journal of Communication 34: 176-182.

MILAVSKY, J. R., R. C. KESSLER, H. H. STIPP, and W. S. RUBENS (1982) Television and Aggression: A Panel Study. New York: Academic Press.

SCHRAMM, W., J. LYLE, and E. B. PARKER (1961) Television in the Lives of Our Children. Stanford, CA: Stanford University Press.

SINGER, J. L. and D. G. SINGER (1981) Television, Imagination, and Aggression: A Study of Preschoolers. Hillsdale, NJ: Lawrence Erlbaum.

STIPP, H. H. (1975) Validity in Social Research: Measuring Children's Television Exposure. Ph.d. dissertation, Columbia University.

WELLS, W. D. (1973) Television and Aggression: Republication of an Experimental Field Study. Chicago: University of Chicago, Graduate School of Business. (unpublished)

PART II

Mounting Large-Scale Field Studies

A TALE OF TWO SURVEYS:
LESSONS FROM THE BEST AND WORST OF TIMES
IN PROGRAM EVALUATION

Ronald M. Andersen
Lu Ann Aday
Gretchen Voorhis Fleming

"It was the best of times, it was the worst of times, it was the age of wisdom, it was the age of foolishness" (Dickens, 1859). Charles Dickens's famous characterization of the late eighteenth century in England and France in *A Tale of Two Cities* seems an apt description of evaluation research today. It is the best of times for researchers because of the increasing salience and relevance of evaluation research to policy development and program implementation. It is the worst of times because of budgetary constraints and pressures to compromise the research process that attend evaluating real world experiments.

This chapter describes evaluations of two demonstration programs, the Community Hospital Group Practice Program (CHP) and the Municipal Health Services Program (MHSP) carried out by the Center for Health Ad-

AUTHORS' NOTE: An earlier draft of this article was presented at the NSF Conference on Improving Data Collection in Program Evaluation, March 29-31, 1984, Amherst Massachusetts.

ministration Studies (CHAS) over the past six years. Both are considered in our efforts to abstract lessons learned about data collection in program evaluation for a number of reasons. These two evaluations have jointly consumed a large majority of CHAS's research effort for a substantial period of time. Contrasting their similarities and differences aids us in drawing implications. Two observations, although not ideal, are certainly better for external validity than a single case study. Finally, although largely concurrent, CHP started more than a year before MHSP. Some effort was made to apply lessons learned from CHP to MHSP.

In the following sections we will consider the demonstrations and the designs to evaluate them, data limitations and our efforts to deal with these problems, the validity of the results, and the "ideal" design to address remaining data limitations.

DEMONSTRATIONS

The CHP program was a product of the mid-1970s when access to medical care was still the primary concern in health services delivery (Aday et al., 1978). It was sponsored by the Robert Wood Johnson Foundation (RWJF), the purpose of which was to stimulate the development of primary care group practices in community hospitals. These practices were expected to relieve community access problems and promote a type of medical practice emphasizing prevention, continuity, and ambulatory services while deemphasizing inpatient and emergency room care. Ultimately, 53 programs were funded for planning and start-up costs to a maximum of $500,000 each for a period of six years (Aday et al., 1984a).

The MHSP program was conceived in the late 1970s, when emphasis was shifting from access to controlling costs of medical care. Again, RWJF was a major sponsor, but was joined by the Health Care Financing Administration (HCFA) (Andersen et al., 1982).

In 1977, RWJF requested proposals for MHSP from the 50 largest cities in the country to develop a plan for a network of at least three clinics. Each clinic would centralize in one community location the existing categorical programs of public health departments and primary medical services which are traditionally available through the municipal hospital outpatient departments. Grants of approximately $3 million per city covering six-year periods were given to five cities: Baltimore, Cincinnati, Milwaukee, St. Louis, and San Jose.

Many of the purposes of MHSP were the same as those for CHP. In addition, HCFA provided a waiver of certain Medicare regulations for patients going to these primary care centers. It promised cost-based rather than fee-for-service reimbursement to the new clinics, eliminated patient payments of coinsurance and deductibles under Medicare, and added services to Medicare coverage including prescribed drugs, preventive services, dental care, dentures, and one-half the cost of eye glasses. Similar waivers also were provided in some locations for Medicaid patients. The hope was that MHSP would reduce patients' use of expensive hospital inpatient and outpatient services so that, even though more services are covered under the waiver, total costs and HCFA's overall costs actually would be reduced.

EVALUATION

Both CHP and MHSP had two-pronged evaluations. For CHP, RWJF provided grants to the University of Washington to study the organizational and financial viability of the group practices and to CHAS to evaluate the groups' impact on access to medical care in the communities they were intended to serve. In the case of MHSP, the Conservation of Human Resources Center of Columbia University had a grant from RWJF to document changes in the organization and financing of municipal health services that were necessary for the implementation and maintenance of the MHSP in each municipality. In addition, CHAS had a contract from HCFA (supplemented later by a grant from RWJF) to evaluate the impact of the MHSP on the access to and expenditures for medical care by persons in neighborhoods served by the program. This chapter focuses on the social survey-based evaluations done by CHAS in each demonstration.

DESIGN

The originally proposed design was similar in both evaluations (Aday et al., 1978; Andersen et al., 1982). It was essentially a before-and-after measurement with a nonequivalent control group replicated across a number of sites. Service areas were to be defined for each primary care practice to be evaluated. Social surveys would be undertaken in each service area before the primary care practice became operational. A follow-up survey two years later would document changes in the health care experience of those who became users of CHP and MHSP practices versus those who did not. Various statistical controls would be introduced in an effort to reduce some of the threats to internal validity, such as patient selection into the CHP and MHSP programs. We also expected to pool data across sites for some analyses to increase degrees of freedom and ability to detect program effects.

The initial CHP design called for a sample from the universe of hospital-sponsored group practices as sufficient resources were not available to study them all. The MHSP design included surveys in all five cities. However, there were multiple primary care centers within each city (three or more). Limited resources necessitated the selection of one site for evaluation within each city. The selection was not random, but was based on the start-up time of the site, ease of defining a service area, and potential of the site to affect the access measures used in the study.

DATA SOURCES

Both surveys included dual-frame sampling of community residents and program patients (Aday et al., 1984a; Fleming and Andersen, 1984). The field work was carried out by Chilton Research Services. In the 12 sites selected for CHP, multistage area probability samples of households were taken in each site. A randomly selected adult was chosen for face-to-face interviews within each household. In addition, if children (17 and under) resided in the household, the most knowledgeable adult provided information concerning a randomly selected child. The second part of the frame for CHP came from lists of CHP patients living within the service area of the CHP group practices. These patients were interviewed fact-to-face in their own homes. The interviews averaged about 35 minutes.

Telephone interviewing was chosen in the MHSP study primarily to reduce data collection costs. Random-digit dialing was employed for the community survey including screening questions on residence to exclude residences outside the service area. In addition, telephone numbers of MHSP patients were secured from sites to increase the yield of MHSP users. The interviews in MHSP were for the entire family, conducted with the most knowledgeable family member. The average interview time was about 50 minutes.

The target for CHP was to complete 850 to 900 individual interviews at each site for each time period. The adjusted response rates for the follow-up community surveys varied from 72 percent to 90 percent and averaged 82 percent. The patient samples yielded response rates from 65 percent to 93 percent and averaged 81 percent.

The goal for the MHSP survey in the "before" period was to complete 1200 family interviews in each site. Due to higher than anticipated costs, the sample sizes were reduced in the follow-up surveys to 1000 completed interviews per site. The completion rates in follow-up surveys varied from 69 percent to 81 percent with an average of 73 percent. In addition to the social surveys, a number of other data sources were employed in the MHSP evaluation. These included medical care use and payment records from Medicare and Medicaid as well as records from MHSP sites and some municipal hospitals.

DATA LIMITATIONS AND RESEARCHERS' RESPONSES

Tables 5.1 to 5.3 catalog some potentially serious data limitations and how we attempted to deal with them. The limitations are listed chronologically, according to whether they were anticipated in the planning stage (Table 5.1), uncovered during the study implementation (Table 5.2), or identified in data analysis (Table 5.3). Contrasts are also made between data limitations and responding strategies in CHP and MHSP. Time and space limitations precluded discussion of all the limitations and responses in these charts. We will mention briefly issues which appear least self-explanatory or require elaborations. All of the issues are treated in more detail in the final reports (Aday et al., 1984a; Fleming and Andersen, 1984).

ANTICIPATED LIMITATIONS

Documenting Successful Sites—CHP (3)

The funders and administrators of CHP were particularly anxious to use the evaluation resources to document the experiences of those hospitals expected to organize effective and financially viable group practices and have a measurable impact on access to medical care in the community. They were less anxious to expend evaluation resources on hospitals they considered less likely to succeed. The evaluators argued that the funders' strategy would seriously impair the external validity of the evaluation. The compromise was to stratify the CHP grantees according to CHP program administrators' estimates of probability of success (most, in between, least). The strata then were sampled with differential probabilities of selection. Those judged most likely to succeed were over sampled. Consequently, more of the sites expected to be "stars" were documented, while those judged to have less potential were still represented in the sample.

TABLE 5.1

Data Limitations Anticipated in Planning and Researchers' Responses

Limitation	Response
CHP	
Year recall period*	Validity check, comparison with external sources
High cost of collection	Sampling the sites
Documenting "successful" sites	Differential sampling according to estimated success
Missing data	Imputation program
Limited number of observations	Supplemental family questionnaire
Identifying future users of CHP in before survey*	Seek predictive information on potential users and drop full panel design
MHSP	
Collecting medical care cost information	Estimation program, use of record data sources
High cost of collection	Telephone interview and selection of single site within city
Reaching inner city residents	Telephone interview, incentive payments
Decay in large family interviews	Limit to five family members for whom detailed data are collected
Limited number of observations	Family interview
Limited phone coverage in service areas	Effort to adjust weights for nonphone coverage
Separating organizational effect from waiver effect	Using price data to estimate waiver effect

*Similar limitation for MHSP

Sample Size—CHP (5) and MHSP (5)

There was initial concern in both evaluations about the power to detect certain kinds of program effects such as impact on hospitalization. A random sample of individuals within households was used in CHP, supplemented by a short family questionnaire. The latter gathered limited information including hospital experience about all family members, increasing the degrees of freedom for the hospital-use analysis. In MHSP, the decision was made to use a family questionnaire to maximize the data collected. This strategy provided complete information on all family members, allowing more detailed analyses on hospital use than was possible in CHP.

Identifying Potential Users—CHP (6)

The plan for a regular panel survey with before and after measures had to be revised in both evaluations. Future program users could not be identified readily in the before survey. Furthermore, the program penetration rates in most sites were not expected to yield sufficient program users in the follow-up survey to allow user/nonuser comparisons. The revised plan included oversampling of households (CHP) and telephone numbers (MHSP) from the initial surveys in the follow-up surveys, but no effort to identify the same individuals for interviews in both surveys.

Use and Evaluation of Information—MHSP (1, 7)

A major purpose of the MHSP evaluation is determining the impact of the MHSP organization and the HCFA waiver on expenditures for medical care. Survey respondents have difficulty reporting some medical care expenditures, particularly components paid for by third parties. To increase the validity of expenditure information, we relied heavily on expenditure estimation programs similar to those used in earlier studies that appear to have some validity (Andersen et al., 1979). The costs of services received by respondents are estimated using external sources to provide medical care prices. Sources include the American Hospital Association, the American Medical Association, the Bureau of Community Health Services, the National Center for Health Services Research, and public facilities in the cities under study. An additional approach to cope with the limitation of survey expenditure data was to do supplementary expenditure analysis using Medicare and Medicaid records.

Method of Data Collection—MHSP (2, 3)

Telephone interviewing was selected in MHSP with the expectation that one-third of the data collection costs of face-to-face interviewing could be saved. Furthermore, we judged telephones to have a particular advantage in inner city areas where interviewers are less willing to go and respondents less likely to open their doors. The fact that phone coverage in these areas may be limited is a potential disadvantage. To compensate for limited phone coverage, we attempted to adjust the sample weights using comparisons in other studies of respondents with a phone and those without.

LIMITATIONS DISCOVERED DURING IMPLEMENTATION

Defining Survey Groups—CHP(1) and MHSP (5)

A requirement of the grant proposal from hospitals was that service areas for the hospital-sponsored group practices be defined. As these service areas were crucial to the survey design, we attempted to validate them. The pro-

TABLE 5.2
Data Limitations Discovered during Implementation
and Researchers' Responses

Limitation	Response
	CHP
Difficulties of sites in defining services areas	Special patient origin surveys and questionnaires used
Problems locating persons on patient list	Additional resources in follow-up and procedures for estimating characteristics of those not located
Low response rates in some sites	Add incentive payments for respondents and interviewers, use telephone follow-up
Sites closing or changing locations	Substitution of other sites
	MHSP
Low yield of MHSP users from site phone list	More emphasis on directional and pooled analysis
Low response rates	Additional call backs, intensive effort on sample of nonrespondents
Language problems	Special training of interviewers speaking several languages
Expansive field procedures	Reduced sample size and additional funding from RWJF
Some service areas defined too narrowly	Service areas adjusted for follow-up survey
Difficulties in obtaining information from secondary sources	Reduce analysis scope, emphasize data sources most readily available

posal definitions did not generally appear to be reliable. Additional information from administrators and providers at the group practice, as well as patient-origin studies conducted on site, were necessary to define the appropriate service area. Even with this additional effort, validation before the follow-up survey occasionally showed a considerable discrepancy between the defined service area and the actual location of patients' residences. In such cases, the service areas were adjusted for the follow-up survey. There were similar experiences in the MHSP evaluation.

Defining Service Area—CHP (4)

In one instance, a hospital initially selected for the evaluation made a decision to change the location of its group practice. The uncertainty about defining the relevant service area led to the decision to drop the site from the study. In a second case, a hospital in the evaluation dropped out of the CHP program shortly after the first survey. The evaluation team argued that the follow-up survey should be conducted as part of a "natural experiment" to document the impact of a site closing on community access. The funders argued that evaluation monies should not be spent on an explicit failure. In this case, the funders prevailed. No follow-up survey was done in the service area of the closed group practice. Rather, another hospital, which had a successful track record along with several satellite group practices in operation or planned, was added to the evaluation. This nonrandomly selected observation was classified by the evaluation as a separate case study; yet in many parts of the analyses, this nonrandomly selected site was not distinguished from the other sites.

Low Yield of Users—MHSP (1)

The list of phone numbers of patients provided by the MHSP facilities generally did not yield as many MHSP users as we had hoped. Some numbers were inaccurate; respondents might not recall or admit any family member visiting the MHSP facility; or while visiting the facility, family members reported other regular sources of care. The relatively low yield of users caused us to rely more in the analysis on directional findings (when there was not sufficient power to detect significant differences). We also relied more on summary or pooled measures, even though there was considerable heterogeneity among MHSP facilities.

Limited Availability of Preexistent Data—MHSP (6)

An expected strength of the MHSP analysis was the multiple data sources. The social surveys were to be supplemented by Medicare and Medicaid reports and patient records from municipal hospitals and MHSP facilities. Although some of the sources were very cooperative, others were not. The evaluation effort had low priority compared to administrative activities. Also, sources that perceived little direct benefit to themselves from MHSP were slow to cooperate. After considerable negotiation and expenditure of time and energy, we decided to cut our losses. The scope of the secondary analysis was substantially reduced.

LIMITATIONS IDENTIFIED IN DATA ANALYSIS

Determining Sources of Care—CHP (1)

Although the panel analysis design was dropped, the before and after samples were correlated in both evaluations because households and phone numbers used in the before samples were disproportionately represented in the follow-up samples. The most direct way of finding out where program users received care prior to the demonstration was to examine where the joiners of the program facilities previously received care. We used matching

TABLE 5.3
Data Limitations Identified in Data Analysis
and Researchers' Responses

Limitation	Response
CHP	
Determining prior sources of care	Developing matching program for limited panel analysis
Separating selection from program effects	Using multiple analytic approaches including synthetically constructed experimental and control groups from initial survey
Heterogeneity of programs*	Rely primarily on site-level analysis rather than pooled analysis
Difficulty in generalizing to programs not in sample	Effort to compare sampled to non-sampled sites on known characteristics and estimate unknown characteristics for nonsample sites
MHSP	
Separating selection from program effects	Using multiple analytic approaches including two stage multivariate analysis for isolating selection
Limited number of MHSP users from selected site in follow-up survey	Include users from nonselected m MHSP sites sampled sites
Generalizing to city sites not included in program	Compare selected sites to other sites on known characteristics and estimate unknown characteristics on nonsampled sites

*Similar limitation for MHSP

programs that included as criteria name, sex, and age to find people interviewed in both surveys.

Separating Selection from Program Effects—CHP (2) and MHSP (1)

Separating selection effects from program effects emerged as the main analytic challenge. Our response in both evaluations was to explore a wide variety of options (Berk, 1983; Heckman, 1979; Rubin, 1973). In each evaluation multiple strategies were selected. Our hope was that the different analytic approaches would yield similar conclusions about selection and program effects, thus increasing confidence in the main conclusions of the study. Fortunately, that was generally the case with CHP (Aday et al., 1984a, 1984b). The final results are still pending in MHSP, but the preliminary findings also suggest similarity of conclusions based on different approaches.

Heterogeneity of Programs—CHP (3)

Originally, we had hoped to pool data from the service areas in both studies. This strategy served to increase the degree of freedom and provide explicit summary measures of the overall program effect. As we proceeded in the data collection and analysis, it became clear that neither MHSP nor CHP was a homogeneous program. The organization and delivery of services varied considerably from setting to setting and the populations served were very different. Consequently, we relied much more than originally planned on comparisons of program users and nonusers within each site in our analysis. The results suggest distinct differences, but definite patterns and similarities also emerged. In subsequent secondary analyses, we hope to return to more pooled analyses taking into account when possible the heterogeneous aspects that our primary analysis uncovered.

VALIDITY OF RESULTS

To what extent do the data limitations affect the validity of conclusions? We will consider selected issues related to construct, statistical conclusion, and internal and external validity (Cook and Campbell, 1979). First, however, what are the most important conclusions resulting from the CHP and MHSP evaluations?

The CHP impact on access to medical care generally appears to be positive but limited—possibly because the communities served were not particularly disadvantaged ones to begin with (Aday et al., 1984b; Loevy et al., 1983). CHP users tend to have shorter waiting times and be more satisfied with the convenience of care. CHP users are more likely to see a physician although they do not average more visits per year. They also tend to have few visits to hospital outpatient departments and emergency rooms. In most communities, hospital inpatient use appears lower for CHP users. The differences in hospital use at the community level generally appear substantively important but not statistically significant.

The MHSP program also appears to have accomplished some of its purposes, but, again, access problems in central city areas served may have existed to a lesser extent than had been assumed (Fleming and Andersen, 1984). The physician visit patterns for MHSP users generally were not different from the comparison groups. MHSP users did use outpatient departments and emergency rooms relatively less than the community as a whole. The hospital inpatient use rate appeared lower for MHSP. Here, too, the significance of the differences is questionable due to the limited number of MHSP user observations. Although access seems reasonably good for MHSP users, they do not appear particularly well-satisfied, especially with the convenience of their care. Per person cost of care for MHSP users does appear to be generally lower both in total and for Medicare, but not for Medicaid. The differences found are primarily attributed to lower hospital inpatient use by MHSP users.

CONSTRUCT VALIDITY

Construct validity is a complex topic, but for our purposes relates to the extent to which the data collected allows us to measure the important topics we wish to measure. Probably the biggest limitation relates to the lack of cost data in the CHP evaluation. With the increasing emphasis on efficiency, competition, and cost constraint in medical care, policy-relevant evaluations of access must explicitly consider the trade-offs with cost. Although we have attempted to employ use measures as proxies for cost or resource consumption, the evaluation would be more salient today with more expenditure data.

Another issue of construct validity in both evaluations concerns the previous medical care experience of CHP and MHSP patients. As both demonstrations progressed, increasing interest developed on the part of funders, providers, and evaluators concerning whether the program facilities were serving previously needy people and where the program patients received care before the programs began. We collected limited data on these issues directly in the survey. Our panel analysis of people joining the sites only partially answers the question.

STATISTICAL CONCLUSION VALIDITY

A major issue in statistical conclusion validity is the impact of random error on the certainty that the observed differences are "real" differences. This is a particular limitation in both the CHP and MHSP evaluations of program impact on hospital utilization. A pressing policy question is whether we can have good medical care access while containing medical care costs. Possibly the greatest potential for achieving this ideal situation is by emphasizing primary ambulatory services and reducing costly inpatient services. Both CHP and MHSP suggest reduced hospital utilization. However, we lack sufficient observations, given the magnitude of the differences, to have the certainty we would like. Statistical conclusion validity poses a special problem for hospital use because of the large proportion of persons that have no inpatient services in a given year. Furthermore, the distribution of hospital expenditures is skewed to a great extent with relatively few outliers accounting for a sizeable proportion of all hospital expenses. Despite the efforts made to deal with this issue, the power we have to detect differences is much less than optimal.

INTERNAL VALIDITY

As the CHP and MHSP evaluations are not inherently strong designs, numerous threats to internal validity are possible. We would hope that the responses previously discussed have taken into account many of the rival hypotheses that might account for the observed results other than the program itself. Two threats to internal validity are of particular concern in both CHP and MHSP. The first problem is one of selection, resulting from a lack of random assignment of patients to the demonstration practices. The second problem deals with diffusion of treatment, which would be a threat even with random assignment.

Problems in diffusion of treatment arise from the uncontrolled or unknown timing of beginning the experimental programs and lack of control over who is exposed to these programs or something like them. These problems arise for a number of reasons. In some instances, it is not clear just when the program started. MHSPs sometimes are made up of some components that previously existed, such as a maternal or child health unit or outpatient department. It is sometimes unclear as well just when to classify a person as a user, as there is no specific enrollment in either CHP or MHSP. Some patients use multiple sources of care, including both demonstration sites and other sources. Finally, there is a general trend toward organized units delivering ambulatory care of the CHP and MHSP variety. These HMOs, primary care centers, community health centers, and larger private group practices represent a diffusion over time, making it more difficult to sort out CHP and MHSP effects.

Selection is a continuing major concern when examining the impact of the organization and financing of medical care on use and expenditures. The fundamental question is whether we observe differences caused by organization and financing per se, or whether certain kinds of people who are predisposed toward certain use and expenditure patterns are attracted also to certain kinds of medical care programs.

The most important selection factors are self-perceived and provider-determined health status and need for medical care. There is some evidence that CHP users perceived themselves to be sicker than others in the community, but this was not true of the MHSP users. In any case, primary attention focused in both evaluations on controlling for these possible differences between site users and comparison groups. Even so, the conclusions still can be challenged on the grounds that important unobserved differences between site users and comparison groups remain, which account for observed utilization and expenditure differences.

EXTERNAL VALIDITY

Both CHP and MHSP were conceived as national demonstrations. The goal of these demonstrations was for government, other third-party payers, and providers to identify successful elements of the program for implementing other large-scale programs and programs run by individual provider organizations throughout the nation. Clearly, the external validity of the demonstrations—the extent to which the results can be generalized to other settings—is an important ingredient in both CHP and MHSP evaluations.

Because external validity is important, we must note the limitations which exist in the generalization of both evaluations. In CHP, the assessment is limited to those hospitals which applied for the grant and were subsequently judged by the CHP Advisory Board to represent a service area with a need for primary care and to have the organizational and financial capability to make the group practice a success. Furthermore, only 12 of the 53 funded hospitals were included in our evaluation. Finally, for those hospitals with multiple CHP facilities, only one facility was chosen. Similarly, in MHSP, the demonstration was limited to those large metropolitan areas which responded with a grant proposal and, from these, the five judged most capable of carrying through on the MHSP purpose. All of the selected MHSP cities had multiple health centers, yet our evaluation was restricted to one of these. Although comparisons of study facilities with other hospitals and cities suggest that the findings have relevance for a broad cross section, the nonrandom selection of study facilities judged most likely to be successful and the limited number evaluated necessitate that generalizations be made with caution.

"IDEAL" EVALUATIONS

In the "best of times" how might one deal with the data collection limitations encountered in these two evaluations? How could the various types of validity be improved? Under "ideal" circumstances the evaluator does not have resource or time constraints, can directly influence the planning and implementation of the demonstration project, and determines the evaluation design and data collection.

CONSTRUCT VALIDITY

First, with the benefit of hindsight, the evaluators of the CHP might have prevailed upon the funders and administrators of the demonstration to support the collection of cost data and possibly more information on the quality of care. This could have increased the current relevance of the evaluation by balancing improved access with cost control objectives and the benefits to the patients of the services being delivered. Cost data were collected in the subsequent MHSP evaluation, making such evaluations possible.

In both evaluations some data should have been collected on people's previous sources of medical care. Such collection is feasible and would have enhanced evaluations of program success in serving previously needy people.

STATISTICAL CONCLUSION VALIDITY

Larger samples would have increased our power to detect program effects. Detecting differences in hospital utilization was a particular problem. It appears that the programs reduced hospital utilization in both evaluations. However, because of the importance of this issue, we would have preferred greater certainty that the differences existed and that we could precisely estimate the magnitudes. One approach might have been to screen samples to increase inpatient users. However, the sampling designs already were sufficiently complex, suggesting that additional components might have introduced major operational problems.

INTERNAL VALIDITY

Internal validity would certainly be improved in both evaluations through random assignment of patients to the programs and control groups. One must question whether, given the nature of both the CHP and MHSP programs, such assignment is feasible, even under ideal circumstances. The programs were voluntary. Even after an initial visit to a program facility, patients could choose to go to another source of care during the study period. It is not clear how to take advantage of randomization at the individual patient level without radical change in the program structure and purpose.

Randomization at the facility level appears more feasible. It is conceivable that some hospitals which applied to CHP and were judged acceptable might not be funded on a random basis. An incentive to participate in the project might be funding in a subsequent time period. These hospitals then could serve as controls. It is also possible that certain hospitals with multiple site facilities could initially have received some funding while others did not based on some random selection basis. Key issues in either case would be defining service areas and patient populations for the comparisons. The key comparisons would be based on service area rates for those with a CHP facility versus those without. This design would require that the experimental CHP practices have sufficient penetration rates (i.e., that there are enough CHP users) in the service area by the time of the follow-up surveys to make possible the detection of program effects at the community level.

Similarly, in MHSP it is conceivable that random allocation of accepted cities or of primary care facilities within cities could be made to experimental and control groups. The process of detecting program effects would be the same as in CHP.

EXTERNAL VALIDITY

Data collection approaches in both CHP and MHSP limit generalizations that can be made. These limitations relate to generalizations about the impact of the programs in all demonstration locations and to generalizations for the broader universes of hospitals and municipalities that might attempt programs similar to CHP and MHSP.

Only one-fifth of the CHP demonstration hospitals were included in the community survey evaluation. If more or all of the 53 hospitals had been included, much more could be said about the overall impact of the program and the kinds of hospital-sponsored group practices that are most likely to improve access to medical care. Although efforts were made to select 11 or 12 hospitals to maximize the ability to generalize, we still are hampered by this limited number of observations.

MHSP municipalities started at least four ambulatory care centers. Even within cities, these centers varied considerably in their organization and the populations they served. If we were able to include more than one location in each city in the evaluation, our ability to describe the overall MHSP impact would be enhanced considerably.

Generalizations to a larger population of hospitals and municipalities is limited considerably by the selection process for the demonstrations. For both CHP and MHSP, we only have data on the kinds of hospitals and municipalities eligible for the programs, writing grant proposals, and receiving awards. If any replication is expected to follow a similar selection process, the limitation is not such a major one. However, it seems unlikely that the complex selection process will (or possibly could) be followed extensively. Therefore, in the ideal evaluator's world it would be beneficial for purposes of external validity to have documented program experiences for sites representing the largely excluded populations. It would be particularly useful to include in the demonstration those hospitals and municipalities which expressed interest in the programs but were not funded. We know that, among grant winners, the ability of program administrators and consultants to predict which sites would be the most successful was somewhat limited. It would be useful for external validity to have some knowledge about how potential applicants excluded by the selection criteria would fare with program support.

CONCLUSIONS

Is it more than an exercise in fantasy to consider ideal circumstances to improve data collection in evaluation research? The remedies we have suggested generally imply the need for more money, time, and/or intrusive evaluator involvement. In fact, CHAS received between $2.5 and $3 million dollars and six years to do each evaluation. These figures do not include the budgets for the other evaluation teams or costs of administering and carrying out the demonstrations. General predictions seem to be that evaluators may expect less rather than more resources in the future. Finally, funders and administrators might well argue that it is naive in large national demonstrations for evaluators to expect control of scheduling or selection criteria or random assignments of subjects.

Indeed, the best of all possible evaluator worlds may not be possible. But a good case can be made that stronger evaluations are feasible, even to the extent of random assignment, and that they benefit other interested parties as well as evaluators (Riecken and Boruch, 1974). Furthermore, although the costs of strong evaluations in health care delivery may appear large, the costs of not using evaluations clearly have proven to be much higher.

REFERENCES

ADAY, L. A., R. M. ANDERSEN, S. S. LOEVY, and B. KREMER (1984a) Hospital Sponsored Primary Care: A Study of Impact on Community Access. Ann Arbor, MI: Health Administration Press.

— — — (1984b) "Hospital sponsored primary care: impact on patient access." American Journal of Public Health 74: 792-798.

ADAY, L. A., R. M. ANDERSEN, G. V. FLEMING, G. CHIU, V. DAUGHETY, and M. J. BANKS (1978) "Overview of a design to evaluate the impact of community hospital sponsored primary care group practices." Medical Group Management 25 (September/October): 42-46.

ANDERSEN, R. M., J. KASPER, and M. R. FRANKEL (1979) Total Survey Error: Application to Improve Health Surveys. San Francisco: Jossey-Bass.

ANDERSEN, R. M., G. V. FLEMING, L. A. ADAY, S. Z. LEWIS, L. A. BERTSCHE, and M. J. BANKS (1982) "Evaluating the Municipal Health Services Program." Annals of the New York Academy of Sciences 387: 91-109.

BERK, R. (1983) "An introduction to sample selection bias in sociological data." American Sociological Review 48 (June): 386-398.

COOK, T. D. and D. T. CAMPBELL (1979) Quasi-Experimentation: Design and Analysis Issues for Field Settings. Chicago: Rand McNally.

DICKENS, C. (1859) A Tale of Two Cities. London: Hatton and Cleaver.

FLEMING, G. V. and R. ANDERSEN (eds.) (1984) Improving Medical Care Access While Reducing Costs? Results from the Municipal Health Services Program. Chicago: Center for Health Administration Studies.

HECKMAN, J. J. (1979) "Sample selection bias as a specification error." Econometrica 45: 153-161.

LOEVY, S. S., R. ANDERSEN, and L. A. ADAY (1983) "Potential patients and loyal users: access to care in community hospital sponsored group practices." Journal of Ambulatory Care Management 6 (November): 43-57.

RIECKEN, H. W. and R. F. BORUCH (eds.) (1974) Social Experimentation: A Method for Planning and Evaluating Social Intervention. New York: Academic Press.

RUBIN, D.B. (1973) "The use of matched sampling and regression adjustment to remove bias in observational studies." Biometrica 29 (March): 185-203.

FIELD SAMPLING PROBLEMS IN DATA COLLECTION FOR EVALUATION RESEARCH

Sandra H. Berry

Most data collection carried out today is intended to provide information about the thoughts and behavior of a particular group of people. As these groups typically are quite large, most research requires sampling a representative subset of the group and querying them. Error in estimates obtained through the use of sampling can be calculated and taken into account when they are applied to the population as a whole. The use of such sampling is as common in evaluation research as it is in political polling or academic surveys.

Theoretically, the use of these well-accepted procedures requires that an unbiased sample of the population of interest be drawn, based on a complete and accurate sample frame, and that data be obtained from each element in the sample. Attempting to come as close as possible to the theoretical ideal of these requirements has led to extensive development of procedures for drawing national and small area probability samples of households for personal interviews and, more recently, of telephone numbers for telephone surveys. There also are well-established techniques for selecting samples from lists. Procedures for obtaining the cooperation of selected sample subjects are not

Reprinted by permission of the Rand Corporation.

AUTHOR'S NOTE: My thanks to Diane Schoeff for sharing field experience and to Jeffrey Garfinkle for programming assistance.

as clearly defined, but there is considerable research and a large amount of lore dealing with these problems. Although certain aspects of these procedures remain problematic, the resulting samples usually are considered to be sufficiently unbiased to make them useful for analytic purposes.

The same basic procedures of establishing a complete and accurate sample frame, drawing a sample from it, and obtaining data from the selected subjects are used extensively in evaluation research. But the problems encountered frequently are more idiosyncratic than those encountered in general population surveys. Typically, the sample consists of the beneficiaries of the program being evaluated, and for comparison purposes it may include others who serve as "controls." In many cases the limits of these populations are difficult to define. (For example, how long must someone be receiving benefits in order to be considered part of the enrolled group?) In other cases the populations are not only hard to define, but also difficult to locate, such as eligible nonrecipients who might serve as controls for an enrolled group. However challenging, these problems lend themselves to solution, given clear analytic plans and sufficient resources.

Other problems of carrying out a sample design are more difficult for the researchers because they contain elements that are beyond their control. This chapter concerns situations in which significant portions of the sampling operations (as distinguished from the design of the sample) are in the hands of someone other than the researcher. This may be for reasons of cost. For instance, it may be simply too expensive for the researchers to travel to the locations of the sample to oversee selection. In another situation, the sample may not exist in one place at one time, necessitating that it be recruited at a slow rate over a long period of time. In the latter case, it would be unfeasible for the researcher staff to do it. In other situations, the researcher may be unable to control sampling for reasons of confidentiality. For instance, in certain cases the researcher cannot gain access to the names and addresses of potential respondents until they have already consented to participate in the research.

This chapter examines several aspects of problems that arise when the actual tasks of selecting and obtaining data from samples were not carried out by researchers directly. These tasks include the selection of samples from lists, recruitment of sample subjects by mail or in person, and carrying out a randomized treatment. Having these research tasks carried out by nonresearchers may have serious negative effects on the quality of the performance of the tasks and potentially serious effects on the data collected. Focusing on three different studies, this study addresses two questions: (1) how well was the sampling task carried out by the nonresearchers? and (2) what effect, if any, did the quality of their performance of these tasks have on the data?

PROBLEMS IN WORK DONE BY NONRESEARCHERS

It may not be obvious why having nonresearchers perform research tasks is any problem at all. The task could be specified completely to a nonresearcher, compensated for his or her time. The researcher, on the other hand, could instruct the nonresearchers, solve any problems that arise, and check the quality of the results. In theory, this line of action should work. In practice, however, several problems arise: The nonresearcher may not have the time, resources, or necessary skills to do the work, or may be unmotivated to do it properly or at all.

Nonresearchers chosen to perform research tasks may be employees of the institution or program being evaluated. Alternatively, they may be employees of agencies or businesses that are not being evaluated, but are in contact with the subjects of the study. In either case, these people simply may be too busy during normal working hours to give adequate time to the research tasks, even when they are compensated. Doing the work after hours may not be possible for administrative reasons or because staff are not available. They may lack resources, such as typing support or access to telephones for follow-up contacts, or they may lack the necessary skills. (For example, they may not be accustomed to highly structured sorting and counting or may feel uncomfortable asking subjects to participate. See Weiss, 1975; Haug, 1971.) If nonresearchers are employees of the organization being evaluated, they may view the evaluation as irrelevant or threatening and give the extra tasks low priority; they may attempt to sabotage them or manipulate the outcome (Form, 1971; Borgatta, 1971; Haug, 1971; Weiss, 1975). Even if they are not directly concerned with the outcome of the evaluation or are favorable toward its goals, they simply may view participation in the research as a low priority compared with their usual tasks. In this case, the researcher operates as a "guest," who can make limited demands based on a "fund of good will" that easily can be exhausted (Form, 1971: 19). In short, researchers' control over the way in which nonresearchers carry out these tasks is imperfect, at best.

STUDIES OF THE QUALITY OF PERFORMANCE

It is difficult to find studies in the professional literature that examine how well nonresearchers perform research tasks. This problem exists in part because the data generally are not collected to evaluate the success of field procedures. The present study focuses on three studies that have been made, two of which were carried out at the Rand Corporation. The studies are described below:

Prescription Drug Information Study

This study evaluated how providing systematically varied patient package inserts (PPIs) affected patient knowledge, attitudes, and behavior toward the 2000 drugs which they were given. In a randomized field trial patients enrolled through 69 cooperating pharmacies over a period of eight months. Patients were surveyed by telephone and mail (for details, see Berry et al., 1981; Kanouse et al., 1981a).

Evaluation of the 1977 Commodity Transportation Survey (CTS)

This study is a methodological evaluation of an ongoing U.S. Census survey of U.S. manufacturing establishments. The survey intended to provide data on transportation modes for manufactured goods. In part of the survey, businesses were instructed to sample and abstract their own shipping records (for details, see Tupek and Perez, 1979).

Study of Diabetic Patient Knowledge, Attitudes, and Behavior Regarding Self-Care

To assist in the evaluation of diabetic patient education, this study sought to develop reliable measures of patient performance in managing the disease, knowledge of treatment tasks, and attitudes toward carrying them out. Diabetic subjects for the study were located through private medical practices and medical institutions. These patients were asked to complete mail surveys for the study (for details, see Marquis and Ware, 1979).

SELECTING SAMPLES FROM RECORDS

Compared to the task of identifying eligible subjects as they appear and persuading them to enroll in a study, selecting a sample from existing records seems simple. Tupek and Perez (1979) conducted a study to evaluate the accuracy with which 308 (out of 20,000) manufacturing establishments sampled records for a mailed U.S. Census survey. After normal data collection was complete, census field representatives visited the firms to obtain a subjective measure of their understanding of sampling procedures and to select an independent sample of their records.

Census field representatives found in the subjective evaluation and independent sampling that more than half of the 308 firms had errors in sampling. The types of errors broke down as shown in Table 6.1. They concluded that although some of these errors were not preventable due to the system of recordkeeping used by the firms, a large percentage could have been avoided if the respondents had followed the sampling instructions.

TABLE 6.1
Errors in Sampling Records by 308 U.S. Firms
in U.S. Census CTS Survey

Type of Error	Percentage of Errors
Undersampling	72
Oversampling	5
Haphazard "random" or purposive sampling	14
Undercoverage	42
Overcoverage	5
Multiple major problems	2
Minor counting problem	18
Other minor errors	9
Total firms with errors	160

SOURCE: Tupek and Perez (1979)

RECRUITMENT OF SAMPLE SUBJECTS BY MAIL OR IN PERSON

Two recent Rand studies have faced problems of having to obtain subjects indirectly. In the first case, the Diabetes Study, the sample design called for examination of medical records to select a sample of diabetic patients stratified by age, sex, and insulin dependency. Once identified, these patients were to be mailed a survey by Rand and normal follow-up procedures were to be carried out to minimize nonresponse.

Assistance was formally requested from four hospitals and four private diabetes clinics. One hospital and two clinics refused to participate on any basis and another hospital consented too late to be included in the study. Cooperating institutions required major changes in sampling procedures. In both cases clinic staff paid by Rand selected the stratified sample and carried out mailing and telephone follow-up, also supported by Rand. Although initial sampling and mailing were carrried out adequately, both clinics underestimated the amount of work involved and follow-up was hit or miss. In Hospital 1, Rand staff working at the hospital had access to names of patients who had visited the clinic within a certain time period—no stratified selection was possible. Telephone follow-up was carried out by the hospital and was hampered by difficulties obtaining telephone numbers and an extremely short time period allotted to the task. In Hospital 2, a retired employee sat in the clinic and personally enrolled patients and distributed surveys. Although no stratification was possible, Rand was able to carry out normal follow-up by mail and telephone directly. The results are shown in Table 6.2 (taken from Schoeff, 1981).

TABLE 6.2
Percentage of Diabetes Surveys Completed by Institution

| | Type of Institution | | | |
	Clinic 1	Clinic 2	Hospital 1	Hospital 2
First mailing	25	35	37	57
Final rate	52	54	51	85
Initial sample of patients	200	300	214	150

SOURCE: Schoeff (1981)

The problems that arose from these circumstances were significant. Clearly, the procedures required by participating institutions in order to maintain the privacy of their patients had a major effect on the sample. The resulting sample was not stratified, as called for in the research design, and the overall response rate was only 56 percent. This reflected in part the inability of researchers to conduct a complete follow-up of nonresponses. The fact that dealing with the institutions required vast amounts of time and patience was another impediment of the study.

The second Rand study for which subjects were identified and recruited indirectly is the Prescription Drug Information Study. This study called for patients filling prescriptions for one of three drugs in retail pharmacies to be identified and, if eligible, enrolled. Enrolled subjects were given a PPI explaining the drug according to a predetermined randomized assignment plan and were later surveyed by telephone and mail.

About 1300 Los Angeles area pharmacies initally were categorized by their status as chains or independents and by demographic characteristics of their customers. For the study, 196 were selected to participate. Of these, 88 accepted and only 69 enrolled at least one subject. The high initial refusal rate was partially caused by the pharmacists' negative attitudes toward PPIs, which were at the time about to be required by the Food and Drug Administration. Many pharmacies dropped out of the study because of their lack of success in enrolling subjects. Yet comparing customer characteristics of participating and nonparticipating or drop-out pharmacies showed no significant differences.

Participating pharmacies were provided with detailed instructions and prearranged packets of materials for enrolling customers. Pharmacists were trained at the beginning of the study and visited weekly for the collection of materials for enrolled subjects, dealing with problems, and encouraging continued efforts.[1] The disappointingly slow rate of enrollment (a mean of 1.9 cases per pharmacy per week) indicated that pharmacies were not enrolling all eligible customers.

To obtain information about the eligibles not being enrolled, we placed a checklist in each pharmacy for a randomly selected week during the study and asked the pharmacist to record information about *every* customer who presented a prescription for one of the three study drugs. Ninety percent of the pharmacists claimed to have achieved total coverage on these checklists. The checklist indicated the drug, sex, and approximate age of the customer, and whether or not the customer was asked to participate. If the customer was not asked, we requested a reason. If asked, we requested the result.

Using the checklist data we found that 79 percent of the customers who were not asked to participate were legitimate ineligibles. The rest, 21 percent, should have been asked, but were not because the pharmacist was too busy or because of some characteristic of the customer (too old, too difficult to deal with, in a hurry, etc.) Although they were not popular with the pharmacists, the checklists had the serendipitous result of stimulating enrollments (to a mean of 3.2 per week) so the above figures understate the number of cases "missed" during normal (nonchecklist) weeks. Assuming that the number of eligible customers and the percentage who agreed to participate when asked (about 56 percent) remained the same during normal weeks, the study estimates that the pharmacists approached only about 50 percent of eligible customers overall. Based on the checklists, no significant differences were found between the eligibles who were and were not asked to enroll on the basis of sex or age. However, females were more likely to agree to participate than were males.

Thus, relying on the pharmacists to enroll customers resulted in a very slow enrollment process that required considerable effort on the part of study staff to carry out. It also resulted in the loss of about half of the customers who were eligible to participate through failure to be asked.

CARRYING OUT A RANDOMIZED TREATMENT

Difficulties with carrying out randomized designs has been well documented by Conner (1977). Pharmacists in the Prescription Drug Information Study performed this function, but in a simplified way. Packets of enrollment materials, including one randomly selected version of the PPI, were placed in folders by drug. The packets were in random order so the pharmacist's task was simply to give out the first packet in the folder each time he or she enrolled a participant.

Errors nevertheless occurred. About 22 percent of the packets were distributed out of order. Because one error caused subsequent packets for the week to be counted as out of order, only an upper bound on the number of errors can be assigned. Interestingly, although there was no evidence of differential errors among different versions of the PPIs, the pharmacists were significantly more likely to *underassign* the no-PPI control cases. We speculate that despite the fact that we attached an explanatory notice to these packets, the pharmacists quickly pulling a packet without a PPI may have assumed there was a mistake and assigned the next case or may simply have preferred to give out PPIs.

Thus despite the simplicity of the tasks and attempts to monitor performance on a regular basis, using a nonresearcher to carry out randomized assignment resulted in significant departures from the desired result.

EFFECTS OF THE QUALITY OF PERFORMANCE OF SAMPLING TASKS

In many studies it is not possible to go beyond a brief discussion of the problems encountered in indirect sample selection. Either the data to assess their significance could not be collected (e.g., characteristics of nonparticipants) or the problem was recognized too late to make such data collection feasible. In two of the studies described above, however, strenuous efforts were made to analyze the effects of errors in carrying out procedures.

ERRORS IN SAMPLING FROM LISTS

In census evaluation of the 1977 Commodity Transportation Survey, researchers analyzed the results obtained from the original sample drawn by firms from their own records and the second sample drawn by census field representatives. The study found significant differences that could not be attributed to sampling variability. As shown in Table 6.3, the error was overwhelmingly in the direction of overestimating the weight of goods shipped by various methods. Based on their results, the researchers recommended a careful study of procedures for the CTS in order to modify or replace existing methods.

DIFFICULTIES IN RECRUITING SAMPLE SUBJECTS

As mentioned above, the use of checklists in the pharmacies participating in the Prescription Drug Information Study stimulated the pharmacies to increase their solicitation of eligible customers from an estimated 50 percent to nearly 90 percent. Thus, the customers enrolled during the weeks when checklists were in the pharmacies provided a special subsample of cases for which the pharmacists' possible selection effects on enrollment were mini-

TABLE 6.3
Discrepancies in Estimates of Total Weight Shipped
by U.S. Firms by Mode of Transportation

| | Weight in 100s of Tons | | |
	Original (in millions)	Evaluation (in millions)	Evaluation as a Percentage of Original
Rail	0.4	0.2	56
For hire – ICC	0.3	0.3	79
Private truck	0.9	0.4	42
Water	1.1	1.5	135
Pipeline	1.4	0.7	50

SOURCE: Tupek and Perez (1979)

mized. Comparing this subset of cases with the rest of the sample gives us an opportuntiy to assess the effects of pharmacists' selection on the data.

Data were drawn from the completed telephone interviews for 1821 cases, of which 193 were recruited during checklist weeks. The researchers compared demographic characteristics of patients for checklist and non-checklist weeks for each of the three drugs included in the study.[2] The samples were then compared along the dimensions of sex, age, education, race, and setting in which they usually saw their doctor (clinic, private office, etc.). Using an inclusive significance level of p < .10, the existence of significant differences were noted between the two samples in only 2 of the 15 comparisons. (For details, see Berry et al., 1981.) The flurazepam sample included more older patients during the checklist weeks—a mean age of 61 rather than 54 years (p < .01). The estrogen sample included more clinic patients in the checklist weeks—12 percent compared with 6 percent (p < .01). It is not difficult to believe that the excluded patients were the kinds of patients whom pharmacists were likely to perceive as more difficult to enroll or less desirable candidates for the study.

Although demographic differences are interesting, there is a more subtle dimension of possible pharmacist selection effects. Pharmacists may have selected customers to enroll based on their beliefs about whether the customer would be likely to accept. If they did, and if they could predict successfully who would and would not enroll, and if propensity to enroll was associated with variables of interest in the evaluation, for example, likelihood of reading the PPI or evaluations of its usefulness, sample selection problems would directly affect the results of the evaluation.

In fact, Ramsey (1982) found just such a problem with research on compliance with hypertensive treatment. Patients who were diagnosed as hypertensive and who agreed to be treated were significantly more likely to have demonstrated a past history of compliance with recommendations for clinic visits for follow-up appointments than those who refused to participate. Although compliance with one recommendation does not always generalize across other recommendations (Marquis and Ware, 1979), it is worrisome, especially when the two measures seem closely linked at an intuitive level, as they do in the PPI evaluation.

To assess this problem the researchers compared the checklist and non-checklist samples for each of the three drugs for a number of behavioral and attitudinal variables reflecting evaluation of the PPIs; this comparison is shown in Table 6.4. (For complete descriptions of the variables, see Kanouse et al., 1981b.) For two of the three drugs, erythromycin and estrogen, there is a fairly clear pattern of effects, although only one measure reaches statistical significance. All but 3 of the 11 (or 10 for estrogen) measures for each drug show that the sample obtained during the weeks when the checklists were in place was less favorable toward the PPIs than the rest of the sample. These results, although weak, support the hypothesis that the pharmacists were influencing the enrollment process by selecting participants who would be more favorable toward both the study and the leaflets. However, an opposite pattern emerges for the flurazepam sample. For this group, the pattern of results is completely consistent, and 3 of the 11 comparisons reach statistical significance. But the sample obtained during the checklist weeks is more favorable toward the PPIs than the rest of the sample. These results do not support the hypothesis that pharmacists were selecting customers who favor the PPIs during the nonchecklist weeks.

The results of this analysis are not definitive for the weeks when pharmacists were doing a more complete job of enrolling customers; the study does not show any strong, consistent tendency for the subsample of respondents selected to be any less favorable toward PPIs than respondents selected during the remaining weeks. In fact, the more significant results pointed in the opposite direction. Taken in conjunction with the results of the demographic comparisons of the two samples, the researchers concluded that pharmacists sometimes did produce significant effects in the sample selection process, but there is not strong indication of consistent bias in the study results for evaluation of the PPIs.

ERRORS IN CARRYING OUT
RANDOMIZED ASSIGNMENTS

Errors in assigning the PPIs are regrettable, but not particularly troubling, unless they indicate that systematic pharmacist control has been substituted for experimental control over assignment. For example, misplacing a packet in the folder creates errors, but not systematic errors. Examining a

TABLE 6.4
Percentage of Cases Indicating Positive Response to Leaflet by Drug and Checklist Status in Prescription Drug Information Study

	Type of Drug					
	Erythromycin		*Flurazepam*		*Estrogen*	
Checklist Status	*Yes*	*No*	*Yes*	*No*	*Yes*	*No*
Reports of Behavior						
Read PPI	71	74	89	67*	61	75
Read before taking drug	61	62	74	55*	51	56
Read again	34	43	32	32	–	—
Kept PPI	75	73	85	82	46	45
Showed PPI to someone else	37	33	32	23	7	15
Sample size[a]	85	692	38	296	57	512
Attitudinal Reports about PPI						
Gave new information	70	75	70	56	20	27
Helped understand the drug	90	93	100	88*	77	79
Helped follow doctors' orders	71	76	70	70	60	47
Helped understand drug effects	78	90*	94	88	91	83
Helped know when to take drug	72	76	79	67	37	40
Produced worry	20	19	36	23	23	27
Sample size[b]	60	512	33	197	35	363

SOURCE: Tabulation by author.
*Chi-square significance at $p < .05$, df = 1.
a. Sample includes those who received a PPI. Sample sizes vary slightly across measures due to missing data.
b. Sample includes those who received a PPI and reported reading it. Sample sizes vary slightly across measures due to missing data.

packet and deciding not to give it out because it was or was not appropriate for a particular customer, however, can create systematic error.

To determine whether error in carrying out random assignment was systematic, the researchers compared the samples of respondents receiving each of the PPI variations (9 for each drug plus a no-PPI control) on the dimensions of age, sex, race, education, and medical care setting. With an alpha level set at an inclusive level of $p < .10$, no significant differences were found. Repeating the comparison specifically for PPI versus no-PPI cases, a similar result was obtained. (These results are presented in more detail in Berry et al., 1981.)

CONCLUSIONS

Evaluation research frequently is conducted in field settings in which it is not possible for all phases of the research to be under the direct control of the researcher. Carrying out research indirectly presents significant hazards. This study examined the difficulties posed in sample selection and random assignment when these processes were carried out by nonresearchers in three studies. The hazards included the following:

- significant levels of error introduced into the procedures, which, in some cases, resulted in demonstrable negative effects on the quality of the results and, in others, introduced a strong element of doubt
- substantial changes in the research design resulting in reduced analytic power
- considerable expenditure of time and resources to obtain the cooperation of nonresearchers and maintain the quality of such indirect efforts

The following advice to evaluators with similar problems is suggested (the advice partially echoes Weiss, 1975). First, reduce the tasks to the essentials, even if this requires a brutal sacrifice of elegance in design for simplicity in implementation. Second, think about the problem of motivation on several levels. What can you do to make the tasks easier and more relevant for the people who have to do them? For example, while paying pharmacists directly for participating was useful and important, paying their customers a token amount to participate in the research also made it easier for the pharmacists to ask customers to participate. Furthermore, not all pharmacists responded to payment. Some, although needing to be paid in recognition of their efforts, were also strongly motivated by a sense of participation in the research. Third, be prepared to do enormous amounts of handholding and cheerleading, in addition to doing as much of the actual labor as the situation permits. Finally, think in advance about what can go wrong and design ways to estimate, not only the magnitude of the errors (which can be frightening), but also the effects on the results.

NOTES

1. Pharmacists were paid $3-$5 for enrolling each eligible case. A periodic study "newsletter" and visits to Rand for participating pharmacists were also used to maintain continued interest in the study.

2. These drugs, erythromycin (an antibiotic), flurazepam (a sleeping pill commonly known as Dalmane), and conjugated estrogen (for symptoms of menopause), are taken by different segments of the adult population.

REFERENCES

BERRY, S. H., D. E. KANOUSE, and W. H. ROGERS, with J.B. GARFINKLE (1981) Sample Selection for the Prescription Drug Information Study: N-1657-FDA. Santa Monica, CA: Rand.

BORGATTA, E. R. (1971) "Management and tactics of research," pp. 185-197 in R. O'Toole (ed.) Organization, Management, and Tactics of Social Research. Cambridge, MA: Schenkman.

CONNER, R. F. (1977) "Selecting a control group: an analysis of the randomization process in twelve social reform programs." Evaluation Quarterly 1 (May): 195-244.

FORM, W. H. (1971) "The sociology of social research," pp. 3-42 in R. O'Toole (ed.) Organization, Management, and Tactics of Social Research. Cambridge, MA: Schenkman.

HAUG, M. R. (1971) "Notes on the art of research management," pp. 198-210 in R. O'Toole (ed.) Organization, Management, and Tactics of Social Research. Cambridge, MA: Schenkman.

KANOUSE, D. E., S. H. BERRY, B. HAYES-ROTH, and W. H. ROGERS (1981a) Design of the Prescription Drug Information Study: N1552-FDA. Santa Monica, CA: Rand.

— — — and J. D. WINKLER (1981b) Informing Patients About Drugs: Summary Report on Alternative Designs for Prescription Drug Leaflets: R-2800-FDA. Santa Monica, CA: Rand.

MARQUIS, K. H. and J. E. WARE (1979) Measures of Diabetic Patient Knowledge, Attitudes, and Behavior Regarding Self-Care: Summary Report: R-2480-HEW. Santa Monica, CA: Rand.

RAMSEY, J. A. (1982) "Participants in noncompliance research: compliant or noncompliant?" Medical Care 20 (June): 615-622.

SCHOEFF, D. A. (1981) "Using hospitals and clinics to draw patient samples: diabetes project. (1979)." (memo)

TUPEK, A. R. and A. M. PEREZ (1979) "Can U.S. businesses take a sample of their own records?" pp. 188-193 in Proceedings of the American Statistical Association, Business and Economic Statistics Section. Washington, DC: American Statistical Association.

WEISS, C. H. (1975) "Interviewing in evaluation research," pp.355-395 in E. L. Struening and M. Guttentag (eds.) Handbook of Evaluation Research. Beverly Hills, CA: Sage.

CHAPTER

7

MEASURING UNFILED CLAIMS IN THE
HEALTH INSURANCE EXPERIMENT

William H. Rogers
Joseph P. Newhouse

National health policy-making depends partly on accurate medical care use statistics. Use projections show the social cost (or resource cost) of alternative health financing proposals, as well as existing programs such as Medicare and Medicaid. But a simple measure of dollars paid out by an insurer would fail to include resource costs for services when reimbursement claims

Reprinted by permission of the Rand Corporation.

AUTHORS' NOTE: We are grateful to Glen Slaughter and associates for their skillful fieldwork and claims processing, Kent Marquis for early analysis that led to this work and his assistance in the experimental design, Ken Krug for his tireless attention to fielding decisions, Joan Keesey for her programming and linking of the claims data, and Naihua Duan for several discussions early in this work. We also are grateful to George Goldberg, Ellyn Bloomfield, Rae Archibald, Marie Brown, Maureen Carney, Sherry Trees, Bryant Mori, Bob Young, and Darlene Blake for administrative and data processing assistance. The research reported was performed pursuant to Grant O16B8O from the U.S. Department of Health and Human Services, Washington, D. C. The opinions and conclusions expressed are solely our own and should not be construed as representing the opinions or policies of any agency of the United States government.

were not filed. Actual use, not claims filed, determines the need for health care facilities and training programs. For these reasons, the Rand Health Insurance experiment (HIS) has sought to measure use rather than claims for reimbursement under the experimental insurance policies.

Nevertheless, data from claims for reimbursement provide such a convenient way to measure medical care use that the initially reported results from the Rand study employed them. A working assumption has been that the "error," or difference between claimed expenses and actual expenses, is small. Ideally, this difference would be unrelated to plan. If the difference is small, any resulting bias in the estimated plan response would be small. But if the difference is large and systematically related to plan, the study's estimate of response to plan (Newhouse et al., 1981) could be seriously overstated. In this chapter we test our working assumption.

This chapter is concerned with any systematic error or "bias" introduced by analyzing claimed expenses instead of actual expenses. In theory, whenever expected reimbursement was small, participants or their providers might have chosen not to file the claim. If this happened systematically for less generous policies, it would be possible to confuse the reporting effect with price response to insurance. The experiment implemented three major procedures to assure claim filing. First, participants were told at the outset that it was important to file every claim. Second, all plans were structured to pay at least 5 percent of every claim. Specifically, we paid this 5 percent even if a deductible had not been reached. Third, provider visit information was collected in a biweekly health diary. Participants were prompted to provide claims whenever a visit was reported in the health diary for which a claim had not been filed within a certain time interval.

Were these procedures sufficient, or did claim underreporting nonetheless occur? To address this question, we undertook a separate survey of provider billing records in four of the six study sites. The results of this survey are interesting from both methodological and substantive viewpoints.

METHODS

THE RAND HEALTH INSURANCE EXPERIMENT

The fee-for-service portion of the experiment ran from November 1974 through January 1982 and enrolled 5712 people in 2005 families. (These values exclude those families enrolled in a prepaid group practice, in which use data were abstracted from medical records. Thus, any underreporting in the fee-for-service portion of the experiment would also bias the comparison of prepaid group practice fee-for-service plans.) Seventy percent of the sample participated for three years and the remainder for five years. Families lived in one of six sites (Dayton, Ohio; Seattle, Washington; Fitchburg or Franklin County, Massachusetts; and Charleston or Georgetown County, South Carolina). Participants were representative of the general population of the areas in which they lived, except for certain intentional differences. Very high income families, military personnel, Medicare-eligible persons, and institutionalized persons were excluded. The income exclusion applied to one percent of the households contacted.

Families were assigned to one of 14 experimental insurance plans by a random sampling technique that matched family characteristics across plans (Morris, 1979). Any family assigned to an experimental plan that offered less coverage than its current insurance plan was reimbursed an amount at least equal to its maximum possible loss. The reimbursement did not have to be spent on medical care and had a negligible effect on use (Newhouse et al., 1981).

For this analysis, each of the 14 experimental insurance plans was assigned to one of four categories (two with higher filing incentives and two with lower filing incentives) as follows: (1) the free plan, under which the family was reimbursed for all filed claims; (2) nine intermediate coinsurance plans, under which the experiment reimbursed 50 or 75 percent of claims until the family had spent 5, 10, or 15 percent of its income or $1000, whichever was less ($750 in some sites and years); (3) three income-related catastrophic plans under which the experiment paid 5 percent of claims up to 5, 10, or 15 percent of its income or $1000, whichever was less; or (4) the individual-deductible plan, under which the experiment paid 5 percent of outpatient claims up to a maximum of $150 per person ($450 per family) and all inpatient claims. Above the maximum, all medical care was free to the participant.

Participants were further randomized to a "no health diary" group for the first year of participation (25 percent). This group did not submit a health diary; the remainder submitted the health diary. For the survey described in this chapter both groups also were randomized to an "unmentioned" group described below.

Interim results based on claims filed show that cost sharing affected expenditures (Newhouse et al., 1981). For ambulatory visits, expenses on the income-related catastrophic plans were about two-thirds of expenses on the free plan.

THE PROVIDER BILLING RECORDS SURVEY

The provider billing records survey covered 2082 participants in four sites—all participants in Fitchburg or Franklin County, Massachusetts; and five-year participants in Charleston or Georgetown County, South Carolina; South Carolina participants between the ages of 14 and 18 at enrollment were excluded for reasons related to South Carolina law. Tables 7.1 and 7.2 display characteristics of the sample.

The survey covered a 27-month period (7/1/76 to 10/1/78 in the two Massachusetts sites and 11/1/76 to 2/1/79 in the two South Carolina sites) including the first two years on study for each participant. The survey was fielded in October 1979.

Providers surveyed included all locatable outpatient physicians in the immediate geographic area of the sites, as determined by claim records and local telephone directories. Hospital or clinic patient records were sampled for outpatient visits only; inpatient records were considered in a later similar study, which has not yet been analyzed.

In principle, we could have sampled the records of each provider for each participant. The sampling frame used (with hypothetical data) has the following appearance:

| | Participants | | | | |
| | Family 1 | | Family 2 | | |
Provider	A	B	C	D	E
1	0	0	65	10	0
2	72	0	0	0	0
3	0	30	0	0	14
4	0	0	0	0	0
...					

Medical Expenses by Provider-Participant Pair ($)

The sampling unit is a provider-participant pair (whether or not they had a relationship).

Although convenient for analysis, a random sample from this frame would have yielded too little information and too much provider response burden. As in the example above, the typical matrix would be filled with

TABLE 7.1
Number of Participants by Plan and Site

Number of Participants by Plan	
Free plan	701
Intermediate coinsurance	516
Income-related catastrophic	352
Individual-deductible	513
Total	2,082
Number of Participants by Site	
Fitchburg, Massachusetts	723
Franklin County, Massachusetts	889
Charleston, South Carolina	208
Georgetown County, South Carolina	262
Total	2,082

TABLE 7.2
Sample Characteristics of Participants

3-year enrollment (vs. 5-year) (percentage)	
Massachusetts	74
South Carolina	0
Took physical exam at enrollment	74
No health diary	24
Average education of decision-maker (years)	
Massachusetts	12.2
South Carolina	10.8
Percentage with existing public insurance	
Massachusetts	10.1
South Carolina	4.9
Percentage with existing private insurance other than their employment	
Massachusetts	15.4
South Carolina	22.0
Percentage with existing private insurance through their employment	
Massachusetts	77.0
South Carolina	73.4
Average income (1983 $)	
Massachusetts	22,400
South Carolina	21,000
Person's family size (average)	3.9
Age < 14 at enrollment (percentage)	43
Male (percentage)	49

zeroes. Finding the provider who served a given patient is like searching for the proverbial needle in a haystack. Instead, we chose a three-stratum sampling technique based on known utilization. The three strata were "mentioned pairs," "family-mentioned pairs,"and "unmentioned pairs." A pair was classified as "mentioned" if the participant had named this provider on the preexperimental baseline survey or if claims in hand at the time of the fieldwork indicated the participant had visited the provider during his or her first two years in the study. The participant was called "family-mentioned" if mentioned by any family member (known to us as of mid-1979). The "unmentioned pair" category included all other pairs.

Consider possible data from the above sampling frame. Previously received claims might indicate $30 of expenses for pair C1 and nothing for D1 or E3. Then pair C1 would be called mentioned, pair D1 family-mentioned, and pair E3 unmentioned.

The three groups were sampled at different rates. For each provider, we sampled (1) all mentioned pairs (rarely more than five for each provider), (2) all family-mentioned pairs, except those on intermediate coinsurance plans, and (3) unmentioned pairs combining the provider with members of the unmentioned participant sample, up to a maximum of 150 names for each provider. The same unmentioned participant names were used throughout each site, but the order of the names sent the provider was random with respect to the three groups.

For each participant listed (identified by name and birthdate), the survey form asked whether the participant was a patient. If the answer was yes, the form requested date of service and amount billed for each date of service. The form also asked if the participant had generated any bad debts in 1977. The survey normally was filled out by an employee in the provider's office; the provider was paid a fixed fee depending on the number of dates of service we thought he or she would need to provide. With implementation of standard follow-up procedures, provider response was fair, with 57 percent returning our questionnaire.

Prior to matching claims, we eliminated certain claims that could not be confused with outpatient visits (i.e., dental claims and hospital bills). Billing records were matched to claims for each participant using provider, date, and cost. Date errors were accepted within limits (within 8 weeks, eight months for maternity cases, or off by a digit error). We also allowed provider errors (e.g., a physician practicing in two clinics) and cost errors (e.g., including a lab test in the billing record but not on the claims, or vice versa), individually or combined with date errors. Excluding zero-cost visits, 9361 visits were reported in the billing records survey, of which 7.0 percent were unmatched, 55.8 percent were perfectly matched, 10.1 percent contained date error, 20.1 percent contained cost error, 6.0 percent contained provider error, and the remaining 1.0 percent contained a combination of errors. These matching rules were considered aggressive; we verified by manual examination that other match types (e.g., provider and cost errors) would not be productive.

In addition, we eliminated certain classes of visits that might contribute bias or noise to the results. We restricted the analysis file outpatient physician visits, including psychiatric visits, with positive charges. Although we were interested in no-charge visits, we were interested primarily in accurate expense measures. We excluded visits outside the experimental period or the reference period, yielding a period of 24 to 27 months immediately after enrollment. Claims or billing records for periods after a participant's attrition from the experiment were excluded. The only claims considered were those that the participant was supposed to have filed according to his or her agreement with the experiment.

For any specified match rule, including the one given above, there are eight possibilities:

	The visit existed		The visit did not exist	
	Claim	No Claim	Claim	No Claim
Record	Match(A)	Underreport(C)	Fraud(F)	Record Error(H)
No Record	Lost Record(B)	Undetected(D)	Fraud(G)	— — —

One category makes no sense—visits that were neither claimed nor recorded, and that did not exist. They are represented by a dash in the table.

The above diagram applies to visits, but dollar amounts were analyzed. Claims were matched dollar for dollar with billing records. Excess amounts were recorded separately from missing claims (C+H) and billing records (B+G).

We assumed that record error is independent of plan, that fraud is small compared to correctly matched visits, and that billing records examined by the survey are typical of those not examined. That is, if the visit existed, finding it with the record is independent of finding it with the claim. This assumption could be violated if the survey accessed a nonrepresentative set of records, such as those pending third-party payment (we do not think this

happened because physicians tend to keep billing records in a uniform way).
Mathematically, these assumptions are as follows:

(1) $E(H) = c$ independent of plan (mainly name and clerical errors)
(2) $[E(F)+E(G)] / [E(A)+E(B)+E(C)+E(D)] << 1$
(3) $E(C)/E(A) = E(D)/E(B)$

The viability of assumption 3 could be verified by reference to a third source
of data, such as the health diary.

Failures to match identical visits would introduce data in both the lost record (B) and underreport (C) categories. Matching nonidentical visits would
reduce data in these categories. Both of these effects would lead to positive
association between unmatched claims and records. However, we do not observe such positive correlation in the data.

For each participant-provider pair, we calculated five variables. Average
values for participant totals of the variables are given in parentheses.

(a) ($53.88) Matched billing record and claim, amount of expenses. (This in-
cludes the matching part if one amount exceeds the other.)
(b) ($37.51) Matched billing record and claim, amount claim exceeds record.
(c) ($2.77) Matched billing record and claim, amount record exceeds claim.
(d) ($96.51) Unmatched claim, amount of claim.
(e) ($6.50) Unmatched billing record, amount of billing record.

Variable e combines unmatched mentioned provider expenses (el =
$2.88), family-mentioned provider expenses (e2 = $0.78), and unmentioned provider expenses (e3 = $2.84). The last is the average for the un-
mentioned participant sample only. The large dollar amount of unmatched
claims (category d) comes from providers who did not participate in the survey and from providers who were included to facilitate matching. The first
group includes out-of-area providers (e.g., for participants who moved) as
well as providers who failed to respond to the survey. On this basis, we ignored excess claims (c) and unmatched claims (d). These variables were further examined as predictors of unmatched billing records, however.

This leaves two comparisons worthy of further analysis: unmatched billing records (e) with matched claim-billing records (a), and excess billing
records (c) with matched claim-billing records (a).

STATISTICAL METHODS

The data were analyzed using two different techniques. First, we computed simple averages of a-d and e1-e3 taking into account the different par-

TABLE 7.3
Average Unmatched and Matched Billing Records

	Massachusetts				South Carolina			
	Free	Int.	Cata.	I.D.	Free	Int.	Cata.	I.D.
Summary of Results								
Mentioned (e1)	2.44	2.38	3.27	3.43	1.50	3.31	2.97	4.49
Family (e2)	0.96	0.00	1.13	1.06	1.09	0.00	0.69	1.22
Unmentioned (e3)	0.98	2.13	5.43	3.39	2.07	3.94	3.17	1.85
Total	4.38	4.51	9.83	7.88	4.66	7.25	6.83	7.56
(se)***	(0.91)	(1.27)	(2.52)	(1.48)	(1.35)	(1.84)	(1.84)	(1.65)
Total, pooled by incentive	4.42			8.38*	5.57			7.23
	(.74)			(1.27)	(1.09)			(1.23)
Compared to free and intermediate				3.96				1.66
				(1.47)				(1.64)
Disposition of Claims**								
Matched (a)	73.91	62.20	42.18	46.70	50.85	22.66	27.32	18.58
Unmatched (d)	131.55	84.16	65.24	120.12	85.05	34.62	44.03	42.06
Excess (b)	51.59	44.50	33.80	40.59	22.58	6.86	5.36	4.30
Excess billing (c)	3.04	2.90	2.21	2.99	2.79	1.90	3.04	0.99

SOURCE: Billing records survey and preliminary claims file.

NOTE: (a) - (d) and (e1), (e2), and (e3) refer to definitions in text. All amounts listed are in current dollars.

*Significant, z = 2.7. Pooling across sites gives $4.71 for the free and intermediate coinsurance plans, $7.78 for the catastrophic and individual-deductible plans, z = 2.8 (p < .001 in each case).

**Note these are partial claims covering the same reference periods (27 months) as the billing records survey.

***Standard errors are computed assuming independence. Intrafamily correlation was insignificant in this dataset.

ticipant groups to which e1-e3 apply. For example, e3 was only collected on 600 participants, and e2 was not collected for participants on the intermediate plans. Table 7.3 presents analysis based on the sum of these average values for the various sites and plans.

The second analysis attempts to adjust for demographic and other available data and takes into account the fact that both quantities (e) and (c) are zero for most of the sample. We use a two-part model, where

$$E(Y) = P(Y > 0) * E(Y \mid Y > 0)$$

We modelled the first part using logit analysis and the second using a least squares regression of log dollar unmatched billing records on a set of covariates. In both parts, the independent variables included the experimentally determined insurance plan, other experimental variables, and participant characteristics.

The analysis of unmatched billing records (e) takes account of the stratified sampling design. That is, unmatched billing records from unmentioned providers are analyzed only for the unmentioned participant sample for that provider; the mentioned participant sample by definition had a claim filed with the mentioned provider.

RESULTS

RELATIONSHIP WITH INSURANCE PLAN

Table 7.3 shows average values of unmatched and matched billing records by site and plan. Dollar amounts of unmatched claims probably are inflated by errors in the billing records survey. However, differences across plans are meaningful. In Massachusetts we observed an average of $3.96 ($8.38-$4.42) more unreported expenditures on the low-incentive plans and in South Carolina an average of $1.66 ($7.23-$5.57) more. These figures are, respectively, 9 and 7 percent of the matched claims for the low-incentive plans in these sites.

A slightly different picture emerges with a combined-sample regression analysis. If we begin with site and plan effects, we cannot reject the hypothesis that plan effects (in dollars) are the same across sites. Assuming that there is no interaction, this model estimates that the predicted difference between the lower-incentive plans and the higher-incentive plans is $2.42, which is about 5 percent in Massachusetts and 11 percent in South Carolina. This variation between sites reflects the different levels of outpatient service utilization in the two areas.

TABLE 7.4
Regression Equations for Mentioned Provider Underreporting

Variable	Logit Coefficient	Conditional Log Regression
Low-incentive plan	0.44*	0.08
3-year term	0.06	0.23
Took physical exam	−0.23	−0.14
No health diary	0.04	−0.08
Education (effect of 4 additional years)	−0.33*	−0.22*
Log income (change in income by factor of 2)	−0.10	0.03
Public insurance	0.55*	−0.03
Log family size (change in family size by factor of 2)	−0.03	−0.05
Child	−0.24	−0.25*
Male	0.18	0.12
Log preexperimental visits (change in visits by factor of 2)	0.20*	0.03
Education x plan	−0.00	0.23

*Significant at $p < .05$.

RELATIONSHIP WITH OTHER VARIABLES

In the regression models, several participant characteristics were evaluated simultaneously. Other participant characteristics predicting unsubmitted claims included low education, adulthood versus childhood, existing public insurance, poor mental health, and utilization prior to the study. Franklin County had significantly lower levels of unsubmitted claims than the other three sites. Characteristics not appearing to affect unsubmitted claims included income, gender, enrollment term, the physical exam, presence of the health diary; no education-plan interaction was apparent. In a separate analysis, matched claims had a positive effect on unsubmitted claims, but unmatched and excess claims had negative effects.

Table 7.4 includes the regression models for mentioned provider verification. Results for unmentioned providers are similar, but more random, due to the larger amount of randomness in that data.

CONCLUSIONS

The observed reporting differences between the low-incentive and higher-incentive plans are small, relative to insurance effects previously reported by the experiment (Newhouse et al., 1981). These diverge by approximately 50 percent. Thus, qualitative conclusions drawn there appear valid.

The principal reasons for not submitting claims appear to be lack of incentive (represented by plan) and personal disorganization (suggested by the effects of low education and poor mental health). One important result for the study was the small and insignificant effect of the health diary. No effect of diary on expenditures has been found in other research. At the outset of the study, considerable resources were spent prompting for claims on the basis of the diary; this effort was discontinued in 1977. According to field records, about 0.2 percent of claims were received as a result of prompting. This is considerably less than our point estimate of the effect, but clearly within a 95 percent confidence interval.

One must be cautious about extending these results to other types of claims, such as hospital, pharmacy, or laboratory claims. The effort and organization required to file claims in these cases could be different, leading to different amounts of underreporting by plan.

IMPLICATIONS BEYOND THE HEALTH INSURANCE EXPERIMENT

Administrative records, such as insurance claims, can be a very accurate source of evaluation data. However, one must expect biases that are associated with reasons for their existence. A high-quality evaluation project should search for these sources of bias, rather than assuming they do not exist. In the Health Insurance Experiment, this billing records survey is one of many attempts to evaluate Hawthorne effects and other data collection biases (see Newhouse et al., 1979).

Assessing data collection bias with an independent check design can be effective. Although literature on its use dates back to ChandraSekar and Deming (1949), it mostly has been used to evaluate interview quality (e.g., Balmauth, 1965; Cannell, 1965; Cannell and Fowler, 1965; and Madow, 1973). Check designs also can be ineffective (see Marquis et al., 1976). Because the HIS was a designed experiment, we only needed to compare underreports across treatments, not estimate actual dollar amounts. This point was crucial for the success of this analysis. Also, our ability to match individual claims rather than expenditure totals greatly improved our precision. One error source, unknown record survey error, applied to all plans and so canceled in plan comparisons. Without individual claim matching, it would have been impossible to separate excess claims (mainly from providers who did not cooperate in the billing records survey) from much smaller, unmatched billing records totals; the results would have been dominated by kinds of claims that we did not effectively sample.

Attempts to model underreporting from claims information alone would have yielded problematic results. Standard selection models require a positive indicator of non filing, which was not available as decisions about each claim could be made independently. Economic models of rational claim filing suggest that busy, high-income families would not file, missing entirely the sociological "personal disorganization" aspect. Given that claims are a central focus of study in this experiment, methods for studying them should be distribution-free wherever possible. The independent record check design meets this requirement.

REFERENCES

BALMAUTH, E. (1965) "Health interview responses compared with medical records." National Center for Health Statistics Series 2, 7.

CANNELL, C. F. (1965) "Reporting of hospitalization in the Health Interview Survey." National Center for Health Statistics Series 2, 6.

—and F. FOWLER (1965) "Comparison of hospital reporting in three survey procedures." National Center for Health Statistics Series 2, 8.

CHANDRASEKAR, C. and W. E. DEMING (1949) "On a method of estimating birth and death rates and the extent of registration." Journal of the American Statistical Association: 101-115.

MADOW, W. G. (1973) "Net differences in interview data on chronic conditions and information derived from medical records." National Center for Health Statistics Series 2, 57.

MARQUIS, K. H., M. S. MARQUIS, and J. P. NEWHOUSE (1976) "The measurement of expenditures for outpatient physician and dental services: methodological findings from the health insurance study." Medical Care.

MORRIS, C. N. (1979) "A finite selection model for experimental design of the Health Insurance Study." Journal of Econometrics 11:43-61.

NEWHOUSE, J. P., W. G. MANNING, C. N. MORRIS et al. (1981) "Some interim results from a controlled trial of cost sharing in health insurance." New England Journal of Medicine 305:1501-1507.

NEWHOUSE, J. P., K. H. MARQUIS, C. N. MORRIS, C. E. PHELPS, and W. H. ROGERS (1979) "Measurement issues in the second generation of social experiments." Journal of Econometrics 11:117-129.

ISSUES OF DATA COLLECTION IN ASSESSING PROGRAMS INVOLVING CRIME REDUCTION: THE JOB CORPS AND SUPPORTED WORK EVALUATIONS

Charles Mallar
Irving Piliavin

The specific issues raised in this chapter relate to problems associated with obtaining evaluation data when a socioeconomic model is used to assess a public program. In the context of specific evaluations, these problems involve a broad array of difficulties, including the following: (1) failure to obtain quantitative measures consistent with the models of socioeconomic behavior that underlie the empirical work; (2) failure to carefully delineate and measure variation in program implementation; (3) failure to develop data on the attributes of program participants that could influence their responsiveness to programs; and (4) failure to identify, monitor, and record the complexities involved in participant querying, program start up, and program monitoring. These matters often are overlooked or, perhaps more of-

AUTHORS' NOTE: We wish to thank Craig Thornton for helpful comments on an earlier draft of this chapter and for his valuable contributions to our previous work on the Job Corps and Supported Work evaluations which motivated this work.

ten, placed on the back burner until the time of project reporting, when they are resurrected as issues to be considered in future evaluations.

The data collection problems cited above are similar to problems noted by other researchers that involve the failures of data collectors to take necessary precautions in gathering information. In this case, however, the villains are neither staff nor respondents, but the project investigators themselves. The "sin" originates in a failure to apply sufficient and substantial theory to their evaluations. As a result, project investigators simplify program assessment, often overlooking important substantive results as well as problems of bias and data confounding. In the discussion to follow, we will illustrate these points with examples from the evaluations of two major employment programs undertaken during the 1970s. We then briefly take up the elements of a program for evaluation research that offers promise for mitigating these problems and enhances our ability to produce evaluations that can better contribute to the development of more effective programs and implementation strategies. To do this requires breaking no new ground, but, rather, a guide to evaluation researchers how some recent empirical innovations can enable us to apply principles for learning more from program evaluations.

THE SUPPORTED WORK AND JOB CORPS EVALUATIONS

During the 1970s, the Supported Work demonstration and the Job Corps program were two major employment and training programs, sponsored by the United States government, which had objectives of reducing crime. The operational costs of the Supported Work program were over $80 million for a five-year period, approximately $10 million of which was spent on program evaluation. The operational costs of the Job Corps averaged over $200 million per year. Outlays for its evaluation totaled over $2 million.

Evaluations of both programs were rigorous. The Supported Work evaluation was based on an experimental design. The Job Corps evaluation used a quasi-experimental comparison group design. Samples in both projects were large and interview data were collected by trained, well-supervised staff. Data analyses in both projects were, and remain, representative of the state of the art in statistical techniques (Hollister et al., 1984; Mallar et al., 1982). Given these advantages, one might expect such evaluations to provide definitive information on program impact within the bounds of the populations sampled and the program stimulae utilized. But, as we shall demonstrate, this conclusion is not so certain in some areas, and the shortcomings noted can point the way to more definitive findings in future evaluations.

SUPPORTED WORK

In general form, the Supported Work program was not distinguishable from other job provision programs of the 1970s. The jobs provided were of limited duration, the wages were relatively low, and the work itself was typically unskilled. The program was thought to be different, however, in that it incorporated peer group support, graduated stress, and close supervision of participants. Peer group support consisted of assignment of program participants to work in teams in which members had similar backgrounds. It was assumed that this structure would provide a supportive environment for individuals who were having difficulty entering (or reentering) the labor market. Graduated stress was predicated on the belief that program participants could not, at the time of their enrollment, meet the performance standards of the regular labor market. Thus, Supported Work jobs were structured so that initial performance demands were modest but were gradually increased until they resembled those which participants would face in nonprogram employment. Increased demands were accompanied by increased wages to maintain incentives for work. Close supervision was provided so experienced supervisors would teach participants better work skills and habits.

Unfortunately, in practice it was difficult to determine the thoroughness and consistency with which these features were realized.[1] Supported Work was implemented in 15 communities throughout the United States, with initial enrollees coming to the program in March, 1975. Evaluation of the program in terms of its impact on those believed to be high crime risks was carried out in nine of these sites. Three high crime risk populations were singled out by program operators as being appropriate targets for the program. The crucial identifying characteristics of these populations for the purposes of Supported Work recruitment included the following: adult offenders, individuals at least 18 years of age who had been released from jail or prison within six months of application to Supported Work; adult drug addicts, individuals at least 18 years of age who had been enrolled in drug treatment programs within six months of program application; disadvantaged youth, 17 to 20 years of age, school dropouts, half of whom had a history of prior delinquency arrests. Program eligibles also had to have at best marginal employment records prior to their Supported Work application. Adult offenders participated at seven program sites, addicts participated in four locations, and youth at five. The period over which sample members were followed ranged from 18 to 27 months, and target group sizes were large; thus, it was possible to carry out detailed analyses with a potential reliability and precision not realized by prior studies.

The findings from the Supported Work experiment indicated that the impact of employment on individuals' subsequent criminal activities was selective and lagged. Addicts, older criminals, and previously arrest-free youths were among those most likely to restrict future crimes after program exposure. But all those who appeared to reduce their criminal activities were most likely to do so after leaving Supported Work and after their overall employment advantage relative to controls had been largely eroded. As suggested by this overview, the early and significant employment advantage of participants relative to controls, resulting from the former's in-program job guarantees, almost disappeared over time. Significant experimental employment advantages continued within various subgroups, but these were generally not the same groups in which crime reductions among experimentals were found.

JOB CORPS

This program provided, and continues to provide, economically disadvantaged youths between 16 and 21 years of age with basic education, vocational training, and related services in a residential setting. The program's objective is to help these youths become more productive workers, improve their lifetime earnings prospects, and help them become more responsible citizens. Job Corps is designed to serve youths who currently live in such debilitating environments that they must be relocated to residential centers and provided with residential support in order to benefit from basic education, vocational training, and ancillary services.

The Job Corps evaluation was designed to provide the Department of Labor with a comprehensive evaluation of the economic impact of the Job Corps program. The first detailed personal interviews were conducted in the spring of 1977 with a sample of Corps members then participating in the program and with a comparable group of disadvantaged youths who had not attempted to enroll in Job Corps. At periods 9, 24, and, most recently, 54 months after the baseline survey, reinterviews were conducted with all of the youths in the comparison group and with Corps members who had been out of the program for a sufficient length of time to provide the needed postprogram information.

In terms of size and statistical significance, some of the most noteworthy estimated effects of Job Corps on the behavior of former participants are as follows (on a per Corps member basis, including military jobs, and averaged over the four-year postprogram observation period):

- increase in employment of over three weeks per year
- increase in earnings of approximately $655 per year, in excess of a 15 percent increase (controlling for nonlinear time trends)
- substantial increase in the probability of having a high school diploma or equivalent degree (a fivefold increase)
- higher college attendance
- decrease in high school attendance associated with the effects of high school degrees obtained in Job Corps
- better health, with a reduction in serious health problems on average of over one week per year
- reduction in the receipt of financial welfare assistance, amounting to an average of over two weeks per year
- reduction in the receipt of Unemployment Insurance of nearly one week per year

The crime effects as measured by arrests are erratic over the postprogram period and, in aggregate over the entire period, show no effect; however, there is a significant shift from more to less serious crimes.

The positive overall impacts generally persist throughout the four years of postprogram observation. The trend over the four-year postprogram observation period appears to be an increase in program benefits during the first few months (especially for employment and earnings during the transition from center life to reentering the regular labor market) and then relatively stable effects throughout the rest of the four-year period.

DATA PROBLEMS

MEASURES OF CRIMINALITY

Both the Supported Work and Job Corps analyses relied heavily on self-reported arrests as a measure of criminal behavior. In fact, for the Job Corps evaluation, only arrest data were obtained as measures of criminal activity. This was based largely on a belief that arrests would be more accurately reported than actual incidents of crime. Furthermore, arrests are more readily verifiable measures because they can be compared to records from the criminal justice system.

There are, however, serious and well-known validity problems in individuals' self-reports of their past experiences. Respondents may not remember past events well; they may be ashamed to confess their faults; they may be concerned about the uses to which their information will be put. These problems are nowhere more severe than in regard to information supplied by individuals regarding their past criminal activities. In the Supported Work and Job Corps evaluations, the decision to use self-reporting of arrests rather than official records, as the primary source for data on criminal history was dictated by cost considerations and (as it turned out, well-founded) expectations that governmental agencies would not uniformly comply with project requests for officially recorded data on sample members' arrest and adjudication histories. There is little doubt that official arrest data would have been used to record sample members' criminal arrests had it been available at reasonable cost.

In order to assess and, if necessary, make allowance for self-reporting bias, Supported Work evaluators compared officially recorded and self-reported arrest histories for a subsample of observations—participants at three sites at which criminal justice agencies did cooperate with the project team (Schore et al., 1979). The results of the comparison were encouraging. Despite a general tendency for sample members to underreport arrests after entering the Supported Work sample, there were no significant underreporting differentials between experimentals and controls. This result led program evaluators to regard self-reported arrest data as providing unbiased information on sample members' criminal activity.

A problem that was not addressed was that arrest information may not accurately reflect criminal involvement. Arrests are related to the skill at committing crimes and factors other than the systemic concept of criminality in the underlying socioeconomic models. An example of potentially severe problems is suggested in some initially overlooked data on self-reports of crime that were also obtained from Supported Work sample members throughout the course of the evaluation.

Self-reports of crime were not used in the evaluation because their validity could not be directly assessed and because arrest data were considered by project staff to be an acceptable indicator of illegal activity in the evaluation of crime control programs. But preliminary analyses undertaken early in the Support Work project indicated that self-report data on criminal involvement led to different results from those provided by self-reports of arrest. Given the demonstrated absence of bias with self-reported arrest data, this discrepancy was attributed to likely validity problems with self-reported crime. No further evaluation of Supported Work was carried out using the crime reports. Recent research has raised serious questions about the presumed superiority of self-reported arrest data relative to criminal activity for indexing criminal involvement. This research involves our use of data from two waves of the Supported Work evaluation to test some recursive models of crime based on economic and related theories of deterrence.

These deterrence models initially employed an unmeasured crime factor as the dependent variable for which self-reported crime and self-reported arrest reports were assumed to be observable indicators of this same systemic concept. The models fit the unrestricted covariance matrix significantly less well than models in which self-reported arrest and self-reported crime were treated as separate but correlated observables. Furthermore, the models based on self-reported crime as the key dependent variable fit the data much better than did models based on self-reported arrests, and the parameter estimates in the former models were more in accord with theoretical expectations than were those in the latter models (see Figures 8.1 and 8.2 and related discussion in Appendix A).

These various findings have disquieting implications for previous evaluations. Researchers have assumed that self-reports regarding crime provided invalid information because program evaluations based on this measure were inconsistent with evaluations based on a measure whose validity for experimental-control comparisons was supported by official arrest records. What was not seriously considered by the researchers is the implication from the subsequent study that self-reported arrests and self-reported crimes measure different albeit related phenomena. Clearly, a major problem with arrest as a measure of crime is its endogeneity in models of criminal behavior—being arrested may connote nothing more than ineptness in committing a crime. Furthermore, it is not strictly true that self-reported criminal activity is beyond validity check. The economic models of deterrence we have been examining in recent research do, in fact, provide a form of validity test that goes by the term "construct validity". Assuming the models estimated are specified properly (at least approximately), the fact that the models based on self-reported crime provide a better fit with theoretical expectations suggests that self-reported crime data are more valid an indicator of illegal activity than self-reports of arrests. The most serious immediate implication of this is that the "criminal participation" findings of previous evaluations may be in error.

It may be argued that our finding on the relative merits of crime measures reflect procedural artifacts or a chance finding. This is a less likely possibility, considering that this finding was observed in models based on three independent samples (i.e., offenders, addicts, problem youth), and that respondents' reports regarding the criterion measures were obtained nine months after they provided information on the other variables used in the models. Thus, the findings appear to be relatively stable and such contaminating factors as response set and recall do not seem to be likely contributors to the relationships observed.

VARIATION AMONG PARTICIPANTS IN PROGRAM EXPOSURE

Because of their large scope, certain analytic advantages were to be found in the Supported Work and Job Corps evaluations. Foremost among these was the opportunity to study whether theoretically or policy relevant subgroups might respond differently to program exposure. Although such detailed study seems an obvious necessity in program evaluations, it rarely has been undertaken because evaluation samples have been too small. The Supported Work and Job Corps samples proved less limiting as they were diverse in character and numbered approximately 6000. Indeed, the detailed analyses conducted in the course of the program's evaluation suggested that certain groups were more likely than others to benefit from this work experience.

Unfortunately, the large size of the evaluation also posed data collection problems with potentially serious implications for analysis. For example, at any given time during the Supported Work demonstration, there was a set number of program participant slots to be filled. These slots were distributed across several communities or sites. Whenever a slot opened because a program participant withdrew or graduated, the slot was filled by a randomly selected program applicant. At the same time, a new member of the control group was added by the same process. Participant and control slots were filled in this manner over a 28-month intake period. As a result, program participants differed in three important ways that could confound efforts to isolate program impacts. They varied in the type of employment, the program site, and the time at which they came into the demonstration. Controls could differ along the latter two dimensions. All three of these confounding elements proved impossible to disentangle for Supported Work, and similar problems occurred for the Job Corps evaluation.

Program Assignment

Although the presumed stimulus in the Supported Work demonstration was employment, the jobs to which participants were assigned varied greatly. Some jobs approximated "make work" whereas others required a modicum of skill training; whereas most jobs offered no transition to permanent employment, a few did. These and other variations were not in the data base used by researchers. It may be that for the purposes of programming, such detailed accounting would be difficult to implement. Yet there are propositions in social and behavioral science that speak to the importance of task content and reward structure for shaping behavior. The failure of Supported Work to track these features clearly limits and perhaps distorts the analysis of the program's impact.

Program Site

The regression models that were estimated to assess participants' responses to Supported Work include interactions of site with experimental status. These interactions indicated that experimental-control differentials were much more favorable in some sites than others. Unfortunately, individual programs in Supported Work evolved partly in opportunistic fashion with only loose central guidance; careful multidimensional classification of the programs was never made. In any case, the number of programs was too small to permit meaningful groupings. Furthermore, the basis for referral to individual programs was not monitored or well understood. Thus, although significant variations in site achievements were observed, it could not be ascertained what distinguished the more successful programs or, in fact, whether the achievements were somehow related to the basis by which individuals were led to apply to Supported Work. These problems were even greater with Job Corps because of the greater dispersion of enrollees' home and program sites.

Time Of Sample Entry

Enrollment in the Supported Work demonstration took place over a two and a half year interval. Because of cost considerations, it was not possible to extend the evaluation sufficiently to follow all sample members over an equal period of time. To deal with this problem, the evaluation sample was divided into three cohorts, each distinguished by the calendar time interval in which its members enrolled in the demonstration. The earliest cohort was given five interviews at intervals of nine months over a 36-month period; the middle cohort received four interviews over 27 months; and the late cohort had three interviews over 18 months. Analysis of arrest patterns within these cohorts suggested that experimental-control differences in the addict and offender target groups differed for different cohorts. In particular, at each follow-up interview experimentals in the earliest cohort reported a cumulative percentage arrest rate lower than that reported by controls. In the middle cohort, the patterns were mixed and in the late cohort, experimentals reported slightly higher arrest rates than controls (see Table 8.1).[2] Although

TABLE 8.1
Differences in Percentage with Any Arrests by Cohort

	Months 1-18		Months 1-27		Months 1-36	
	Experimental Minus Control Differential	Control Group Mean	Experimental Minus Control Differential	Control Group Mean	Experimental Minus Control Differential	Control Group Mean
18-Month Cohort						
Addicts	3.1	31.4	*	*	*	*
Offenders	2.3	45.0	*	*	*	*
24-Month Cohort						
Addicts	−9.5**	32.8	−9.4	42.1	*	*
Offenders	1.1	45.5	2.8	50.6	*	*
36-Month Cohort						
Addicts	−17.3**	38.4	−14.2**	46.1	−18.1**	53.1
Offenders	−5.2	53.5	−10.3	63.5	−8.0	64.8

NOTE: The data presented are regression–adjusted estimates that control for sites and personal attributes.
*Not available.
**Statistically significant at the 5% level.

the differences were not always statistically significant, the cohort variations were sufficiently large that they could not be ignored. Various explanations could be put forth to account for them. In view of the procedures by which the Supported Work sample was selected, the possibility could not be excluded that the variations stemmed from shifts in sample selection procedures. It also was possible that they resulted from artifacts associated with program start-up or routinization. Although it also could be argued that members of the early cohort were more or less likely to distort criterion information to evaluators, this possibility was considered unlikely as no cohort effects were observed in the aforementioned study of self-report arrest bias (Schore et al., 1979). Efforts to discover what might have led to the different patterns among the 36-month cohort took two forms. One entailed locating and testing the consequences of individual attributes that differentiated the three sample cohorts. The second sought to determine whether the cohort effect reflected the different impacts of programs operating at different sites. The first analysis failed to find an array of individual attributes that distinguished early and successful participants from all others. The second indicated that the cohort effect existed at virtually all sites. Because of limitations in our data, we could pursue the question no further. As a result, it still is not clear that the positive impacts found among Supported Work participants represent anything more than experimental artifacts or some unknown time-interaction between program content and participant attributes.

MODELING PROGRAM PARTICIPATION
IN QUASI-EXPERIMENTAL DESIGNS

If program participation can be modeled and statistically identified vis-à-vis the other behavior of interest, consistent estimates of program impacts can be obtained from quasi-experimental designs (see Appendix B). In order to statistically identify the model, we need to have variables that can reasonably be assumed to affect participation but not the other behavior.[3] With the Job Corps evaluation it was possible to develop such variables for evaluating the overall program. Specifically, the evaluators used proxies for knowledge of the program and proximity to Job Corps centers as variables that affect program participation, but not employment and related variables (see further in Appendix B). However, in this evaluation it was not possible to extend the approach to estimate the differential impacts of different kinds of program treatment because program operators and participants engaged in unknown processes leading to the latter's allocation to treatments. Not enough was known beforehand about selection into different kinds of programs to statistically identify appropriate models.

CONCLUSIONS

Some of the major problems of data collection in evaluation studies are of researchers' own doing. For example, evaluators fail to control or develop data that could enable them to identify and explain variations in their findings that may arise from inconsistencies in program implementation or from variation over time in populations that are being recruited. Researchers may not consider whether their collection of data provides adequate indicators of the phenomena they wish to examine. The cases discussed here involved an indicator that was a primary criterion for assessing program success.

Lack of attention to these matters may seriously confound evaluation findings. The reasons that these matters have been given so little previous attention by evaluation researchers do not include ignorance of the problem. A substantial literature, part of which is found even in basic research methodology texts, brings these problems to the attention of investigators and even identifies some by name as, for example, halo effects, placebo effects, program decay effects, experimenter demand effects, specification error. Given this recognition, why are these problematic influences on evaluation studies so often ignored by researchers? First, the control of contaminating influences of the type discussed here through sample intake procedures, project design, program monitoring, and other techniques often is not possible and, in any event, is expensive. Second, accounting for the effects of these phenomena through statistical techniques requires large samples, is time consuming, complicates analyses, and also is expensive. Finally, because research on these matters is rare, there may be only a partial "payoff" from these control and accounting efforts. Researchers, as in the case of the Supported Work example, may simply be left with unexplained effects.

Attending to the contaminating influences discussed here therefore may be seen to bring much expense and little reward. The problem of researchers' use of flawed indicators also may be a matter of time and expense in data development. But as suggested above, it may also reflect a misguided belief that a flawed indicator which is demonstrably consonant with recorded fact is to be preferred to another indicator with apparent face validity but which is not demonstrably consonant with recorded fact.

Efforts to mitigate these problems require more ambitious research endeavors than are generally undertaken. The requisites comprise a familiar listing. In addition to the usual procedures associated with sound research design, evaluation samples and data bases must be, respectively, large enough and oriented to permit identification of confounding influences in results. Indicators of key criterion variables, at least under certain circumstances, need to be better validated. Program implementation must be better monitored and conceptualized. The expense in time and money of such efforts is substantial and no doubt poses a major obstacle to their initiation. However, the costs entailed by the absence of this work potentially are much greater. At best, otherwise valid results of many evaluation efforts will have an air of indeterminancy; at worse, the results will be biased.

APPENDIX A

RECURSIVE MODELS OF CRIME AND ARREST WITH SUPPORTED WORK DATA

Figures 8.1 and 8.2 portray the estimated recursive models linking the first nine-month follow-up crime and arrest experiences of adult addict sample members to their demographic backgrounds and attitudinal characteristics as reported at time of sample entry. The background and demographic attributes are treated as exogenous in each model. The initial numerical entries adjacent to the boxed exogenous variable entries and along the arrowed paths are structural regression coefficients representing the estimated impact of the variable at left on the probability of reported crime or arrest at nine months. These entries are followed, in parentheses, with these associated t-statistic values. The exogenous variables are assumed to be intercorrelated as are the two risk factors and the relative earnings and criminal opportunity measures. Although coefficients linking the exogenous variables to the various attitudinal measures have been estimated, they are omitted from Figures 8.1 and 8.2 because they are not relevant to the subject matter of the chapter and, furthermore, their inclusion would seriously clutter the diagrams. We also exclude the variable MINPAY from our discussion because its predicted effect is not clear and the coefficients relating this variable to crime or arrest never approached statistical significance. The theory predicted signs of the other attitudinal variables in the propensity to commit crime unambiguous are as follows:

Variables	Sign
CRIMEFFIC	+
RELEARN	+
CRIMOP	+
PERSONAL RISK	–
FORMAL RISK	–
NETOCC	–

As can be seen from the models portrayed, the signs of four of the six predictor variables are in the predicted direction (three being statistically significant) using reported crime as the dependent variable, whereas only two are in the predicted direction (one bordering on statistical significance) using reported arrests as the dependent variable. These findings essentially are replicated using the two other samples available from the Supported Work demonstration.

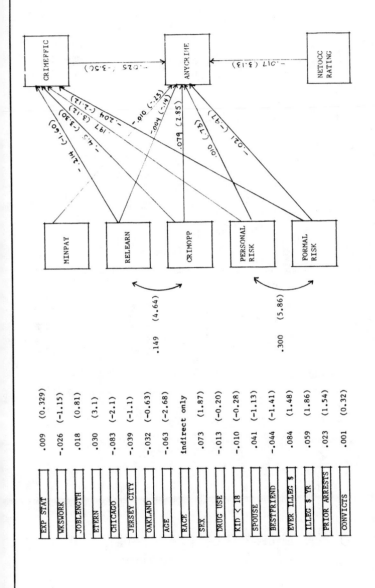

Figure 8.1   Estimated Recursive Model of Crime at 9 Months for Addicts

149

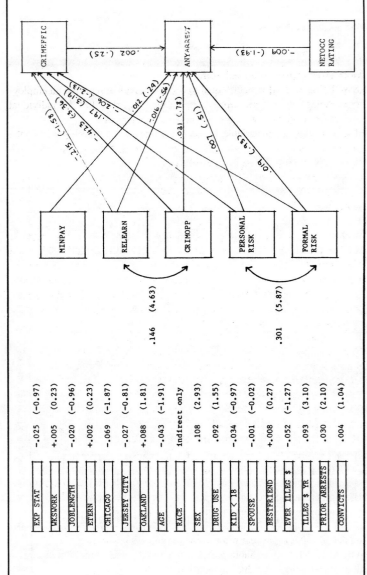

EXP STAT   -.025   (-0.97)
WKSWORK   +.005   (0.23)
JOBLENGTH   -.020   (-0.96)
ETERN   +.002   (0.23)
CHICAGO   -.069   (-1.87)
JERSEY CITY   -.027   (-0.81)
OAKLAND   +.088   (1.81)
AGE   -.043   (-1.91)
RACE   indirect only
SEX   .108   (2.93)
DRUG USE   .092   (1.55)
KID < 18   -.034   (-0.97)
SPOUSE   -.001   (-0.02)
BESTFRIEND   +.008   (0.27)
EVER ILLEG $ -.052   (-1.27)
ILLEG $ YR   .093   (3.10)
PRIOR ARRESTS   .030   (2.10)
CONVICTS   .004   (1.04)

Figure 8.2   Estimated Recursive Model of Arrest at 9 Months for Addicts

DEFINITIONS OF VARIABLES USED
IN THE SUPPORTED WORK ANALYSIS

BACKGROUND VARIABLES

EXP STAT:a dummy variable equal to 1 if an individual was in the Supported Work experimental group and 0 otherwise.

WKSWORK:an ordinal variable equal to 0 if an individual reported no employment during the year preceding sample entry; equal to 1 if the individual worked from one to nine weeks; and equal to 2 otherwise.

JOBLENGTH:an ordinal variable equal to 0 if an individual reported no job in the two years prior to sample entry; equal to 1 if the individual reported a job lasting 1-6 months; and equal to 2 otherwise.

FTEARN:a continuous variable measuring the individual's average legal income (in dollars) per month, during the time they were not incarcerated in the last year.

SITE:dummy variables equal to 1 if an individual was enrolled in the Supported Work program in that city. Four sites, Atlanta, Hartford, Jersey City, and New York, were included in the structural models for the youth group; Philadelphia was the excluded site. Three sites, Chicago, Jersey City, and Oakland, were included in the exaddict structural models; Philadelphia was the excluded site. Six sites, Chicago, Hartford, Jersey City, Newark, Oakland, and Philadelphia, were included in the exoffender structural model; San Francisco was the excluded site.

AGE:a continuous variable equal to an individual's age in years.

RACE:a dummy variable equal to 1 if an individual was black, 0 otherwise.

SEX:a dummy variable equal to 1 if an individual was male, 0 otherwise.

DRUG USE:a dummy variable equal to 1 if an individual reported ever using opiates prior to sample entry, 0 otherwise.

KID 18:a dummy variable equal to 1 if an individual reported living with a child under 18 years of age, 0 otherwise.

SPOUSE:a dummy variable equal to 1 if an individual reported living with a spouse, 0 otherwise.

BESTFRIEND:a dummy variable equal to 1 if an individual reported having a straight best friend (i.e., not involved in any "hussles" or crime), 0 otherwise.

EVER ILLEG $:a dummy variable equal to 1 if an individual reported ever having made money illegally, 0 otherwise.

ILLEG $ YR:a dummy variable equal to 1 if an individual reported making money illegally in the year prior to sample entry, 0 otherwise.

PRIOR ARRESTS:a continuous variable equal to the total number of arrests an individual reported ever having incurred.

CONVICTS:a continuous variable equal to the total number of convictions an individual reported ever having received.

RISK VARIABLES

PERSONAL RISK:a factor whose indicators are individuals' scores (1=low, 3=50/50, 5=high) on two risk variables: risk of losing friends if imprisoned and risk of losing spouse if imprisoned.

FORMAL RISK:a factor whose indicators are individuals' scores (same as PERSONAL RISK) on five risk variables: risk of being seen; risk of being reported if seen; risk of being arrested if reported; risk of job loss if arrested; and risk of imprisonment if arrested.

RELATIVE VALUE AND MONETARY RETURN VARIABLES

MINPAY:a continuous variable indicating an individual's estimate of the minimum weekly pay he or she would accept from a legitimate job.

RELEARN:a dummy variable equal to 1 if an individual expected greater or the same earning potential from illegal activity, relative to a legitimate job, 0 otherwise.

CRIMOPP:a dummy variable equal to 1 if an individual perceived frequent opportunities to commit crime, 0 otherwise.

NETOCC RATING:a continuous variable equal to the difference between individual's mean occupational respect rating (on a scale of 1-100) for six legitimate occupations (house painter, postal worker, factory worker, construction worker, car washer, and cleaning person) and his or her mean occupational rating for seven criminal occupations (numbers runner, gambler, hustler, cocaine dealer, purse snatcher, numbers of banker, and pimp).

CRIMEFFIC:an ordinary variable, based on individual's estimates of the time required for them to earn $1,000 from crime: 1=within an hour; 2=from 1-3 hours; 3=from 4-24 hours; 4=from 1-3 days; 5=4-7 days; 6=from 1-3 weeks; and 7= 4 or more weeks.

CRIMINAL BEHAVIOR VARIABLES (DEPENDENT VARIABLES)

ANYCRIME:a dummy variable equal to 1 if an individual reported committing at least one crime in the period between sample entry and the 9-month interview, 0 otherwise.

ANYARREST:a dummy variable equal to 1 if an individual reported experiencing at least one arrest in the period between sample entry and the 9-month interview, 0 otherwise.

APPENDIX B

CONTROLLING FOR UNOBSERVED DIFFERENCES BETWEEN CORPS MEMBERS AND COMPARISON YOUTHS

For the Job Corps evaluation, in addition to controlling for observed factors that affect the behavior of interest, an econometric methodology was used that controlled for unobserved differences between samples. Specifically, in this application, statistical techniques were used to control for unobserved differences between youths in the Job Corps and comparison groups (for example, unobserved differences in employability, trainability, and motivation). With the technique used, the basic procedure entailed modeling and estimating program participation and then including in the regression equations a control variable that is a function of the estimated probability of program participation.

The socioeconomic model used in this analysis suggests that the behavior of interest (e.g., employment, crime) is affected by the Job Corps treatments, other observed explanatory variables, and unobserved factors. This can be approximated by a linear regression model, as follows:

$$\gamma_{it} = \beta' X_{it} + \delta' T_{it} = \epsilon_{it} \qquad [1]$$

where it is the socioeconomic behavior of interest for the ith individual during the tth time period, the T's are program-treatment variables, the δ's are program effects on the behavior of interest, the X's are observed variables (other than program treatments) that explain the behavior of interest, the β's are coefficients representing the effects of the explanatory variables, and ϵ is an error term including unobserved factors.

With a nonrandomized control group (a comparison group), the program-treatment variables, T's, in equation 1 potentially are correlated with the error term, ϵ. Many important unobserved variables that affect the economic behavior of interest also are likely to affect individual decisions about whether to participate in the program and, hence, the T's. Therefore, the T's are potentially endogenous with respect to the behavior of interest, in which case least squares (LS) regression estimators generally will be biased.

As an example, variables such as innate ability and motivation are not observed directly; however, they undoubtedly affect both employment-related behavior and the decision about whether to participate in the Job Corps or similar programs. If youths are motivated to maximize their incomes, any variable that affects employment and income also will affect decisions about whether or not to attempt to participate in the Job Corps. Thus, the same unobserved variables can be important elements in the error terms for both γ and the T's with a comparison group. This is in contrast to the situation with a randomized control group, in which unobserved as well as observed variables should tend to be orthogonal to, or uncorrelated with, the T's. When a comparison group is used, the T's generally will be correlated with ϵ, and the program variables should be treated as endogenous. Furthermore, LS estimators generally will be biased when endogenous variables are included in regression equations, unless the correlation between the endogenous variables and the error term (ϵ) can be partialled out.

Different procedures for selecting comparison groups in the absence of randomization will lead to varying levels of (1) statistical inefficiency from correlation between the X's and T's, because the program and comparison groups do not match with respect to observed variables; and (2) LS bias from correlation between the T's and ϵ when the groups do not match with respect to unobserved variables and when program effects (γ) are estimated via LS. Some procedures that have been used to obtain comparison samples yield poor matches and, hence, lead to inaccurate estimates for the γ's with either difference-in-sample-means or LS estimation procedures (e.g., evaluations using the preenrollment experience of participants as a comparison and rely on before-after comparisons for youths or other new entrants or reentrants to the labor force; evaluations using individuals who enrolled but did not show up for the program; and evaluations using individuals who dropped out of the program soon after entering).

However, the comparison group procedure outlined above should be relatively efficient and have relatively little LS bias. If, as designed, comparison group members differ from Corps members primarily in terms of random access to information about the program and random proximity to the program, then the X's and T's and the T's and ϵ should be weakly correlated. In this case, estimates of program effects will not differ much, depending on whether we control for observed differences between the Job Corps and comparison groups, unobserved differences, both (observed and unobserved differences), or neither.[4]

Even with the rigorous comparison group procedures that we developed, interview data and any available secondary data should be used to control for both observed and unobserved differences that remain between the comparison and program participant groups. Only in that way can we ensure against bias in the estimates of program effects. In principle, consistent estimates of program effects can be obtained by controlling for observed differences directly and for unobserved differences indirectly through a model of the participation decision.

If a normal distribution is assumed for the error term in equation 1, that error term can be decomposed into two components—an estimable component correlated with the T's and another component uncorrelated with the T's which has the properties of an LS error term. Thus, equation 1 can be rewritten as follows:

$$\gamma_{it} = \beta' X_{it} + \gamma' T_{it} + \delta \lambda_i + \omega_{it} \qquad [2]$$

and

$$\lambda_i = P_i \frac{f(a'Z_i)}{F(a'Z_i)} - (1 - P_i) \frac{f(a'Z_i)}{1 - F(a'Z_i)} \qquad [3]$$

where P_i is a binary program participation variable that equals 1 for Corps members (0 otherwise); $f(\cdot)$ denotes the standard normal density function for program participation; $F(\cdot)$ denotes the standard normal distribution function for program participation; the Z's are explanatory variables that affect program participation; and δ and the a's are coefficients.

We can estimate λ for each individual youth (Job Corps or comparison group) by estimating the a's with a probit equation for participation in Job Corps. The estimated values of λ will be close to 0 for Corps members who have a high estimated probability of participation in Job Corps and for comparison youths who have a low estimated probability of participation. In other words, λ will be close to 0 for cases that are correctly classified by the participation model and, thus, that have small errors in the probit equation estimated for P.

The estimated values of λ will become progressively larger positive numbers for Corps members who have lower estimated probabilities of participation (i.e., youths who participate in Job Corps for unobserved reasons) and, hence, who have larger positive errors in the probit equation estimated for P. Similarly, the estimated values of λ will become progressively more negative for comparison youths who have higher estimated probabilities of participation (i.e., youths who do not participate in Job Corps for unobserved reasons) and, hence, who have more negative errors in the probit equation estimated for P.

The sign of δ is determined by the correlation of the errors (e.g., from omitted variables) in the underlying equations for Y and P. If the estimated value for δ is positive, it indicates that individuals who have higher values of γ and are more likely to participate in Job Corps for unobserved reasons will also have higher values of Y, on average, for unobserved reasons. Therefore, when δ is positive, the failure to adjust for sample selectivity (i.e., unobserved differences) will bias program effects in a positive direction for Y, because youths with high Y's for unobserved reasons will tend to be program participants for unobserved reasons.[5] Similarly, if the estimated value for δ is negative, it indicates that individuals who are more likely to participate for unobserved reasons will have lower values of Y on average for unobserved reasons, in which case the failure to adjust for sample selectivity will bias program effects in a negative direction for Y.

As previously noted, when estimating Job Corps effects on employment and related activities, the bias stemming from the failure to adjust for sample selection could be in either direction. A positive δ and positive (i.e., upward) bias for the γ's from omitting λ will occur for employment and earnings if there is a predominance of youths with higher unmeasured abilities who are more likely to participate in Job Corps (e.g., because they benefit more from training opportunities). A negative δ and negative bias for the γ's from omitting λ will occur for employment and earnings if there is a predominance of youths with lower unmeasured abilities who are more likely to participate in Job Corps because it costs less (i.e., fewer opportunities outside of Job Corps).

If a consistent estimate of F($\cdot$) is obtained through probit procedures, consistent estimates for all of the coefficients in equation 2 can be obtained from LS by substituting the resulting predicted values of λ into equation 2. However, the standard errors and t-statistics for the estimated coefficients might be biased slightly if the predicted λ's are used in a typical regression package. The typical regression programs will not account for the implicit heteroscedasticity involved in controlling for unobserved differences between Corps members and the comparison sample via the Heckman (1979) approach of using predicted λ's. In practice, however, the standard errors and t-statistics from the typical regression packages are usually close to their unbiased counterparts, especially when the coefficients for the adjustment variables are small and/or statistically insignificant (which is often the case with our estimates).

Therefore, the standard errors and t-statistics from typical regression packages are approximately accurate and indicative of the true values of these statistics. Maximum likelihood estimates could yield some gains in

terms of (1) the statistical efficiency for coefficient estimates and (2) un-
biasedness for estimates of the standard errors. With our large sample sizes,
however, maximum likelihood estimation would be prohibitively expensive
for gains that are likely to be small.

Another issue that arises when using the above procedures to control for
unobserved differences between program and comparison groups is whether
equation 2 is statistically identified when predicted values of λ are used, as
they must be because λ is inherently unobservable. Conceptually, as suggested by Barnow et al. (1980), equation 2 is statistically identified by the
inherent nonlinearities in the model for λ and Y, even if the X's and Z's are
identical. In practice, however, these nonlinearities by themselves often turn
out to be ineffective for statistically identifying behavioral models, and they
can lead to multicollinearity if used alone.[6] Parameter restrictions are necessary for ensuring identification in models such as those represented by equation 2. The parameter restrictions amount to obtaining Z variables that can
reasonably be modeled as affecting the decision to participate in Job Corps,
P, but that do not directly affect the behavior of interest (i.e., are not among
the X variables in equations 1 and 2).

Variables associated with youths' knowledge about Job Corps (information, perceptions, etc.) are potential candidates for identifying the employment and related behavior of interest to this study. Differential knowledge
about Job Corps undoubtedly will affect youths' decisions about whether or
not to participate in the program. By itself, such knowledge should not have a
direct effect on employment and related behavior. Based on our earlier findings that recruitment for Job Corps differs substantially across geographic
areas (see Kershaw, et al., 1976) and that friends and relatives are by far the
most important sources of information about Job Corps (see Kerachsky and
Mallar, 1978), we developed two proxy variables for knowledge of Job
Corps from the preenrollment addresses of Corps members and comparison
youths. These two proxy variables (#JCMEM-75 and %JCMEM-75) indicate, respectively, the number and fraction of youths from preenrollment
neighborhoods who participated in Job Corps during the period just before
our sample was deciding whether or not to attempt to enroll in Job Corps.
More specifically, these two knowledge proxies are obtained from data on
Job Corps enrollments by three-digit ZIP code areas during fiscal 1975.

The greater the number of previous Corps members from a youth's neigh-
borhood, the more likely it was that the youth knew about Job Corps and,
hence, would participate in the program. Therefore, these knowledge proxies should be important variables for explaining observations about whether
or not youths participated in Job Corps.[7] Furthermore, the amount of Job

Corps participation in youths' preenrollment neighborhoods, per se, should not have a direct effect on their postprogram employment and related behavior.[8] So it is plausible to exclude #JCMEM-75 and %JCMEM-75 from the list of X variables. Therefore, #JCMEM-75 and %JCMEM-75 appear to satisfy the properties of variables to identify equation 2—they belong in the set of Z variables but not in the X variables.

Even if these knowledge proxies or other characteristics of preenrollment neighborhoods are added to the estimating equations for employment and related behavior, they generally will not affect the estimates of Job Corps impacts.[9] By design, the preenrollment neighborhoods of Job Corps and comparison youths should be similar in terms of the labor market characteristics and other relevant factors for the employment and related behavior of youths.[10] Our previous findings (see Kerachsky and Mallar, 1977) substantiate these expectations of labor market similarities. First, the earlier findings show that the preenrollment neighborhoods of the Corps member and comparison samples are on average similar with respect to important dimensions, such as population density, local youth unemployment, numbers of youths, income, nonaged welfare dependence, education, and race/ethnic composition. Second, the earlier findings indicate that the omission of characteristics of preenrollment neighborhoods from the equations for employment and related behavior will not affect the estimates of Job Corps impacts.

For estimating Job Corps impacts, the preenrollment labor markets can be viewed as similar across observations, and the lack of explanatory variables to control for differences in preenrollment labor markets cannot be used as an argument to include in the employment and related equations local variables—such as #JCMEM-75 and %JCMEM-75—that do not otherwise belong there. Because the local proxies for knowledge of Job Corps are not expected to affect the employment and related behavior of youths directly, they can be omitted from the employment and related equations. Thus, by providing a comparison sample with preenrollment labor market backgrounds that are similar to those of Corps members, our comparison group design helped ensure the plausibility of the one critical assumption used in our empirical model to control for unobserved differences between Corps member and comparison youths[11]—namely, that #JCMEM-75 and %JCMEM-75 can be omitted from the employment and related equations.

The other explanatory variables used in the Job Corps participation equations are similar to those used in the equations for employment and related behavior (identical, except for slight differences in functional form). The primary difference between the Job Corps participation equations and the equations for employment and related behavior is that the proxy variables for knowledge of Job Corps are included as explanatory variables in the Job Corps participation equations but are omitted from the equations for employment and related behavior. Thus, the proxies for knowledge of Job Corps help to statistically identify the employment and related equations, in addition to the statistical identification provided by the inherent nonlinearities in the model.

With the econometric procedures outlined above, we should obtain consistent estimates of the impact of Job Corps on participant behavior. Thus, in principle, the estimates of Job Corps effects are based on differences between groups of Corps members and comparison youths that have similar compositions in terms of both observed and unobserved characteristics. These procedures also should enable us to obtain unbiased estimates of what Corps members' activities would have been had they not participated in Job Corps, by netting out (i.e., subtracting) estimated Job Corps effects from the observed sample means for Corps members.

NOTES

1. For instance, the various sites in which Supported Work was located were periodically visited by monitors, but their visits typically took place less than once a month and did not permit full program assessment.

2. These comparisons were not reported for the 36-month youth cohort because of its small size (N=79).

3. Relying on the inherent nonlinearities in the model usually proves to be unstable and/or sensitive to the functional relationship that is assumed.

4. Some of the discussion is phrased as if there were only one (binary) program variable, which might or might not be the case. However, the results generalize to multiple T's, as is the case for our application (see below), as long as the selectivity being modeled is only between the Job Corps and comparison groups. It becomes more difficult, in practice, to control for selectivity into various types of program treatments. Often, the same factors affect the decisions about whether different program services are received; hence, the statistical identification of models of selectivity into multiple components of programs is almost always difficult and often impossible.

5. Another way to see the direction of LS bias from not controlling for unobserved differences between Corps members and the comparison group is to note that a positive correlation exists between T's and λ. Therefore, if δ is positive (negative) and we do not control for unobserved differences—the $\delta\lambda i$ term is omitted from equation 2—then part of the positive (negative) effect of the unobserved differences—the omitted term, $\delta\lambda i$—will incorrectly be attributed to the T's.

6. The λ function is nearly linear across a broad range of probabilities, P (from approximately 0.2 to 0.8).

7. The high correlation between the knowledge proxies and Job Corps participation for our sample is partly an artifact of the sample design (i.e., Job Corps saturation areas proximate to

centers were not allowed to be comparison sites). However, that statistical artifact has only a positive effect on the suitability of the knowledge proxies as identifying variables.

8. The postprogram period is 2 to 6 years later, and most of the Corps members no longer even lived in these neighborhoods.

9. However, the standard errors of impact estimates would be larger if the knowledge proxies were added to the equations for employment and related behavior, because only slight nonlinearities in the probability equation would be statistically identifying the model.

10. The local comparison sites were drawn randomly but with systematic procedures that helped to ensure comparability to the neighborhoods of Corps members in terms of population density, geographic dispersion, nonaged welfare dependence, and race/ethnicity.

11. The other assumptions or maintained hypotheses of our model are more commonly used in econometric analysis—the explanatory variables included in equation 2 other than λ, the normality of error terms, the error-components model of the correlation of individuals' error terms across time periods, and so on.

REFERENCES

BARNOW, B. S., G. G. CAIN, and A. S. GOLDBERGER (1980) "Issues in the analysis of selectivity bias," pp. 42-59 in E. W. Stromsdorfer and G. Farkas (eds.) Evaluation Studies Review Annual. Beverly Hills, CA: Sage.

HECKMAN, J. (1979) "Sample bias as specification error." Econometrica 47: 153-161.

HOLLISTER, R., P. KEMPER, and R. MAYNARD (eds.) (1984) The National Supported Work Demonstration. Madison: University of Wisconsin Press.

KERACHSKY, S. and C. MALLAR (1978) An Examination of Jobs Corps Participation. Princeton, NJ: Mathematica Policy Research.

— — — (1977) Interim Report for the Impact of the Jobs Corps Program. Princeton, NJ: Mathematica Policy Research.

KERSHAW, T., C. MALLAR, and C. METCALF (1976) Technical Study Design for the Evaluation of the Economic Impact of the Job Corps Program. Princeton, NJ: Mathematica Policy Research.

MALLAR, C., S. KERACHSKY, C. THORNTON, and D. LONG (1982) Third Follow-Up Report for the Evaluation of the Economic Impact of the Job Corps Program. Princeton, NJ: Mathematica Policy Research.

SCHORE, J., R. MAYNARD, and R. PILIAVIN (1979) "The accuracy of self-reported arrest data." American Statistical Association Proceedings of Section on Survey Research, 1979: 384-387.

SOME FAILURES IN DESIGNING DATA COLLECTION THAT DISTORT RESULTS

Albert J. Reiss, Jr.

Our failures in data collection often are a consequence of our models and the concepts embedded in them. These data collection failures, in turn, provide misleading results. Their correction requires reconceptualization and often new modes of data collection as well. Because our concepts are part of a socially constructed and changing reality, they are themselves subject to change; those changes, in turn, complicate the problems of data collection for overtime measures. Often there are no simple solutions as the problems stem from a paradoxical relationship between concepts and their measures or from the dynamic nature of populations and changing social organization. This chapter explores some of these problems in data collection by way of several examples.

MISLEADING MEASURES AND CONCEPTS

In social experiments and other evaluations of social programs, data are collected to measure the rate or amount of change due to the program. For example, whether a crime prevention program has any effect on the crime rate may be of interest. In this case, an assessment of program impact might require precise estimates of the "true" crime rate for a population before the change was introduced and any change in this rate.

For most empiricists, official statistical measures of crime (such as crimes or arrests known to the police based on police agency data collection procedures) do not measure a true rate of crime or the prevalence of offenders. Police records do not include some criminal incidents revealed by other methods of data collection, such as self-reports either of samples of offenders about their offending behavior (Short and Nye, 1957, 1958; Reiss and Rhodes, 1959) or of victims about their victimizations by offenders (Biderman et al., 1967; Ennis, 1967; Reiss, 1967; NCJISS, 1976; BJS, 1982).

Discrepancies in magnitude of crime events and offenders obtained from police statistics compared with the self-reports of offenders and victims typically are attributed to the way that police agencies collect crime statistics. In particular, official statistics include only those crime events that become known by police (Reiss and Bordua, 1967:40-48). The difference between the total volume of crime measured by official statistics and by self-report victim surveys then is defined as a measure of the "dark-figure" of crime—or of "unrecorded criminality" or "unregistered criminality" (Antilla, 1964).

There are grounds, however, for questioning the simple assumption that survey data measure the true rate of crime because they yield a higher rate. Over fifteen years ago, Biderman and Reiss (1967:9) pointed out that, historically, there had been two positions on what is the true rate of crime. The "realists" contended that the prevalence of victims and criminals, and the crime events in which they were involved, are the true measures of crime; the "institutionalists" argued that institutional validation by criminal justice processes is required for inclusion in prevalence measures. Biderman and Reiss concluded that both of these positions lead one astray because they neglect the fact that there are only socially organized ways of knowing. Objective reality is shaped by the organization of each particular mode of data collection or registering knowledge (Biderman and Reiss, 1967:14).

Apart from directly questioning the notion of obtaining a true rate on the grounds that it can only be approximated by any particularly socially organized means of knowing, there are other reasons to doubt that the larger of any two independent estimates of a rate measures a true rate. A main reason for having such doubts is that each mode of data collection has its own error structure; ordinarily, error profiles are not identical for independent modes of data collection.

To return to our example of measuring crime rates, it is clear that surveys of victims, self-reports of offenders, and the case report method of data collection employed by the police have different error structures. Each may over- and underestimate different kinds of events. Both victim and offender surveys often have incomplete sampling frames, have refusals to cooperate in data collection, and fail to locate some respondents known to the police. They also are less likely than are the police to learn of crimes which offenders, victims, or both define as noncriminal events. The definition of assaults within the family as "fights" is a common example.

Certain survey omissions undoubtedly come to the attention of the police because their case reports come from different proactive and reactive strategies of law enforcement. Police learn about crime events, their victims, and their offenders in more ways than do survey interviewers, who are limited to victim respondents. Police are more likely to learn of them from witnesses to such events, from informants with whom they have regular contacts, and from police observation during the course of their work.

Surveys of people as victims, moreover, give inadequate coverage to crimes against, and in some cases by, organizations. Although attempts have been made to develop surveys that measure organizational victimization by crime, these surveys are beset with major problems because of incomplete sampling frames from which to draw a population of organizations, inability to locate respondents who have the information essential to reporting on an organization, and the lack of organizational intelligence systems that accurately record information on victimization by crime. A major attempt to measure victimization of U.S. business organizations by burglary and robbery not only disclosed these major problems, but indicated that the estimates were not substantially larger than those obtained from the police case report method (Penick and Owens, 1976:70-71).

Although the larger estimates obtained by the self-report as compared with the case report method were attributed to unregistered criminality or unreported crimes initally, no attempt was made to identify which cases in an aggregate estimate of the crime rate were unreported to official law enforcement agencies and how the reported differed from the unreported. Some victimization surveys, including the National Crime Survey (NCS), did so by including questions on whether or not the police were informed about the self-reported victimization incident (NCJISS, 1976; BJS, 1982).

Analysis of NCS data on whether the police were informed about the victimization shows considerable variation by type of major crime measured in the NCS. In 1980, for example, reporting rates varied considerably by type of crime and the consequences of victimization. Although, in the aggregate, only 33 percent of all crimes against persons and 39 percent of those against their households were reported to police, the more serious the crime in terms of injury to victims and the larger the monetary loss, the more likely it was to become a police case report. Thus, 87 percent of all completed motor vehicle thefts were reported to the police, as were 75 percent of all robberies involving an aggravated assault (BJS, 1982: Table 89). However, only 14 percent of all household larcenies involving losses of less than $50, and but 27 percent of all personal larcenies without contact were reported to the police (BJS, 1982: Table 89). As these latter crimes represent a major share of aggregated personal and household crimes measured in the NCS, overall reporting rates consequently are sharply reduced.

These several different lines of inquiry into the problem of estimating crime rates for a population led to the conclusion that, in all likelihood, no single method was able to collect information on the same set of events that are measured by the other approaches. Methods differ in their organization so that some, such as police case reports, are able to capture information on both persons and their organizations, but others, such as self-report surveys, require different ways of organizing the collection of information when criminal acts victimize persons and organizations. Clearly, each method of data collection adds to the population of known events. None captures all of the events. No method of censusing a population of events is likely to include all the events obtained from any other method.

The obvious conclusion, then, is to pool the information obtained from two or more data collection procedures. Pooling assumes that any estimate ordinarily is an underestimate. The less the overlap between any two methods of censusing, the greater the underestimation of each method. It follows, also, that any method will contribute to the pooled estimate so long as it adds some cases to the pool not obtained from any other method. Logically, one can increase the precision of the estimate by repeated censusing of the same population with the same or different methods until the additions to the pool yield only marginal increases in precision.

THE UTILITY OF MODELS

Once it is clear that pooling information from different methods of censusing is a way to increase the precision of one's estimates, the problem is how to pool it. Fortunately, capture-recapture or multiple capture models (Bishop et al., 1975: 230-231) for estimating the magnitude of animal and human populations are applicable to populations of events such as crimes.

Censusing estimation methods (e.g., capture-recapture or multiple capture models) are one of the two major types of statistical models used to estimate the size of populations. (The other major type is statistical sampling theory.) The early work on capture-recapture models developed multiple re-

TABLE 9.1
The Capture-Recapture Model

Self-Report Survey of Victimizations by Crime	Official Case Reports of Police	
	Present	Absent
Present	Both case report and self-report	Self-report only
Absent	Case report only	Unobserved by either case or self-report methods

capture census methods to estimate the size of animal populations in closed populations (Cormack, 1972, 1973; Fienberg, 1972; Otis et al.,1978). Multiple recapture census models for open populations in long-term studies also have been developed (Seber, 1973). Recently, Pollock (1981, 1982) has questioned the sharp demarcation usually made between open and closed population models, and shows how one may use the methods of both in the same data collection design.

Multiple recapture census models for estimating the magnitude of animal populations also have been adapted to estimate the size of human populations (El-Khorazaty et al., 1977). They are especially useful where there is no complete enumeration of a population but where censusing data collected by several different methods can be used to estimate the size of the population. Recently, Ericksen and Kadane (1983) proposed that multiple recapture methods be used to adjust for the undercount in population estimates arising from implementing the complete enumeration censusing of the U.S. population.

The basic premise of multiple recapture is that information from two or more independent censuses of the same population can be used to estimate either the number of members of that population who are not counted by these censuses (a prevalence measure) or the number of events characterizing its members (an incidence measure). In practice, the information from three of the four cells of a 2 × 2 contingency table is used to estimate the size of the unobservable cell. We may diagram a capture-recapture model, following Bishop et al. (1975: 231), to estimate the incidence of crime victimizations in the U.S. population. The model assumes that the case-report method of the police and the self-report victim survey are independent samples in which victims can be uniquely identified in crime events (see Table 9.1).

There are, in the pooled information of police case report and self-report surveys of victimizations by crime, three subsets of victims: (1) those captured by both methods of data collection; (2) those obtained only by case reports to the police; and (3) those obtained by self-reports only. We already have given reasons why each of these subsets can reasonably be expected. The fourth cell logically consists of those cases that are captured by neither of these methods of data collection.

The multiple capture method of estimation requires that cases be uniquely identified in each census so that those cases common to two or more censuses can be counted. Unfortunately, no national data set exists that makes it possible to match the uniquely identified victims (or their victimizations) of crimes known to police with those uniquely identified in the self-report national victimization survey (NCS). Fortunately, however, the NCS reverse-record check validation studies can be used to estimate the proportion of crimes known to the police that also are reported to survey interviewers. The reader should bear in mind, however, that in the case reporting of the police, the crime events that become known to them are the way they uniquely identify persons involved in crimes, whereas in the NCS, uniquely identified people are used to capture crime events or victimizations by crime. Using the estimates of events that overlap in the reverse-record check studies thus will give us only crude estimates of either the prevalence of victims or the incidence of their victimizations by crime.

Reverse-record checks were conducted in three cities: Washington, D.C. (USBC, 1970a), Baltimore, Maryland (USBC, 1970b), and San Jose, California (NILECJ, 1972). A sample of victims known to the police was drawn and embedded within the probability sample of the population of each of these metropolitan communities. The San Jose data for aggravated assault (NILECJ, 1972) and NCS counts of victimizations by aggravated assault for 1980 (BJS, 1982) can be used to illustrate the utility of the multiple capture model as a means of estimating the incidence of aggravated assault victimizations for the U.S. population in 1980.

Just under one-half (48 percent) of all aggravated assaults included in the police case report subsample also were reported by victims to survey interviewers. Moreover, according to the NCS, only 54 percent of all victims of aggravated assaults said their assault was reported to the police (BJS, 1982: Table 89). Thus, of the 1,661,000 estimated aggravated assaults in 1980 (BJS, 1982: Table 1), only 896,940 were said to be reported to the police. Of these victimizations reported to the police, only 48 percent (or 430,531) were identified by both methods of data collection. The number of victimizations

TABLE 9.2
Estimates of Aggravated Assault Rate for 1980

NCS Self-Reports of Victimization by Aggravated Assault	Estimated Official Case Reports of Aggravated Assault		
	Present	Absent	Total
Present	430,531	1,230,469	1,661,000
Absent	466,409	(1,333,009)	(1,799,418)
Total	896,940	(2,563,478)	(3,460,418)

reported to the survey interviewers that went unreported to the police, then, is 1,230,469. By using these estimates in a multiple capture model, we can estimate the number of victimizations that are not included in these two surveys and the aggregate aggravated assault rate for 1980. The calculated estimates are given in Table 9.2.

Using the two-sample technique (Bishop et al., 1975: 235), the estimate of the expected number of 1982 victimization follows:

$$\hat{N} = \frac{896,940 \times 1,661,000}{430,531} = 3,460,418 \qquad [1]$$

$$SD = \sqrt{\frac{896,940 \times 1,661,000 \times 466,409 \times 1,230,469}{430,531^3}} \qquad [2]$$

$$= 3,226$$

With an asymptotic 95 percent confidence interval and a standard deviation of 3,226, the number of 1980 aggravated assault victimizations is estimated between 3,453,886 and 3,466,950 victimizations. Clearly, the aggravated assault victimization rate is estimated to be substantially greater than that captured by either means of data collection. The estimated crude victimization rate using multiple capture is almost twice as high as that estimated by the NCS and over three times that estimated from police case reports.

There is a cautionary tale here, then, about methods of data collection. There are only socially organized ways of knowing phenomena. Each and every method of data collection produces a biased estimate as it fails to capture all the elements of a population, even by repeated sampling or multiple censusing using the same method. We must be sensitive, then, to the nature and forms of bias in each method of data collection chosen for evaluation.

Several considerations need to be addressed before deciding to base population estimates on multiple capture census models. First, it is necessary to uniquely identify individuals or events for accurate estimates, as only by unique identification can one determine their overlap and, hence, use multiple record systems of estimation.

Second, socially defined barriers to the use of unique identification are more pronounced in some record systems than in others. It is not problematic for police records, in which unique identification exists, but it will be quite problematic for surveys, perhaps even those under government auspices, such as the U.S. Bureau of the Census and the NCS.

Third, each data collection system will need to be designed to increase the accuracy of matching uniquely identified individuals or events. That requirement necessitates reducing the errors in items of information below that permitted under conventional standards in social science research.

Fourth, we will need to depart from single frame sampling schemes in designing our data collection. Minimally, dual frame sample selection is necessary, but where three or more independent sources are available, sampling selection needs to be adapted accordingly.

Fifth, more attention should be paid to increasing the diversity of socially organized systems of data collection to obtain more accurate estimate rates. It is quite likely that each data collection system will add to the magnitude, although not necessarily the precision, of estimates. Where there are substantial numbers of socially organized systems of data collection, we may need to attend to selecting among them, given the cost involved in producing such estimates. That selection may well be on quite deliberate grounds, rather than on notions of sampling such systems of data collection. What perhaps should govern their selection is to maximize their diversity so that one will minimize overlap.

Sixth, although it might seem to follow that when one has only marginal gains in an estimate of the rate, one is approximating the true rate for the population, this is not necessarily the case. It depends, rather, on how close one comes to exhausting the socially organized ways of knowing and the error structure of each.

Finally, when one wishes to compare a rate for two or more points in time, one must be able to know how much the changes in the material and nonmaterial technology of data collection affect both our concepts and their measures. When one moves from in-person to phone interviewing, and from interviewer-based to computer-assisted recording of information, it cannot be assumed that they produce the same results at different points in time. We know that ordinarily both response rates and the productivity of respondents are greater for in-person than for telephone interviews (Groves and Kahn, 1979: 75-76) and that measures are far easier to standardize for computer assisted than for interviewer recording. Where and when such shifts are made, more complex and overlapping designs of data collection are required and their effects need to be evaluated.

There is a cautionary tale here, as well. The problems of how alternative forms of data collection affect both the quality and quantity of our results can no longer be neglected. Until we can be assured that reasonable estimates of properties of data collection that affect our results exist, we will have to design our inquiries to measure those properties.

CHANGES IN POPULATION COMPOSITION IN PANEL SURVEYS

A population is a dynamic and changing entity. One reason for its dynamic character is that it is under continuous replacement by accretions and losses. But there also are other processes going on in human populations that continually and substantially alter their characters and the status of some of their members. Among such vital processes are marriage, divorce, and morbidity. Others with major consequences are changes in employment or educational status. It may well be that whenever a population is selected and followed over time, the dynamic character of that population has consequences for measuring changes in it. To be sure, such changes may perhaps be more consequential for large populations than for very small samples, but they can be consequential for the latter. Where there is high residential mobility and migration, for example, a cohort of students in a school or even a classroom can have turnover or replacement rates of more than 50 percent.

We are well aware of dynamic demographic changes and have learned to take them into account in certain kinds of overtime measurement. Yet it is surprising how rarely we do. Consider how often criminologists are quoted as saying that changes in the birth rate affect the crime rate and use it to account for some particular increase or decrease in the crime rate. Yet it is infrequent that any attempt is made to assess how much of the change in the crime rate is due to the changing age composition of the population—no easy task to be sure. Still, work by Wellford (1973) and others can serve as a model to do so.

Our example of the delayed effect of the birth rate on the crime rate is chosen deliberately to illustrate the point that, ordinarily, we fail to focus on the exogenous or endogenous variables that characterize a dynamic population precisely because our explanatory models fail to take population processes into account. No provision is made, therefore, to collect data to analyze these effects. What follows is an attempt to show how important such dynamic changes in a population can be for understanding changes in the behavior of that population and its members. Both the necessity of taking dynamic processes of populations into account and some of the difficulties encountered in data collection and analysis in doing so are demonstrated.

HOUSEHOLD RESPONDENT STATUS
AS A DYNAMIC PROCESS

The first example illustrates the importance of considering dynamic population processes in evaluating a data collection model and its measurement properties. To redesign the National Crime Survey, a number of quasi-experimental methodological studies were undertaken. In one of these (Biderman et al., 1982), the intent was to determine whether household respondent status affected how its members reported their personal victimizations. Specifically, household respondents were questioned about crime victimization that might aid recall of personal as well as household victimizations; in addition, certain cues in the household screen questions seemed germane to personal as well as to household victimization reporting. To assess these effects, we took advantage of the fact that the NCS sample is divided into six rotation groups, each of which is in sample for three years. To control somewhat for the fact that moving households and individuals are not followed, our examination was limited to a one and a half year period or three interviews at six-month intervals.

Inasmuch as the NCS permits a household respondent to be selected anew each interview, the household respondent could change across the three interviews. With this variation we were able to execute a quasi-experimental design in which eight possible combinations of household respondent status constituted the comparison groups.

In order to construct these groups, however, both the structure of a population of households and changes in their composition can reduce the size of the population considerably. To begin with, it is obvious that, for single person households, the effect of exposure to the household screen and the individual screen questions for reporting household and personal victimizations cannot be measured respectively, as all single person household respondents must always receive both.

Nonetheless, not all single person household respondents remain single, given the dynamic processes of a population (e.g., by marriage or a returning family member). At the same time, some two or more person households become either single person households or two or more households because of processes such as death and divorce. Other households with three or more adults eligible for household respondent status could not be selected during the three-interview interval, necessitating also a control on size of household.

What was surprising was that, given the elementary dynamic processes in a population, more than one-third of all households interviewed at time one were excluded from the experimental design by time three. We were able to exercise some control over these losses by examining time one to time two changes for both persons with two interviews only as well as those who were in for three.

What should be apparent, then, is that changes in status complicate the design of field experiments and analysis of their results. Yet by modeling at least the major dynamic processes for a population, a quasi-experiment can be used to adjust results for some sources of status changes. We were unable to measure the effects of all the different combinations of status changes owing to demographic processes. There appears to be little way of doing so, even in a strict field experiment in which one could systematically expose subjects to victimization screen stimuli. It takes little imagination to see that with 7 household and 13 individual questions to screen for major crime victimizations, some of which have multiple cues, a rigorous control of stimuli in an experiment would require an infeasibly large number of experimental groups.

EFFECTS OF SECULAR POPULATION CHANGES

A second NCS study illustrates how intractable some evaluation measurement problems can be because of population processes. One of the interesting problems in victimization studies is a test of victim proneness or structural determinants of repeat victimizations. From an intervention standpoint, moreover, it is important to test whether particular strategies or tactics have intended effects of reducing victimization by crime. To test such theories or to evaluate interventions, one would want not only to develop stochastic models of repeat victimization but to be able to calculate household and individual risk over time.

We know that risk of victimization by crime varies with respondent and household status. Single young males, for example, are more likely to be victims of assault than are other age-sex-marital status groups. We also speculated that individual probabilities of victimization might well affect household probabilities. Following our interest in population structure, we reasoned that household size might have an independent effect. Interaction effects likewise seemed possible.

Attempts to sort out these effects, however, have proven to be intractable in the short run for several reasons. First, the NCS currently does not follow moving households and individuals and, thus, systematic sample loss occurs. Second, inordinately large samples or their cumulation over time would be required to secure enough cases to take population processes and their effects into account. Third, the processes themselves do not always occur in such ways that their effects can be separated. Finally, not all data collection can be handled prospectively, short of a complete enumeration.

Consider just one example. We noted that single young males had high rates of victimization by assault. Some in the sample will marry or cohabit with a woman. The males will be of different ages at marriage, and the age difference with the spouse also varies—factors that must be taken into account. Clearly, the spouse also changes status. In the example of males marrying, the women who live with them change statuses. Moreover, in forming a new household, at least one party will have to change territorial location, another source of risk of victimization. The chances are great that prior risk information on the spouse will be lacking because the spouse will not be selected from the sample population. Analytically, one would want to calculate the effect on each of those forming the two person household and of their location independent of the others. But, clearly, that is not possible (nor need one slavishly follow such analytical canons).

What should be apparent is that to take changes of risk into account owing to changing one's location in both territorial and social space would require both a different data collection strategy and a complex analytical model. In the NCS, the combination of attrition and replacement of households and persons due to processes of moving households and individuals results in a net loss of those who contribute victimizations. This leads to an artifactual decline in the victimization rate during the time a rotation group is in sample.

In order to correct for such secular population changes, both the sample design and data collection procedures must be changed. Most especially, it requires not only following persons and households as they leave locations but gathering data on those who fill the vacated locations so that one is able to separate location proneness from individual and household proneness.[1]

REEXAMINING DOMESTIC ASSAULT FINDINGS

Again, the lesson seems clear. Attention to the dynamic processes of a population necessitates a different data collection strategy than one would undertake otherwise and, consequently, often different analytical strategies as well. We shall try to illustrate how thinking about such processes when evaluating an intervention can lead one to reconsider the firmness of one's conclusions, absent knowledge of those effects. Modeling the effects of population changes and their attendant social processes requires further testing to determine whether the evaluation results are correctly interpreted. This point is illustrated by reexamining the Minneapolis Spouse Assault Experiment (Sherman and Berk, 1984, also reported elsewhere in this volume). Very briefly, the design of the experiment required police officers to randomly administer one of three treatments when handling simple domestic assaults: separating the parties to the dispute; mediation or counseling; or arrest of the offending spouse. The basic conclusion was that repeat assault of the spouse was significantly lower for the arrest treatment. Absent any other criteria for determining that some other treatment might be effective for members of an identifiable subgroup or of changes in the mode of other treatments to make them more effective, it seemed clear that aggregate spouse assault rates might be reduced by a policy of arrest (Sherman and Berk, 1984: 270).

There are a number of puzzling facts reported about the spouse assault victims and their offenders that raise the possibility that population structure and processes could account for at least some of the observed effects of arrest regarded as deterrent without necessarily reducing the assault behavior of the offender. Arrest may reduce repeated assault on the same victim because arrest leads the offender to vacate the relationship and seek a new partner. If the assault behavior of the arrested persons were to remain constant, the effect of arrest then would increase the number of victims of spouse assault while reducing the individual rate of assault victimization for any particular spouse. There would then be no deterrent effect of spouse assault.

One fact that leads us to speculate along these lines is that only 35 percent of the assaults on women in the spouse assault experiment involved a spouse by marriage, whereas more than 50 percent are assaulted by an "unmarried male lover" (Sherman and Berk, 1984: Table 2). Although precise empirical evidence is lacking, one must conclude that in all these relationships, there is a current rate of dissolution by desertion, separation, and divorce. That should be relatively small for a population in six months. But it may be substantially greater for the unmarried. To be sure, police records showed that 80 percent of these victims had been assaulted by the suspect in the prior six months. That would suggest that mean duration of the relationship is well above six months. Yet assault may be more characteristic of the late than of the early stage of an informal spouse relationship; hence, these high rates might reflect only imminent break-up. Lacking population rates for these statuses, we cannot, of course, determine an expected rate of leaving.

Other data provided on the experiment suggest, however, that the rate of assault in the succeeding six months is well below 80 percent for any treatment, the maximum repeat violence rate in the six posttreatment months is 37 percent of those in the advise treatment condition. Something, then, is accounting for the six-month posttreatment rate of violence known to the police being less than one-half that of the six-month pretreatment rate of violence known to them.

In a fair proportion of cases, the spouse no longer was present at the time of the six-month interview. Perhaps as many as one-third of all the arrested partners had not returned when the six-month interview was taken (Sherman and Berk, 1984: Table 5). If so, the drop in violence rates following arrest might be due largely to the spouse leaving. Indeed, as Table 5 tells us only reunion figures, we do not know how many partners may have left shortly following reunion.

Several possibilities exist then. One is that arrest has the consequence of accelerating the desertion and separation rate. Another is that spouse assault is characteristic of unstable relationships that have a high rate of break-up. Yet another is that arrest has a deterrent effect on assaulting the spouse for which the offender was arrested, but that he leaves and finds another mate who may become his next victim of assault.

Clearly, redesign and additional kinds of data collection are essential if one is to rule out alternative explanations based on group and population processes. Not only data on the rate at which relationships break up are required, but one also would want to follow the offending spouses as well as their victims to learn whether, when they leave, they form other relationships that result in spouse assault. A process model that specifies assault in the later rather than the early stage of that relationship would require a follow-up period well beyond six months. But follow-up designs are not easily executed, especially for arrest populations. Residential transiency is high among that segment of the population most vulnerable to assault. A substantial proportion of the victims of the Minneapolis spouse assault experiment could not be located six months after their reported assault. An even greater proportion of their offending spouses perhaps could not be located; 69 percent of them had a prior arrest record (Sherman and Berk, 1984: Table 2). Indeed, when the assaulting spouse vacates the relationship, often the victim spouse does not know where he has moved.

It is well known that it is difficult to trace underclass offenders over time. Their transiency rate is high even in so short a period as six months. As a great many evaluation studies in criminology require tracking violators over time, attention might well be given to how to design data collection systems to track that subpopulation and to secure their cooperation to collect information.

CONCLUSION

The foregoing examples call attention, then, to the importance of modeling dynamic aspects of populations under investigation in program evaluations. In a more general sense, they call attention to modeling any social process and its effect on variables under observation. By modeling those processes, one may be able to take them into account in data collection and analysis.

NOTE

1. It should be noted that the dynamic processes of residential change, whether those associated with urban decay or with gentrification, must have some effect on location proneness as well. Often, however, such changes, are due to simultaneous changes in the characteristics of occupants and the cumulative and interaction effects of those changes.

REFERENCES

ANTILLA, I. (1964) "The criminological significance of unregistered criminality." Excerpta Criminologica 4: 411-414.

BIDERMAN, A. D. and A. J. REISS, Jr. (1967) "On exploring the 'dark figure' of crime." The Annals 374: 1-15.

BIDERMAN, A. D., D. CANTOR, and A. J. REISS, Jr. (1982) "A quasi-experimental analysis of personal victimization reporting by household respondents in the National Crime Survey." Proceedings of the American Statistical Association, Section on Survey Research Methods 1982: 516-521.

BIDERMAN, A. D., L. A. JOHNSON, J. McINTYRE, and A. WEIR (1967) Report on a Pilot Study in the District of Columbia on Victimization and Attitudes Toward Law Enforcement: Field Surveys I. Washington, DC: President's Commission on Law Enforcement and the Administration of Justice.

BISHOP, Y. M. M., S. E. FIENBERG, and P. W. HOLLAND (1975) "Estimating the size of a closed population," pp. 229-256 in Discrete Multivariate Analysis: Theory and Practice. Cambridge, MA: MIT Press.

Bureau of Justice Statistics [BJS] (1982) Criminal Victimization in the United States, 1980: A National Crime Survey Report, NCJ-84015. Washington, DC: Government Printing Office.

CORMACK, R. M. (1973) "Commonsense estimates from capture-recapture studies," pp. 225-254 in M. S. Bartlett and R. W. Hiorns (eds.) The Mathematical Theory of the Dynamics of Biological Populations. London: Academic Press.

— — — (1972) "The logic of capture-recapture estimates." Biometrika 29: 79-100.

EL-KHORAZATY, M. N., P. B. IMREY, G. G. KOCH, and H. BRADLEY (1977) "Estimating the total number of events with data from multiple-record systems: a review of methodological strategies." International Statistical Review 45: 129-157.

ENNIS, P. A. (1967) Criminal Victimization is the United States: Report of a National Survey, Field Surveys II. Washington, DC: President's Commission on Law Enforcement and the Administration of Justice.

ERICKSEN, E. P. and J. B. KADANE (1983) Estimating the Population in a Census Year: 1980 and Beyond. Department of Statistics Technical Report 260. Pittsburgh: Carnegie-Mellon University.

FIENBERG, S. E. (1972) "The multiple recapture census for closed populations and incomplete 2^k contingency tables." Biometrika 59: 591-603.

GROVES, R. M. and R. L. KAHN (1979) Surveys by Telephone: A National Comparison with Personal Interviews. New York: Academic Press.

National Criminal Justice Information and Statistics Service [NCJISS] (1976) Criminal Victimization in the United States, 1973: National Crime Survey Report SD-NCP-N-4. Washington, DC: Law Enforcement Assistance Administration.

National Institute of Law Enforcement and Criminal Justice [NILECJ] (1972) San Jose Methods Test of Known Crime Victims: Statistics Technical Report 1. Washington, DC: Statistics Division.

OTIS, D., L.K.P. BURNHAM, G. C. WHITE, and D. R. ANDERSON (1978) "Statistical inference for capture data from closed populations." Wildlife Monograph 62.

PENICK, B.E.E. and M.E.B. OWENS [eds.] (1976) Surveying Crime. Washington, DC: National Academy of Sciences.

POLLOCK, K. H. (1982) "A capture-recapture design robust to unequal probability of capture." Journal of Wildlife Management 46: 752-757.

— — — (1981) "Capture-recapture models: a review of current methods, assumptions, and experimental design," pp. 426-435 in C. J. Ralph and J. M. Scott (eds.) Estimating Number of Terrestrial Birds, Studies in Avian Biology 6.

REISS, A. J., Jr. (1967) "Measurement of the nature and amount of crime," in Studies in Crime and Law Enforcement in Major Metropolitan Areas: Field Studies III, Volume I. Washington, DC: President's Commission on Law Enforcement and the Administration of Justice.

— — — and D. J. BORDUA (1967) "Environment and organization: a perspective on the police," in D. J. Bordua (ed.) The Police: Six Sociological Essays. New York: John Wiley.

REISS, A. J., Jr. and A. L. RHODES (1959) A Socio-Psychological Study of Adolescent Conformity and Deviation. Washington, DC: U.S. Office of Education.

SEBER, G.A.F. (1973) The Estimation of Animal Abundance and Related Parameters. London: Griffin.

SHERMAN, L. W. and R. A. BERK (1984) "Deterrent effects of arrest for domestic assault." American Sociological Review 49: 261-272.

SHORT, J. F., Jr. and F. I. NYE (1958) "Extent of unrecorded juvenile delinquency." Journal of Criminal Law, Criminology and Police Science 49: 296-302.

— — — (1957) "Reported behavior as a criterion of deviant behaviors." Social Problems 5: 207-213.

U. S. Bureau of the Census [USBC] (1970a) "Victim recall pretest household survey of victims of crime: Washington, DC." (mimeo)

— — — (1970b) "Household surveys of victims of crime: second pretest: Baltimore, MD." (mimeo)

WELLFORD, C. F. (1973) "Age composition and increase in recorded crime." Criminology 11: 61-70.

PART III

Use of Record Information

PROGRAM EVALUATION
AND THE USE OF EXTANT DATA

Eleanor Chelimsky

Concern about the Reagan administration's recent cuts in federal budgets for administrative and statistical data systems has focused almost entirely on one expected impact of those cuts: that is, a decrease in the amount of information directly available to the public.[1] Researchers, business people, members of Congress, farmers, government planners at federal, state, or local levels, labor unions, and many other groups have expressed fears that they would not continue to find the data they need for performing their various functions. In addition, given the large number of radical changes brought to government programs by the present administration, many data users have been surprised that these cutbacks affect the very quantitative tools that eventually will be needed by the administration both to describe its innovations and to demonstrate their success.

The response of administration spokespersons to this concern is that as particular federal programs are reduced, eliminated, or transferred to the states under its New Federalism initiatives, the administration's policy is to cut back or abolish federal data collection efforts in those program areas and other areas in which the data are not being collected specifically and directly for executive branch policy purposes. They have suggested that, as programs

AUTHOR'S NOTE: The views and opinions expressed herein are my own and should not be construed as the policy or position of the General Accounting Office.

get smaller or disappear from the federal locus of responsibility, the policy makers' need for data in those areas is simultaneously reduced; that much of the federal government's current costly data collection effort is both unnecessary and burdensome. They also have indicated that states, local governments, and business firms easily can fill the federal government's data collection role; that the appetites of data users are insatiable ("policymakers can never have all the data they'd like to have," Schorr, 1983); and that, in any case, special evaluation studies can substitute for existing data systems by conducting original data collection and developing their own independent information.

This chapter will argue, however, the following points:

- Executive branch policy makers are not the only intended users of federal data systems. Federal data systems exist not only to support federal policy-making (which includes both executive and legislative branch policy-making, as well as that of judicial and independent agencies) but also, and especially, to support the advance of knowledge generally for the use of all the citizenry. Indeed, it is this national purpose that has given the federal role in data collection its rationale and public acceptance since the year 1790.
- A major legislative use of executive branch data involves the congressional oversight function; as a result, cutbacks in funding for the executive branch data systems developed over many years—particularly in those areas in which the current administration has reduced, eliminated, or transferred programs— directly impede both legislative oversight of the administration's actions and the public accountability that such oversight was intended to ensure.
- The federal role in data collection cannot easily be filled at subnational levels.
- Funding cutbacks may influence not merely the quantity of data available but the quality of those data.
- Using specially funded evaluations to substitute for existing data systems is problematic because most evaluations depend on existing administrative and statistical data systems. Without those existing systems, evaluations will become less feasible (i.e., more expensive, more laborious, more uncertain, and more time-consuming), less able to pinpoint and address relevant issues or to produce conclusive information, and, hence, of course, less likely be useful.

Reducing funds for data systems therefore can create a kind of double whammy with regard to the information available to the public. Information is decreased not only directly but indirectly, as the very evaluations that are called upon to substitute for the eliminated, truncated, or qualitatively diminished data systems will have lost a large part of the quantitative support on which they rely. The idea that special evaluation studies are autonomous, that they are independent of data systems and can substitute for them, is thus a misconception.

The claim is not being made that all data systems are needed, useful, and untouchable, or that the Reagan administration's policies since 1981 are the only policies that should be questioned. At least some of the data system cutbacks have affected surveys or administrative records that weren't needed or were yielding poor quality information. It is certainly worthwhile to review data collection requirements regularly to ascertain their usefulness and technical adequacy. With regard to Reagan administration policies, it also is true that many recent administrations have manifested only evanescent support for data collection. Since 1970, a number of successive actions taken by different administrations have culminated in major reductions of information quantity, quality, and accessibility.

At present, however, the problem of budget deficits has forced a more comprehensive scaling-back of data systems than any in recent memory. Because it appears that this trend will continue, this chapter focuses, in particular, on current issues and events. It will look, first, at recent funding cutbacks in administrative and statistical data systems; second, at the impacts of these cutbacks on the usefulness and technical adequacy of the data systems involved; third, at the specific ways in which evaluation studies draw support from data systems, using the experience of the Program Evaluation and Methodology Division of the General Accounting Office (GAO); and, fourth, at problems for evaluation studies resulting from inadequacies in those data, along with some suggestions for addressing them.

GOVERNMENT POLICY AND PURPOSES IN COLLECTING ADMINISTRATIVE AND STATISTICAL DATA

The administration's stated intention is to reduce data collection budgets, particularly in those areas in which it is also eliminating federal programs. The impact of these data system cuts has in fact been "concentrated more heavily in agencies that are experiencing cuts in their other programs" (Melnick, 1982: 52). But almost every major nondefense agency of the federal government has felt the effects of the administration's efforts to reduce its expenditures for data collection. The Census Bureau, the Bureau of Labor Statistics, and other units of the Department of Labor, the Department of Energy, the Department of Agriculture, the Department of Housing and Urban Development, the National Science Foundation, the Interior Department, the Department of Health and Human Services, the Department of Commerce, the Department of Education, and many others—even the tiny Statistical Policy Branch within the Office of Management and Budget, which had charge of coordinating and assuring the integrity of the federal government's highly decentralized statistical effort—all have received the presidential order to cut or disband many of their data collection programs. A recent count by a congressional committee provided 58 examples of statistical programs that have been reduced or eliminated (Committee on Government Operations, 1982).

As with many decentralized functions, it is difficult to get a clear understanding of the precise number of existing administrative and statistical data systems across federal agencies. It appears that there are somewhere between 70 and 100 organizations in the federal government with established administrative or statistical data systems; the largest of these organizations together account for appropriations of about $1 billion annually (Subcommittee on Legislation and National Security, 1982: 4), and 36 of them are major programs, developed in 16 agencies (Stanfield, 1981: 2120). However, there are unknown numbers of small, indirect data gathering activities spread throughout the federal government that have grown up around federal programs in many different areas.

The size of the funding cuts made by the administration have been calculated as ranging between 5 percent overall (estimate by the Office of Management and Budget, using current dollars) and 20 percent overall (estimate by private economists, using constant dollars and, hence, controlling for inflation). Cuts for individual agencies, using current dollar estimates, varied from 12 percent for the Bureau of Labor Statistics to 15 percent for Census to 29 percent for the Energy Information Agency.

Regardless of the dimensions of individual and overall cuts, it should be noted that if the data produced by these systems are in fact needed data, even a small cut in funding creates problems. This is particularly apparent when one considers that data systems are labor intensive, making them especially vulnerable to inflation. Increasing labor costs mean that data budgets have to rise with inflation if they are to maintain established levels. But data systems cannot simply stay even; their accuracy and efficiency must be improved constantly, given that all data systems contain some errors. System designs must be upgraded to keep abreast of the state-of-the-art. They must be continually revised to incorporate the most recent data or their quality declines. For example, each decennial census since 1942 has been followed by a survey sample redesign purposes of which are to make use of the most up-to-date census data to revise the sample design, and to incorporate methodological improvements in the survey procedures (Melnick, 1982: 44). Even a small budget cut may mean that for one data system to have the latitude to develop properly and to maintain or improve its quality, another will have to be entirely phased out. This occurred last year at the Census Bureau, when a data series with many users nationwide—a monthly report on regional department store sales—had to be eliminated to allow other series to be maintained adequately. The discontinuation of this series saved the Census Bureau about $200,000, which immediately went to shore up higher priority data systems such as the national income accounts. Yet the eliminated monthly report had been one of the few sources providing an indication of economic trends by major geographical markets, and its demise meant that the analysis of local economic conditions would be rendered vastly more difficult (Crittenden, 1982).

In addition, most data systems take years to build. If phased out, it is not only time-consuming to bring them back, it is very costly—much more costly than maintaining the original systems. Budgetary cutbacks in data systems, therefore, should be considered only after it is established that the data being eliminated are truly no longer needed, and that no future need for the data is likely to force later reactivation of the systems.

The Reagan administration has defended its cutbacks in budgets for data collection with the claim that when federal programs have been reduced, eliminated, or transferred, it is unnecessary to collect data relating to those programs. This argument holds up only if the assumption is made that the exclusive purpose for collecting the data is its use by executive branch policy makers. When we examine the history of government policy from the time of the American Revolution, it becomes apparent that the Reagan administration has introduced a novel interpretation of the role of the government in data collection.

Despite impassioned debate over the appropriate "federal role" since the founding of the Confederation, one rare area of agreement has involved the federal role in data collection. It seems that "federal politics had committed us, from our national beginnings, to a special interest in numbers" (Boorstin, 1973: 168). Census taking is one of the federal government's oldest activities. First begun in 1790 to count only the total population, the census already had expanded by 1800—at the urging of Vice President Thomas Jefferson—to include more details about the lifespan of Americans to be used for social measures to increase longevity. The scope of census subject matter continued to broaden throughout the nineteenth century, and many other data collection activities were added to the federal government's responsibilities (e.g., the general geodetic survey, inaugurated in 1807 and continued by reaffirming legislation in 1878).

It is relevant to note here that when data were collected in 1800 on the lifespan of Americans, no federal programs to increase longevity yet existed, no executive branch policy makers needed the data to guide program operations, and Thomas Jefferson was no advocate of big government. On the contrary, a famous favorite adage of his was "the less government the better" (Hicks et al., 1964:257). What, then, was the purpose of all this data collection and who needed it? Documents of the period make clear that the effort was intended to produce new knowledge for the social and intellectual benefit of the public. To make sure that the knowledge produced was indeed national knowledge, a federal role was mandated to provide the needed uniformity in data definitions and collection procedures.

This concept of the federal role in data collection has changed little over time. A restatement was offered in congressional testimony last year:

> Only the federal government can produce statistical series which are uniform and consistent for the nation as a whole and which are of unquestioned honesty and objectivity. The federal government has a particular responsibility to produce the statistical information it needs for its own use. . . . The federal government also has a responsibility to produce statistical information for which there is a national need even if there is not a direct federal governmental need. State governments need information, uniformly presented, about the states. Private individuals and businesses need uniformly presented information on a wide variety of economic and demographic matters.

> Only the federal government is really well-suited to providing complete, timely, honest, and uniform information to meet federal and national needs. . . . (W)herever there is a need for national uniformity and unquestioned objectivity in information presentation, then it is quite likely that there is a crucial federal role, either in directly producing the information or in enforcing standards for state collection and presentation (Courtney M. Slater, in Subcommittee on Legislation and National Security, 1982: 58-59).

But if it is agreed that the purpose of federal data collection is to benefit the public as a whole, then it is clear that the policy-making data needs of the executive branch are only one component of the total need. Legislative policy makers need executive branch data to monitor the administration's activities, whether in implementing or phasing out programs. Individuals and groups, public and private sectors of the economy, scholars, businesspeople, and many more have legitimate claims on the public data. All the claims, however, may not be consonant with one another.

The head of an executive branch agency, for example, may want to decrease the sample size of a data program in order to hold the agency budget in check. But the Congress may want to increase the sample size to ensure the accurate targeting of billions of dollars in federal funds tied to it because of legislated allocation formulas. Moreover, the fact that a program has been reduced, eliminated, or transferred does not necessarily mean that even executive branch policy makers can do without the data, because the social or economic problem the program was established to address may not have been resolved. Indeed, the fact that the Law Enforcement Assistance Administration (LEAA) was abolished, while funding for its data arm—the Bureau of Justice Statistics—has been maintained, is an excellent example of the contrary.

There are, then, three important reasons why it may be important to maintain data relating to a given eliminated program: (1) the public purpose and use of the federal data collection can thereby be scrutinized: (2) the status of the problem addressed by the eliminated program can continue to be monitored: (3) the merits of eliminating the program can be judged. Even if the administration were uninterested in the status of a problem, the executive branch, as such, would still remain accountable to the legislative branch in the oversight process with regard to the program's elimination. Thus, congressional policy-makers need those data (as do voters, the press, and scholars) which enable them to assess the actions of the administration. The administration's current effort to phase out data collection directly hampers both Congress and the public in their efforts to find out what these effects of eliminating programs may have been.

The administration's claim that agency data collection efforts are superfluous if they benefit states, local governments, or private firms rather than administration policy makers lacks continuity with historical federal policies. For more than 200 years, states, local governments, and private companies have been included as intended users of federal data. It was, in fact, the need of these groups for uniform national data bases that formed one of the major justifications for the federal role in this area from the beginning.

At a congressional hearing in 1982 (Subcommittee on Census and Population, 1982), it was noted that the proposed cutbacks came just as President Reagan's "New Federalism" block grant initiative signified growing, not diminishing, state and federal needs for national data. Numerous witnesses pointed out that moving data collection to the individual states would mean problems of interpretation and aggregation caused by different data definitions and procedures that would preclude comparability across both space (i.e., from state to state or county to county) and time (i.e., from year to year or period to period) and would make sound nationwide assessments difficult if not impossible. Among others, the National Governors' Association has recognized the "state responsibility to report information to the federal government regarding state use of federal funds" and pointed out the puzzling lack of federal reporting requirements related to the administration's block grant programs (Wills, in Subcommittee on Legislation and National Security, 1982:130).

Phasing out the data collection needed to monitor the effects of transferring federal programs to state control directly affects executive branch accountability. It hampers Congress, state government, local government, and various other groups in their efforts to examine the effects of the transfer.

Business firms are no more able to produce the national-level data they need than are states and localities. Although some private sector groups collect marketing data through their own surveys, these usually are local or regional in focus. In addition, the information they produce often is considered proprietary and, hence, both scope and access can be problems to other would-be users. For business groups, as for many other users, the federal role has been indispensable because it ensures wide data availability and maximum usefulness based on the uniform definitions, procedures, and standards that mark federal data collection efforts (Boorstin, 1973:171).

We can see, then, that the administration is not persuasive in arguing (1) that a declining federal program role should be accompanied by a phase-out of associated data systems, (2) that the federal role in generating national-level data can be taken over by states or business firms, or (3) that the data systems it phased out were, in fact, unneeded. Instead, it is clear that the data are needed by a large variety of users and that the administration's cutbacks have caused serious problems to them by affecting both the quantity and quality of the data now available.

IMPACT OF BUDGETARY CUTS ON USEFULNESS AND TECHNICAL ADEQUACY

Perhaps one of the greatest concerns triggered by the administration's reductions in funding is the fear not only of missing data but especially of flawed data and of the potential effects of their widespread use. Looking at policy use alone, it is important to note that the federal government bases some major decisions on federal data series. For example, data on the incidence of poverty in various regions were used in fiscal year 1979 to allocate $122 billion under 150 domestic assistance programs (Subcommittee on Legislation and National Security, 1982). The future accuracy and effectiveness of those targeting decisions currently are brought into question by the administration's data system funding cutbacks. The cutbacks have not merely produced the phase-out of certain data systems, but have also engendered a serious deterioration of data quality in some of the systems that remain.

Continuous improvements of many kinds are needed to ensure steady progress in the usefulness and technical adequacy of the existing data systems that undergird many of the nation's advances in knowledge and major policy decisions. But, instead of moving forward to the improved data systems now realizable, budgetary cutbacks may preclude even the maintenance of data availability to the public and standards of data quality that reflect the achievements of the past.

There are, then, two general impacts that funding cutbacks can have on the data systems they affect: (1) decreased usefulness of the data to those who need it, and (2) decreased technical adequacy of the data. Both of these impacts affect the basic purpose of all federal data collection, that is, to produce new knowledge for the benefit of the public.

Impacts on usefulness—in the form of curtailed publications or cancelled data series, for example—directly and immediately affect the quantity of new knowledge available. Impacts on the technical adequacy of data—in the form of actions or inactions such as reductions in sample size (leading to increased sampling error and decreased data reliability), or failure to update statistics (leading to errors in sampling estimates)—directly and immediately affect the quality and, especially, the conclusiveness of that knowledge.

IMPACTS ON USEFULNESS

In most cases, impacts on usefulness are visible. Cancellations of data series and expected surveys, or delays in the availability of data, are sufficiently obvious and damaging to regular data users (in Congress, in the universities, in private corporations, and at state and local levels of government) that they are not likely to pass unnoticed and may even generate comment in the nonspecialized press. One past example of this type of visibility was a decision by the Eisenhower administration to eliminate the Census of Business. The reaction in the business community was so intense that the census had to be reinstated the next year with consequent increased costs brought on by the disruption. More recently, the Reagan administration decided to phase out the Survey of Income and Program Participation (SIPP), which was intended to collect data focusing on the measurement of income and the effects of the tax transfer system on individuals and families. Here again, the outcry—this time among scholars and researchers rather than business groups—was so unanimous (not only because of the expected value of SIPP for understanding economic assistance to families, but because of the more than $20 million that had already been invested in the new data system) that the administration was forced to change its mind and reprogram funds for the effort (Wallman, 1983).

Agency Responses to Budgetary Cuts

Agencies that collect data have responded in three ways to the Reagan administration's budgetary cutbacks. They have cancelled surveys, censuses, or administrative data collection; reduced the amount of data collected or the frequency of that collection; and delayed reporting of data. These responses directly affect the usefulness of the data. That these responses have been pervasive is quite clear, at least for statistical systems. (Much less is known about what has happened to administrative data systems.)

Cancellations across five major programs (the Census Bureau, the Bureau of Labor Statistics, the National Center for Education Statistics, the National Center for Health Statistics, and the Energy Information Administration) have included the elimination of the Environmental Expenditure Survey; Monthly Department Store Sales Data; Early Data on Corporate Income (for the National Accounts); the Nationwide Personal Transportation Survey; the 1982 National Travel Survey; the Labor Turnover Survey (a leading economic indicator); the Current Population Survey Supplement on Multiple Job Holding; the Nonresidential Buildings Survey (energy consumption by type of structure); the Industrial Sector Survey (fuel prices and industrial costs); Data on the Production and Distribution of Fuels at the state level; the Family Budget Survey; and the Survey of Aid to Families with Dependent Children.

Reductions in the amount of data collected have affected programs such as the following: the Service Industry Data Program; the Wholesale Trade Data Program; the Postcensal Population Characteristics Program; the Survey of Residential Alteration and Repairs; the State Government Employment Survey; Current Industrial Reports; Local Area Unemployment Statistics; and the Survey of Pre-Primary Education Institutions. Reductions in the frequency of observations occurred in such major data sources as these: the National Survey of Family Growth; the National Medical Care Utilization and Expenditure Survey; the National Health and Nutrition Examination Survey; the National Ambulatory Medical Care Survey; the National Nursing Home Survey; the Vital Statistics Survey; the National Longitudinal Survey of the High School Class of 1972; Subcounty Data on

Fertility and Voting; the Occupational Outlook Handbook; the Adverse Effect Wage Rate; and the Annual Housing Survey.

Delays in issuing data have been evident in major postponements for the 1980 Census of Population and Housing (see below), as well as other programs, such as the Commodity Transportation Survey and National Estimates of Personal Wealth. Curtailed publication programs have occurred in many areas, including the Internal Revenue Service's Statistics of Income (many reports cancelled, basic tables reduced by half); 15 Census Reports involving race and ethnic groups, migration, education, employment, and area population characteristics; certain publications of the Department of Agriculture's Economic Research Service; and the Geographic Distribution of Federal Funds.

Decreased Access to Data

Another way in which the usefulness of federal data programs has been affected involves decreased equality of access to the data. The 1980 Census results provide an example of this problem. The Census now costs about $1 billion to produce, a sum paid by the public in the form of taxes. The public also pays the in-kind costs of filling in the Census forms, with about 1 out of 6 persons having to fill out longer Census forms taking a significant amount of time to complete. But as of August 1983, the most complete compendium of Census findings to be published came, not from the Census Bureau, but from a market research firm that sold a 1611-page, 5-volume paperbound set for $395. Following the 1970 Census, in contrast, the Census Bureau had made volumes such as these publicly available by the summer of 1972, at about one-tenth the price. In the 1980 Census budgetary cuts caused major delays in the Census Bureau's publication of 1980 findings; in this situation, private publication became profitable because while timely public access to census information was needed, low-priced public documents were not available.

In this situation, budget cuts necessitated publication delays which produced de facto prioritization of access to publicly owned, publicly funded data. The Census Bureau still will print its major reports at some unclear future date, and the public at large will have to wait until long after special clients have been served. What this means, specifically, in the words of one scholar, is that:

> [I]f a high school student would like figures on the European ancestries of the people in his community, he will be told that these documents are not yet avail-

able. As it happens, such statistics have been in the hands of tape-owners for almost a year (Hacker, 1983).

In so doing, the federal government is not performing one of the services for which such data collection was instituted. As data collection for the census is only possible through public support and cooperation, the failure to provide the compiled information to the public in a timely fashion is especially unfortunate. These budgetary cutbacks have caused problems of individual access to data that compound the restriction, cancellation, and delay problems that already were negatively affecting the usefulness of federal data systems.

IMPACTS ON TECHNICAL ADEQUACY

We have noted that individual government agencies respond differently to budgetary reductions. These responses have direct bearing, not only on the usefulness of data, but on its technical adequacy. One frequent response has been to reduce sample size, which was done in the cases of the Current Population Survey, the Health Interview Survey, IRS Statistics of Income, the Annual Housing Survey, and the Consumer Expenditures Survey. Cuts in sample size create a problem for the technical adequacy of data systems because they lead to higher sampling error and lower statistical power. This particularly affects the reliability of data available for measuring and analyzing changes in subnational areas and in subgroups of the population. For instance, reducing the sample size of the Current Population Survey, which is important in determining federal funds, has reduced the reliability of information at state and substate levels. This reduction in reliability was exacerbated by the simultaneous elimination of a Labor Department program providing assistance to local governments in the compilation of local area employment data. As a result, present and future targeting of federal funds and programs will be much more subject to error. This immediately affects programs such as the Urban Enterprise Zones that must be targeted to areas with high unemployment rates.

Even with the major problems that cuts in sample size engender, they have two advantages over other types of actions that agencies may take which affect the technical adequacy of the data. First, cuts in sample size are more immediately visible to regular users of the data. The second advantage of cutting sample size over other solutions to budgetary problems is that the effects of the sample size are determinable.

These two advantages do not exist when agencies choose certain other methods to respond to budgetary cutbacks. Although delays in survey redesign—such as the ones that have affected the Current Population Survey, the Health Interview Survey, the National Crime Survey, the Consumer Expenditures Survey, and many others—are visible enough, the effects of continuing to use 1970 Census data instead of 1980 Census data as the basis for sample selection are difficult to measure. It is clear that failure to perform this redesign means, for example, that the statistical error for many subgroups will be increased to an undetermined degree.

The obvious problems resulting from delays and cancellations in data issuance discussed above also may seriously affect technical adequacy. When data are not collected, they are lost. If those data are part of longitudinal surveys that produce time series, those time series are broken, to the great detriment of evaluative studies assessing long-term effects of federal policies.

Delaying surveys, or shifting their periodicity, has affected the National Survey of Family Growth, which will now be done every five years instead of every three; the National Ambulatory Medical Care Survey, now every three years instead of every year; the National Nursing Home Survey, now every six years instead of every other year; and the Annual Housing Survey, now every other year instead of every year. Such delays and shifts are as visible as cancellation, but cause immeasureable and often irremediable damage to time-series analyses, which require repeated measurement of the same variables in the same way, over the same time period, on comparable samples of the population.

Other agency responses to budgetary cutbacks may be both invisible (or nearly so) and of unknown magnitude. Such is the case with reductions in pretests, reductions in the quality control of data processing (e.g., coder verification), or reductions in the number of studies examining the quality of data. These reductions are not immediately identifiable by the data user, despite the fact that they would imply a serious loss of technical adequacy in the data of which the user would need to be aware. That loss, even if it were identified, would not be measurable. The danger here is that misinformation would be produced through the unsuspecting use of flawed data.

Even before the administration's budgetary cuts, the federal data system was certainly not perfectly accurate. A number of sources of error were known to exist, such as sampling variability, response error (i.e., the reporting of wrong answers that are assumed to be right answers), measurement error, editing and coding error, and various types of biases (Shiskin, 1970). But steady progress was being made in developing measures of error to determine accuracy and improve research procedures and methodology. But with budgetary cutbacks, many federal agencies are cancelling or deferring methodological research intended to improve data system design and use.

The Census Bureau, for example, will no longer support its statistical methodology information system. The *Statistical Reporter* publication has been discontinued by the Office of Management and Budget. The Bureau of Labor Statistics has eliminated its program, research to improve state and local area unemployment statistics. The National Center for Education Statistics has reduced methodological research and technical development, eliminated technical assistance grants to states, and reduced its projection project and analysis programs. The National Center for Health Statistics has reduced "quality control" in three programs: the Hospital Discharge Survey, the National Ambulatory Medical Care Survey, and the National Health Interview Survey. The Energy Information Administration has reduced its efforts in statistical design, eliminated field audits, and reduced validation and quality assessment reviews of data and models. These reductions represent lost potential improvement. They both affect the quality of current data systems and threaten that of future systems.

It is unfortunate but predictable that budgetary cutbacks should have affected so severely the research activities of the major data programs. These programs are essential to quality in at least three ways: (1) "research groups provide the analytical capabilities for estimating levels of accuracy"; (2) research is needed on a continuing basis to develop methods either for increasing accuracy and utility or for keeping "the same levels of accuracy and utility at lower costs"; and (3) "field statistical operations without strong research auxiliaries are bound to deteriorate over time" (Kruskal, in Subcommittee on Census and Population, 1982:363).

COMBINED IMPACTS ON TECHNICAL ADEQUACY AND USEFULNESS

Other agencies have responded to budgetary cutbacks with staff reductions (i.e., reductions in force, or RIFs, as well as furloughs) and deferral of equipment modernization. Loss of personnel has exacerbated delays of data issuance and increased the numbers of cancellations already scheduled in response to the funding cuts. But the loss of personnel affects the quality of data at least as much as it affects data use. The expertise and experience of federal statistical, research, and evaluative staff are needed for ensuring and maintaining the high quality of the sample, the measurement instruments used, and data processing techniques. These staff members are an integral component of the technical adequacy of data systems. This is another case in which actions are visible but have effects that are not readily or precisely determinable.

Civil Service regulations concerning reductions in force (RIFs) exacerbate this problem. Rules protecting agency staff with seniority result in senior employees "bumping" employees with less seniority. That job is taken by the senior employee, regardless of whether or not the employee has the expertise necessary to perform the new job. It is then possible that people with inappropriate or inadequate skills are responsible for statistical studies, or, as one investigator said, "someone who knows how to estimate state and local population size might be working on the census of commerce and manufacturing; an expert on migration to the Sunbelt might be transferred to the fertility branch" (Cherlin, in Subcommittee on Census and Population 1982:395).

Deferring the purchase of needed equipment sacrifices improvements in productivity that could increase speed, reduce costs, and generally palliate some of the effects of the budget cuts. Everyone recognizes that computer hardware and software have become integral components of data systems. But it is less well known that a good deal of the computer equipment in current use in federal agencies is obsolete, expensive to run, and thus in need of replacement. Current software also needs to be redesigned. Delays in modernizing carry a serious opportunity cost. Although the money for modernization is saved, that saving involves the loss of great potential to improve timeliness, reduce errors, increase accuracy, augment usefulness, and lower costs. Yet much of the equipment used by the Census Bureau is so inadequate and outmoded that many of the 1980 tabulations had to be done by hand (Herbers, 1981). The failure to procure modern equipment is one agency response to the administration's budgetary cutbacks, which will affect the usefulness and technical adequacy of present and future federal data systems.

Finally, many federal and private sector data systems depend on the quality, availability, timeliness, and consistency of the data generated by the major statistical programs; damage to the usefulness and technical adequacy of those programs has a multiplier effect. Because critical 1980 Census data were not available in time, the Department of Defense was forced to delay a manpower recruitment study. The Bureau of Economic Analysis in the Department of Commerce relies for almost all of its statistics on the Census Bureau and the Bureau of Labor Statistics. Figures collected in private surveys often are validated against federal survey data. These private surveys also rely on federal statistics for population controls, for ratio estimates or benchmarks, and for other sample surveys. Given these interrelationships, it is clear that deterioration in the federal data agencies affects the public and private system for producing data.

In summary, the administration's budgetary cutbacks have had major impacts on the technical adequacy and usefulness of federal data. These impacts are likely to extend into the future and to spill over far beyond the boundaries of the federal agencies involved. Reduced reliability, uncertain quality control, and missing data in major federal data programs will weaken any descriptive, evaluative, or planning study that relies on a federal data base to produce its information. What then becomes of the administration's expectation that special program evaluation studies can compensate for the reductions in the availability and quality of federal data?

RELIANCE BY PROGRAM EVALUATORS
ON ADMINISTRATIVE DATA

Program evaluations come in many forms and sizes. Their purposes may include describing a program (process or formative evaluation), analyzing its assumptions and their relationships with program activities (evaluability assessment), identifying program effects (outcome or impact or summative evaluation), comparing alternative programs (comparative evaluation), or synthesizing findings from different evaluations on the same subject (meta-evaluation or evaluation synthesis). In almost every incarnation of program evaluation, and at many different stages in the evaluative process, researchers may rely on existing data from administrative records and statistical programs.

The program evaluation process generally followed in individual studies can be thought of as composed of five phases: review of the substantive and methodological literature, evaluation design, data collection, data analysis, and documentation. Existing data systems can be crucial for all of the first three phases, as is shown by the experience of GAO's Program and Methodology Division (PEMD).

The following discussion of this experience will stress PEMD's use of administrative rather than statistical data, although heavy use has been made of both. This emphasis is chosen because PEMD program evaluation staff use statistical data in typical ways. For example, in an effort to develop a research agenda in the area of retirement policy, the examination of national census data permitted PEMD staff to identify the magnitude of the decline in the "normal retirement age" for males, and the steadiness of that decline, despite major fluctuations in economic conditions. Similarly, projections of trends in labor force participation for women were developed by PEMD staff based on Bureau of Labor Statistics analyses, which, in turn, depended on population estimates made by the Census Bureau. Such use of statistical data is widespread, as is generally understood.

The considerable use of administrative data by program evaluators appears to be less well understood by policy makers and budgetary planners. This is shown by the assumption of the administration, which was already noted, that once a program area loses its federal locus or is eliminated, the administrative data having grown up around the program are no longer needed. It then becomes especially important to understand the extensive use program evaluators make of administrative data.

PREPARATORY STAGES IN
PROGRAM EVALUATION

When PEMD staff begin a program evaluation, a review of the literature always is undertaken to ensure three things: (1) a grasp of the underlying substantive issues that have informed both the program and its legislative history; (2) an awareness of the research methods and measures that previously have been employed to evaluate the program; and (3) a firm basis for estimating the feasibility and usefulness of performing an evaluation in the given program area. Especially with regard to the decision on feasibility usefulness, existing data play an important and almost ubiquitous role.

For example, in a process evaluation now in progress of residential placement for children and youth (USGAO, forthcoming b), the availability of administrative data on the number and types of children in residential care was a major factor in ascertaining that a study in this area would be feasible within time and budget constraints. Had information on the population of children in residential care not been documented, filed, retained, and accessible, it is unlikely that PEMD's study would have been possible.

Grant application forms were the source of information that determined the feasibility of addressing targeting issues in an evaluation synthesis on block grants (USGAO, 1982a). These administrative data were put together by the Department of Housing and Urban Development, using community development block grant applications from a sample of 147 entitlement cities.

In a comparative evaluation assessing the relative cost effectiveness of RIFs, furloughs, and attrition (USGAO, forthcoming a), PEMD staff looked at the range of administrative data collected and available in each federal agency to decide whether it was possible to do such an evaluation and which variables were feasible to examine across agencies.

EVALUATION DESIGN

The existence and availability of administrative and statistical program data is a major consideration when deciding on a particular design. A quantitative case study design, for example, is more attractive when it is possible to use national data to furnish benchmarks against which the case study data can be compared. Although this will not solve the generalizability (or external validity) problem affecting case study designs, it helps to establish confidence in the case study findings.

An ongoing PEMD outcome evaluation using a case study design has taken advantage of just such a situation, using national statistical data as a basis of comparison for the case study results. This evaluation examines the effects of the 1981 Omnibus Budget Reconciliation Act (OBRA) legislation on participants in the Aid to Families with Dependent Children (AFDC) program (USGAO, 1984). The design of this evaluation features two other uses of administrative data. First, published information on characteristics of state AFDC plans were used in the site selection process to ensure that the sites selected would reflect a variety of AFDC program dimensions. Second, county AFDC caseload data also were used in site selection to make certain that the communities chosen would include sufficient numbers of earners (i.e., working AFDC recipients) to allow the detection of OBRA's effects.

Many other PEMD designs have used statistical or administrative data to support site selection and sampling. In the process evaluation examining the residential placement of children and youth (USGAO, forthcoming b), administrative data on the number of facilities per state allowed the selection of three states in which residential care systems were approximately equivalent in size. Without this information, a major data collection effort would have been needed simply to select the sites. Administrative data on the type and location of facilities known to state and county agencies also were essential in developing the universe of facilities in the three states from which the samples could be drawn.

Such dependence of studies on data collected by governmental agencies is widespread. The RIF/furlough/attrition design (USGAO, forthcoming a) made use of agency administrative data on the size, scope, and timing of RIFs to select its sample of agencies for study. A process evaluation on the status of runaway and homeless youth (USGAO, 1983a) made use of grant applications from each funded site for sample selection purposes. The data accessed included site-specific information on the type of community (urban, suburban, or rural), years in operation, years of federal funding, actual federal dollars requested and granted for previous and current fiscal years, administrative affiliations, number of beds, number of clients served, extent of volunteer labor used, major nonfederal contributor, shelter type (center-run, host home, combination), major source of referrals, and degree of networking with other agencies.

In another evaluation now ongoing in PEMD of the national defense industrial base (USGAO, forthcoming c), staff made use of Department of Defense administrative data contained in the Industrial Preparedness Wedge Program, the Master Urgency List, and the Critical Item List to select its sample of case studies.

The comparative design of one PEMD evaluation was based entirely on the existence of administrative data. This evaluation compared two titles of the CETA Program—the traditional Comprehensive Services Program (Title IIB) and the relatively new Private Sector Initiative Program (Title VII)— with regard to targeting, service mix, placement outcomes, and program size (USGAO, 1983b). Because comparable data were available for both titles, it was possible to use a design involving the exploration of similarities and differences between the two programs within the same communities.

Administrative data again furnished the basis for a before/after design in the attrition component of the RIF/attrition/furlough evaluation (USGAO, forthcoming a). If agency attrition data had not existed, it would have been impossible to capture past history in this area. Prior data on attrition also were needed as a baseline from which to assess the need for a RIF.

DATA COLLECTION

Statistical and administrative data have, in some cases, furnished almost the entire basis for an evaluation. For example, a recent PEMD evaluation of state responses to the rising demands and costs of nursing home care (USGAO, 1984a) used federal administrative data to study trends in Medicaid nursing home expenditure by type of service. Expenditure data are disaggregated by type of facility and are reported by the states in January for each prior fiscal year. The administrative data employed covered 1976-1980. Use of the data, much of it unpublished, permitted the examination of expenditure trends for service types over time and between states.

Similarly, program administrative data played a major role in an evaluation synthesis of the CETA program (USGAO, 1982b). Three types of administrative data were used: reports of participant characteristics to address targeting, financial summary reports to address expenditures, and program status reports to address both the mix of services and placement rates. These reports were available from 1976 to 1980 with only minor definitional changes. Prime sponsors (local administering bodies) were required to submit reports to the Department of Labor on a quarterly or yearly basis. Reports were broken down separately for each CETA title.

In other cases, existing data have served to help construct a new data base. AFDC case records were the basis for the bulk of data collection in the AFDC evaluation (USGAO, 1984b), which made it possible to create longitudinal welfare histories for several thousand AFDC recipients. In the same evaluation, monthly reports by the state and county on caseloads and expenditures were used to create time series of up to 46 observations. In a similar vein, the RIF/attrition/furlough evaluation is using agency payroll, personnel, and other records for building the study's data base on costs and savings, as well as the minority status and sex of certain employee populations.

Administrative data records played still another role in the residential placement evaluation (USGAO, forthcoming b), one focus of which was the characteristics of children and youth in residential care. It was possible to focus the study in this way only because facilities had maintained records on their residents. It was from these records that the necessary information was obtained.

The same is true for an evaluation synthesis on access to special education (USGAO, 1981). Administrative child count data, which is submitted annually by the states to the Office of Special Education, were used to answer congressional questions on the numbers and characteristics of children receiving special education. These data were critical in the evaluation's findings, which showed wide disparities across the states in the proportions of mentally retarded children served.

In summary, for PEMD staff or other evaluators to respond in a timely fashion and at a reasonable cost to questions about the status or effectiveness of government programs, data must be readily available and of a high quality. This does not mean that, were these data lacking, there would be no other way to respond to specific Congressional questions. It does mean that the accessibility and adequacy of these systems allows evaluations to be more realistic, more easily and better specified, more rapidly and inexpensively performed, wider in coverage, richer in detail, and more powerful than they could be without them, time and costs being equal. This runs directly counter to the administration's two assumptions that special evaluation studies are independent of federal data systems and can substitute for them and that administrative data have no useful life beyond the life of the federal programs around which they have developed.

POSSIBLE SOLUTIONS

It is important to remember that it always has been necessary to exercise caution in the use of administrative data. Evaluators have had to be on the lookout for changes or differences in definitions of data categories (over time and across space) and in procedures for data collection. This is not a simple matter because, from the beginning, researchers may have to guess at unstated definitions of population and other variables. "Especially when computers are involved, adequate documentation may be hard to obtain since one must know how the data were coded as well as their definition" (Hoaglin et al., 1982:160).

Administrative data have many weaknesses, especially when used alone rather than as adjuncts in the program evaluation process described above. However, these data often are indispensable as aids in determining what evaluation questions are feasible to ask and answer, in designing evaluations that can produce the needed information, and in appropriately structuring data bases to produce it.

In examining agency responses to the administration's budgetary cutbacks, two seem particularly problematic for program evaluation. One is certainly the interruption of time series. A second is the unknown (i.e., invisible and undeterminable) degree of deterioration in the quality of the data made available.

Time series are important to evaluators because they can be used to measure long-term effects of government policies and programs. There are other ways of measuring effects, but none that so efficiently allows the inclusion of lagged or delayed effects which, as we are becoming increasingly aware, are important in evaluating government programs and policies or in thinking about social problems. Time series analyses of the past have had important impacts on the acquisition of new knowledge. Kuznets's longitudinal data series, which, for example, charted the comparative rates of output growth for Western nations (Kuznets, 1956) and showed the relative stability over time of workers' marginal propensity to consume (Kuznets, 1961), shaped much of the current thinking about the success of capitalism. On the other hand, the failure to have good time series data available also has had important impacts. Slater points out that missing data at the beginning of the 1973-1975 recession "concealed a huge inventory buildup, which meant that economic policy planners misjudged the potential for the downturn—a downturn that became the worst since World War II" (Fuerbringer, 1982). Cutbacks that affect time series data, then, are among the most pernicious to evaluators. Such cutbacks deprive evaluators of a critical means by which to understand not only policy or program effects but also the validity of some of the assumptions that undergird those programs and policies.

With regard to the degree of deterioration in the quality of data brought about by the administration's budget cuts, the difficulty of assessing the effects of reductions in quality control already has been discussed. It is clear, however, that at least one of the results of those reductions will be to put an added burden of validation on the evaluator. Establishing the quality of the information contained in administrative records always has been a necessity. Misidentification of individuals, incompleteness of data, double counting, and so forth are common problems that call for careful efforts by evaluators to estimate and understand the dimensions of the potential threat to validity (Roos et al., 1979:243). But with the cutback or elimination of pretesting and quality control in various statistical series, these efforts will need to be heavily extended at considerable cost.

CONCLUSIONS

The existing federal deficits and the administration's extensive budgetary cutbacks in data systems create a climate in which it is difficult to raise issues of needed improvements in statistical and administrative data (that is, to propose expenditures rather than cost savings). Yet if the determination of executive branch accountability via legislative oversight is to remain an important function in government, and if the public use of publicly funded data is to continue, continuing improvements to administrative and statistical data are mandatory.

One of the most important problems encountered by PEMD in using administrative data has been the lack of consistency and uniformity both in terms of the definition of variables and in record keeping. In the RIF/attrition/furlough evaluation, for example, it was found that an employee in one agency who received a general RIF notice and resigned before receiving a specific RIF notice was counted as RIF-affected; in another agency, the employee was not so counted. A low-cost improvement here would be to standardize definitions of personnel actions and the manner in which they are counted. In a more general way, it would be important to encourage not only uniform but constant definitions across programs, at least for reporting demographic characteristics such as age groupings, ethnic/race categories, marital status, income groupings, and so forth.

A second needed improvement concerns the level of data aggregation. In the evaluation synthesis done by PEMD on block grants, for example, the Title XX Social Services program was found to have only state-level data. This level of aggregation is clearly too high for most purposes, making it impossible for PEMD to evaluate the program within congressional time constraints and GAO cost restrictions. Some thought, therefore, needs to be given to the levels of data aggregation appropriate for the different uses and users of public data. Archiving always should be done at the lowest level of aggregation feasible.

A third needed improvement, also involving data aggregation, concerns changes in data records and the way they are made. If new legislation or administrative regulations force modifications in reporting requirements, for example, those modifications should be made in ways that allow the new statistics to be disaggregated back to the original form for at least a reasonable period of time. An example of how this can be done is given by the Department of Labor (DOL), which had to change the definition of "economically disadvantaged" as it applied to CETA participants. Before 1978, economically disadvantaged had been defined in terms of the poverty level as established by OMB. From 1978 on, the definition shifted and referred to the OMB poverty level or 70 percent of the lower living standard income level (Bureau of Labor Statistics), whichever was higher. DOL then had the foresight to require that the reporting system maintain frequencies for both definitions of economically disadvantaged after 1978, enabling comparisons to be made across years before and after the change.

Finally, more thought is needed with regard to the preservation of date. Sometimes management or administrative records are purged so quickly that creation of longitudinal time series or individual client histories may not be possible. Often, this is because the focus of a management information system is likely to be on day-to-day management needs, or because computerized records are no longer archived.

This chapter has analyzed the budgetary cutbacks made in federal data systems by the Reagan administration. It draws the following conclusions:

- The justifications given for those cutbacks are unconvincing in that they distort long-established national policy with regard to the purposes and intended users of federal data collection efforts.
- The cutbacks themselves have been extensive, with severe effects both on data availability and on data quality.
- The idea that major data users, such as state or local governments and businesses, are able to collect their own information is highly questionable.

- The expectation that special evaluation studies can substitute or compensate for cutbacks in federal data systems is illusory, given the use made by program evaluation of those systems, and given the corresponding increases in time and expenditure that would be required to perform evaluations absent those systems.

If, in fact, budget cuts absolutely must be made in federal data systems, then a first step should be to consider all data system needs and users; a second step should be to ensure that the cuts do not result in systematic reduction of access by particular groups. From a program evaluation viewpoint, it would be most important to avoid breaks in time series data and deterioration in data quality, a process whose effects often are neither identifiable nor measurable.

If any new funds can be made available, then four modest improvements are suggested:

- more consistency and uniformity both in the definition of variables and in recordkeeping
- archiving at the lowest level of data aggregation possible
- maintenance of data collection efforts, in the face of definitional and other changes, to allow comparability of the new data with the old
- more attention to the preservation of management data that can be useful for evaluative purposes

NOTE

1. The term "administrative data" as used in this chapter refers to data designed and collected by administrative agencies in the normal course of their work to facilitate the administration of a program (e.g., to guide agency operations and policy decisions). The term "statistical data" refers to data designed and collected to improve scientific knowledge. The distinct purposes of gathering these two types of data have created major distinctions between them in quality and timeliness. "Statistical records and their collection procedures are designed, documented, and controlled to yield the desired statistical results" (Department of Health, Education, and Welfare, 1979:21). Unlike statistical data gathered from surveys and censuses, administrative data often present problems of definition and accuracy. But administrative data may well be more current and offer greater frequency of observation than statistical data. As a result, if data are needed on a regular basis (to construct time series, for example), administrative data records may be the most cost effective information source. If, on the other hand, highly accurate data—at the national, regional, or state level—are needed, then statistical survey data may be the most efficient way to obtain them.

The two types of data may be intermingled in a given study, and statistical use often is made of administrative data records. Some administrative data systems have, in fact, evolved into statistical data systems (e.g., what started out as an administrative data collection effort at the IRS has become the present Statistics of Income file, which is used extensively by researchers to study issues of general statistical or socioeconomic interest). The Census Bureau also uses administrative records in a variety of ways, such as the design of censuses and surveys, identification of sampling universes, and imputations for missing cells.

Another distinction exists between administrative and statistical data files. In censuses and surveys involving the direct collection of data for statistical purposes, assurances usually are provided to respondents that the information they supply will not be used as a basis for administrative action (either against or for them). That, of course, is not the case for administrative data. This situation has led to some consensus among statisticians that it is acceptable to make statistical use of administrative records, but not vice versa.

In summary, the chief distinction between administrative and statistical data is the use to which they will be put. This use implies a prior and "parallel distinction in the degree to which the statistician is in control of the design and collection of the records. Survey records and their collection procedures are designed, documented, and controlled to yield the desired statistical characteristics. When administrative records are used statistically, the statistician must . . . determine their conceptual suitability for the intended use. And the statistician must also devise methods for overcoming technical problems frequently encountered in making new uses of existing records" (Department of Commerce, 1980:19, 27-28).

REFERENCES

BOORSTIN, D. J. (1973) The Americans: The Democratic Experience. New York: Random House.

Committee on Government Operations, U.S. House of Representatives (1982) Reorganization and Budget Cutbacks May Jeopardize the Future of the Nation's Statistical System: House Report 97-901. Washington, DC: Government Printing Office.

CRITTENDEN, A. (1982) "A world with fewer numbers." New York Times (July 11).

Department of Commerce, Office of Federal Statistical Policy and Standards (1980) Report on Statistical Uses of Administrative Records. Washington, DC: Government Printing Office.

Department of Health, Education, and Welfare, Social Security Administration, Office of Research and Statistics (1979) Statistical Uses of Administrative Records. Washington, DC: Government Printing Office.

FUERBRINGER, J. (1982) "Cutting funds for statistics." New York Times (August 2).

HACKER, A. (1983) "Census figures for corporate use." New York Times (August 21).

HERBERS, J. (1981) "Cutbacks hamper Census Bureau: some reports delayed or canceled." New York Times (November 25).

HICKS, J. D., G. E. MOWRY, and R. E. BURKE (1964) The Federal Union. Boston: Houghton Mifflin.

HOAGLIN, D. C., R. J. LIGHT, B. McPEEK, F. MOSTELLER, and M. A. STOTO (1982) Data for Decisions. Cambridge, MA: Abt Books.

KUZNETS, S. (1961) Capital in the American Economy. Princeton, NJ: Princeton University Press.

— — — (1956) "Quantitative aspects of the economic growth of nations: I." Economic Development and Cultural Change 5.

MELNICK, D. (1982) Recent Changes in the Federal Government's Statistical Program. Washington, DC: Congressional Research Service.

ROOS, L. L., Jr., J. P. NICOL, C. F. JOHNSON, and N. P. ROOS (1979) Using administrative data banks for research and evaluation." Evaluation Quarterly 3, 2 (May).

SCHORR, B. (1983) "An administrative lean on statistics." Wall Street Journal (October 5).

SHISKIN, J. (1970) "The trade-off between speed and accuracy in current economic statistics." Presented to the American Statistical Association, January 27.

STANFIELD, R. L. (1981) "Numbers crunch—data funds cut just when more statistics are needed." National Journal (November 28): 2120.

Subcommittee on Census and Population, U.S. House of Representatives, Committee on Post Office and Civil Service (1982) Impact of Budget Cuts on Federal Statistical Programs: House Report 97-41. Washington, DC: Government Printing Office.

Subcommittee on Legislation and National Security, U.S. House of Representatives, Committee on Government Operations (1982) Federal Government Statistics and Statistical Policy: House Report 12-149. Washington, DC: Government Printing Office.

U.S. General Accounting Office [USGAO] (forthcoming a) The Relative Costs and Savings of RIFs, Furloughs, and Attrition (tentative title). Washington, DC: Government Printing Office.

——— (forthcoming b) Residential Placement of Children and Youth (tentative title). Washington, DC: Government Printing Office.

——— (forthcoming c) Shortages in Critical Components, Labor Skills, and Commodities: An Evaluation of Their Impact on Defense and Nondefense Production Needs (tentative title). Washington, DC: Government Printing Office.

———(1984a) Medicaid and Nursing Home Care: Cost Increases and the Need for Services Are Creating Problems for the States and the Elderly. GAO/IPE-84-1. Washington, DC: Government Printing Office.

———(1984b) An Evaluation of the 1981 AFDC Changes: Initial Analyses. GAO/PEMD-84-6. Washington, DC: Government Printing Office.

——— (1983a) Federally Supported Centers Provide Needed Services for Runaways and Homeless Youths. GAO/IPE-83-7. Washington, DC: Government Printing Office.

——— (1983b) Federal Job Training: A Comparison of Public and Private Sector Performance. GAO/IPE-83-5. Washington, DC: Government Printing Office.

——— (1982a) Lessons Learned from Past Block Grants: Implications for Congressional Oversight. GAO/IPE-82-8. Washington, DC: Government Printing Office.

——— (1982b) CETA Programs for Disadvantaged Adults: What Do We Know About Their Enrollees, Services, and Effectiveness? GAO/IPE-82-2. Washington, DC: Government Printing Office.

——— (1981) Disparities Still Exist in Who Gets Special Education. GAO/IPE-81-1. Washington, DC: Government Printing Office.

WALLMAN, K. K. (1983) "Federal statistics: problems, progress, prognosis." Journal of the University of Cincinnati Business School (Fall).

IDENTIFICATION OF TREATMENT CONDITIONS USING STANDARD RECORD-KEEPING SYSTEMS

J. Ward Keesling

In any genuine experiment, the researcher has control over the assignment of "experimental units" to treatment conditions. The experimenter uses this control to assign units to treatment conditions at random, which assures the comparability of treatment conditions under the null hypothesis and makes it possible to compute the probability of obtaining results that contradict that hypothesis. Control also is necessary for identifying the conditions under which each experimental unit is assigned. This enables the researcher to analyze the data at the conclusion of the experiment.

In the nonexperimental setting, the researcher usually must depend on others to provide the information about which subjects participated in which treatment conditions. The evaluator of a social program is most likely to rely on program administrators or archival records. The quality of information in nonexperimental (or quasi-experimental) evaluations often rests on the quality of the record-keeping system, as administrators themselves must rely on record-keeping systems to determine what treatment condition a particular "unit" has received, as well as particular characteristics of that unit that might be useful in evaluating the treatment.

This chapter describes several studies in which it became apparent that the record-keeping systems were flawed. Three problems in the use of record-keeping systems to identify treatment (or pretreatment) conditions are identified:

- Records may not be accurate if there is little motivation to keep them accurately.
- Certain indicators of treatment status may be appropriate for some contexts, but misleading in others.
- Different systems of records about the same units may not have common identifiers.

These problems were evident in federal- and state-sponsored compensatory education projects examined for this study. It is not certain that these examples will generalize to a broader class of interventions which might involve clearer distinctions between the students who are and who are not served and between institutions that do or do not receive funding. The examples in this chapter, however, are cautionary for most evaluators.

MOTIVATION TO MAINTAIN ACCURATE RECORDS

STUDENT RECORDS

Approaching the record-keeping activities of schools as a naive lay person, one might presume that a student's cumulative record would contain a fairly complete history of his or her achievements in school–the grades obtained in various courses, standardized test scores, attendance, any special problems or circumstances, and a record of any special services that were provided and the diagnosis that led to their being provided. One would assume that this information would be useful both for administrators in deciding where to place the student each year and for the teacher who receives the student. In addition, such information would be valuable to evaluators seeking to assess the impact of special programs.

In actuality, administrators and teachers in some schools must make their decisions with less than full information. Administrators are responsible for maintaining student records so the incompleteness of those records must reflect a devaluing of that information. In this example, the differential values placed on certain information will be explored.

In developing a plan for a study of successful practices in the federally sponsored Chapter 1 program in a large, metropolitan school district in the west,[1] the research team (directed by myself) was told that student-level cumulative records would contain attendance data, indications of special programs received, and the scores on the district-mandated tests. Eight schools were chosen to participate in this study and their record-keeping styles ranged from file drawers of unalphabetized folders containing badly dog-eared collections of papers to neat folders alphabetized by membership within each current classroom.

The content of the records also was quite variable. Although annual attendance seemed to be recorded regularly, the provision of special services was not. In our sample the most problematic identifications were for special education and limited-English proficient status. There seemed to be no records kept of students assigned to speech therapy sessions. In addition, these sessions were so short (about 15 minutes) that teachers could not state definitely which students had been absent from their classes to receive the treatment and which had not. Speech therapy apparently is such a common and unobtrusive service that the fact that it is a special education service often is overlooked (McKay and Michie, 1982).

Limited-English proficient (LEP) status is determined by a special test, but it was not clear whether each student in that status had been retested regularly or whether the reclassification was entered on the records properly. We could tell if a student was presently classified as LEP by asking the bilingual coordinator, but we could not always determine when a student presently classified as fluent had first attained that status.

For our purposes, the most troubling failing was the occasional lack of information about whether or not the student had been exposed to Title I (now Chapter 1) services. In our sample of schools this problem was not widespread. When the records seemed incomplete, we were able to obtain information we needed from the Chapter 1 coordinator at the school.

Finding test scores for our study also was troublesome. As a service to the teachers and schools, the district distributes peel-off, gummed labels with the student's name and test scores, so that entering the test scores on the cumulative record does not involve transcribing the information from one sheet to another. In some of the schools, these labels were simply filed as a batch and the cumulative records contained no test information. In others, it appeared that some of the labels had been lost (usually an entire classroom), so some cumulative folders were updated and others were not. For some of the test scores we had to resort to using printed listings of the entire school roster of students and test scores maintained by the district's central evaluation office.

The reason attendance data are kept so well, when the other information is not, is clear. The state reimburses schools on the basis of their daily attendance, so an accurate count of the pupils in attendance and with excused absences is important in determining the resources allocated to the schools. Attendance data are carefully maintained on separate records for each student, with the total absent days recorded on the cumulative folder at the end of the year. One of the ironies of the data collection described above was that the attendance records at one school were audited before they were transferred to the cumulative records. During the audit they were misplaced, so an entire set of students had no attendance data in the study data base.

There are several implications of these findings. First, although we expected to find the data we needed in one place, the cumulative record, it became necessary to search in several places in order to obtain complete data on the students in our sample. This made the data more expensive to collect than we had anticipated. Clerks had to be assigned to collect the data from these records, whereas we had anticipated that the field research staff (regular district employees) would be able to accomplish this task as well as a fairly heavy schedule of classroom observation.

The second implication is that there are so many different data sources involved that the chance for an error in transcription or an erroneous match of names (the district does not assign identification numbers) is substantially increased. It seems likely that if the teachers were keeping the cumulative records in accordance with district policy, there would be less likelihood of such errors and mismatches.

Finally, it seems that the district's own evaluation efforts are compromised by the failure to record uniformly the application of compensatory education programs to students. Although we found few instances of incomplete information on Title I/Chapter 1 services, the district has studied the related problem of identifying Chapter 1 participants on the test forms used to evaluate the program. The district has determined that approximately 17 percent of the schools receiving Chapter 1 funds underreported the number of students being served. Four percent did not identify any Chapter 1 students in either (or both) of the two grades that participated in the testing. If the test scores for some Chapter 1 students are misidentified as belonging to non-Chapter 1 students, and if those scores are distributed in the same way as those for Chapter 1 students, the average score of the non-Chapter 1 group will be lowered. This could tend to make the Chapter 1 program look effective spuriously.

It is difficult to offer hard and fast solutions to this problem. One possibility would be for the researcher to be present at the time of assignment of students to treatment conditions and to keep records outside of those kept by school district personnel. This is an expensive solution and is not possible if it is desired to use the historical records on students covering a period prior to the inception of the research.

Another possibility is for the researcher to obtain corroborating evidence from another source. For example, on state-required tests the students must be classified according to special services received. However, as the district's own study demonstrated, this is not infallible and it also is expensive because it requires searching through voluminous files for these indicators. This searching and matching problem is exacerbated by the district not assigning unique identifying numbers to the students. The matches must be performed on a name basis, which leads to many difficulties as students may change either their surnames or their preferred given names from year to year, or even during one year.

But even if the district-required records were kept perfectly, they may not correspond to the needs of the researcher. In the study referred to above, the observations of the teachers' activities were to be attached to the achievement records of the students. In about one-third of the schools, the students were assigned to a teacher other than the homeroom teacher for reading, math, or both. The district's cumulative record provided only for recording the homeroom teacher. In one of these schools there was another record-keeping system that showed who was assigned where; but in others, these reassignments were based on informal agreements among teachers. The researchers had to go back to the teachers to ask if they remembered which students they had had in prior years.

All of this leads to the uneasy feeling that perhaps five to ten percent of the cases in the study are fundamentally misclassified, not including transcription errors or keypunch errors that might not be caught. As there is no alternative source of identification on these dimensions, it is not possible to determine whether these cases seriously bias the study.

STATE DEPARTMENT OF EDUCATION
EVALUATION REPORTS

The next example comes from an audit of a state's evaluation activities and further illustrates the need for alternative sources to corroborate indicators of treatment conditions in archival records (Keesling and Burstein, 1976).

The Center for the Study of Evaluation (CSE) at UCLA was contracted by the California State Department of Education (SDE), the Office of the Legislative Analyst, and the California Department of Finance to conduct an evaluation of the Early Childhood Education program. As part of that evaluation, an audit of the SDE's own evaluation of the program was conducted. A central part of that audit concerned the receipt, editing, and processing of the evaluation reports sent by the schools to the SDE. Keesling and Burstein (1976) document many types of problems in the treatment of these forms, not the least of which was the fact that the SDE schedule allowed six weeks from the receipt of 40,000 pages of material to the generation of reports on their content. This example focuses on the problems in identifying the programs operating in these schools.

The Evaluation Report (called ER here, although it was known as the E-127-P in California) was the basis on which the SDE determined which sources of funding applied to each school. The audit was concerned with only three of these sources: Title I, the state's Educationally Disadvantaged Youth (EDY) program, and the state's Early Childhood Education (ECE) program. Keesling and Burstein identified several potential problems in using ERs to classify schools as to funding sources:

- Principals may have had difficulty filling out the ER, leading to spurious inclusions or omissions from a program. SDE was not always able to verify these reports.
- A school serving 3 percent of its second-grade students was counted with as much weight as a school serving 100 percent of its students. Test scores were not reported separately by population within each school.
- The amounts of money spent per pupil from each funding source varied greatly. Thus, the treatment in one school might have been qualitatively different from that in another school being funded by the same program.
- The standards for counting pupils as served differed from district to district. Some counted only those students who had been present for at least 80 percent of the instructional days between pretest and posttest.
- There were no uniform standards for reporting the scores of students who were transported from one school to another. In some cases, Title I students were allocated to the schools they attended as a result of busing: in others, they were allocated to their school of origin.

No data were available that could clarify the ambiguities arising from problems of differential funding levels, funds following the students to other schools, or degree of program participation. However, it was possible to check on the degree to which the classification of the second and third grades (the uppermost grades served by ECE and the focus of the audit) with respect to Title I, EDY, and ECE agreed.

For the purposes of the study of ECE, including the audit, a stratified, random sample of 265 schools was drawn from a frame defined by the state's elementary school universe supplemented by information from the applications for services under the three programs involved in the study (Title I, EDY, and ECE). The applications were made on a single form, the A-127-ES. Interestingly, these forms did not include information on the grade levels to be served. Ten schools were drawn into the sample that did not have either second or third grades and were dropped from the study.

The SDE maintained a roster of schools in the ECE program, but it did not maintain a similar roster of schools for the Title I or EDY programs. Thus, the SDE could verify the ECE status of schools, but had to accept whatever was recorded by the principal regarding Title I and EDY. Comparing the ERs to the applications revealed that six percent (of 153) schools that had planned to have Title I projects in operation did not report these services in the second or third grades. Conversely, seven percent (of 102 schools) that did not include Title I in their plan reported such services in those two grades. Slightly smaller percentages of both kinds of discrepancies also were found for the EDY program.

As another check, a special questionnaire was sent to 72 of the sample schools to obtain additional data on program implementation. This information presumably was to be reported by the building principal who was also responsible for filling out the ER; 57 schools returned this questionnaire, and of these, 23 percent indicated a classification different from that derived from the ER data. The most extreme variation was one questionnaire reporting no Title I, no EDY, and no ECE, even though the ER reports showed all three programs in place for three years. Twenty-three percent misclassification is a substantial proportion. It is doubtful that one should attach much meaning to evaluations of program effectiveness based on reports (presumably made by the same school official) that vary so widely regarding the programs providing services to students.

The simplest solution would be for the SDE to maintain records of the historical participation in all of the special programs funded through state or federal sources. This would make it possible to perform several auditing checks on the data as they are processed. Any school that showed a change in status could be checked against a master list of schools funded that year. Even checking the applications against the ERs would have detected some problems that could have been resolved if there were master lists of participating schools. Although Keesling and Burstein (1976) recommended several computerized auditing checks that could be performed (many being modifications of procedures already implemented that would have sharpened and refined them), Keesling (1984) reports that the SDE has scaled

TABLE 11.1
Three-Digit Codes for Status in the
Early Childhood Education Program

Three-Digit Code	1973-1974	1974-1975	1975-1976	No. in CSE Sample
100	F	F	F	42
101*	P	P	P	0
202	P	F	F	26
203+	0	F	F	75
204+	0	F	F	5
205++	0	P	P	0
306	0	0	P	0
307**	0	0	F	0
308**	0	0	F	0
309	P	P	F	10
310	Schools admitted in mid-1975-1976			0
411	Schools admitted for 1976-1977			30
blank	Schools not in ECE and not entering in 1976-1977			67

NOTE: F = fully funded (serving grades K-3); p = partially funded (usually serving grades K-1); 0 = no ECE program; 1973-1974 was the first year of the program.
*These are schools offering only grades K-1. They were fully funded but considered to be partial programs.
**The code 307 is for schools in districts that had ECE schools in previous years. The code 308 is for schools in other districts.
+The code 203 is for schools in districts that had schools in ECE in 1973-1974. The code 204 is for schools in other districts.
++There are not supposed to be any schools in this category.

back on the number of computer checks it performs and now trusts the unaudited reports to a greater degree than before.

MISLEADING INDICATORS
OF TREATMENT CONDITION

The example used to illustrate this problem area is drawn from the same audit of state evaluation practices. The coding scheme used by the SDE to record participation in the ECE program existed in long and short versions. The use of two different versions could lead to different classifications of the schools, as shown below.

ECE was the only program for which SDE had historical information on the implementation of the program at each site. This was represented by a coding scheme given in Table 11.1 (reproduced from Keesling and Burstein,

1976: 15). However, at the time the sample of schools was drawn, only the left-most digit was included in descriptions of the sampling frame. (In this digit, the code 1 means the most exposure to ECE, and the code 3 was supposed to be for schools entering in the third year. The code 4 was developed later, prior to the receipt of the ERs.) The evaluation conducted by the Center for the Study of Evaluation was to focus on the impact of ECE on students who had received the treatment for three, two, or no years at the time they were in second or third grade. After the sample was drawn and the study was underway, it was realized that the three-digit code contained information that would lead to the reclassification of some of the schools. However, the SDE had only entered the left-most digit of the three-digit code onto the ER forms for its own analyses. CSE used all three digits on its records. The two coding schemes clearly would produce different classifications of schools: The SDE's would be related to the number of years of full funding, but not necessarily to the number of years of service received by the students in second and third grade, whereas the CSE's would be related to the number of years of continuous receipt of service.

Clearly, schools coded "blank" or 411 had provided no prior exposure to ECE to the pupils in second or third grades at the time of the study. The schools coded 100 had provided three years of ECE services to their second and third graders as of the 1975-1976 school year. Schools coded 203 or 204 had provided two years of ECE services in the same time span. Codes 202 and 309 were harder to assign.

The typical pattern of funding was to apply partial funding to the kindergarten and first grades, which means that by 1975-1976 the schools coded 202 would have provided ECE services for three years to students in the second and third grades. CSE classified these schools as if they were coded 100 for that reason. SDE classified them as if they had only two years of exposure to the ECE program.

The code 309 required more investigation but, by using the ERs, it was possible to determine that 9 of the 10 schools in the sample had to be classified as three-year schools at second grade, eight of which were unclassified regarding third grade (as ECE had not been offered to these students when they were in the second grade—these schools were not included in analyses of third grade effects). The last of those nine was a three-year school in the third grade, while the tenth school was a two-year school for both grades. It is possible that these classifications could be incorrect because the ERs themselves are not perfect, as demonstrated earlier.

These examinations led to reclassifying 9 schools coded 309 and 26 coded 202 into the category 100 (three years of ECE) with respect to the second grade. The SDE coding scheme (which used only the left-most digit of the three for analytical purposes) classified as two-year or one-year schools nearly 45 percent of the schools in which second-grade students had received three years of ECE treatment. At third grade, the percentage of differently classified schools was close to 35 percent.

The SDE evaluation focused on the years of experience teachers have had instructing under the ECE program. For SDE a three-year school was one in which the second- and third-grade teachers had implemented the ECE program for three years. For CSE a three-year school was one in which the second- and third-grade students had received three years of service from ECE programs. Both analyses proved ambiguous about the impact of the program. The issue of importance was that by reducing the three-digit coding scheme to one, the SDE would be altering the meaning of the categories without explaining this fully. In the previous year, this shorthand had been appropriate for analyses of third-grade outcomes because one year of funding (code 2xx) meant one year of service to third graders and one year of experience for third-grade teachers. But in 1975-1976, the shorthand coding led to an ambiguity about what the focus of the evaluation was to be.

MERGING MULTIPLE DATA BASES
WITHOUT COMMON IDENTIFIERS

As a part of a project for the Department of Education, I was asked to acquire a previously developed data base on the history of the Title VII of the Elementary and Secondary Education Act (known as the Bilingual Education Act), and to merge it with data from the Bilingual Education Management Information System (BEMIS) and with files created by the Office for Civil Rights and the National Center for Education Statistics. The purpose was to compare various indicators of need for bilingual services to one another and to the history of federal support for such services. All of these files use what are known as OE (for Office of Education, the precursor to the Department of Education) numbers to identify districts. But there are patterns of inconsistency in each one that make it difficult to effect a merger of the files.

The "history file" was assembled from project summary sheets onto which the staff constructing the file had added OE codes taken from the 1976 Office for Civil Rights Census. As the history file encompassed projects from 1969 to 1981, there were some districts that could not be given a correct number because there were consolidations and dissolutions before and after the Office for Civil Rights roster was established. Also, there are some types of entities that received funding that were not school districts: Rather, they were consortia of districts or other special administrative arrangements for handling these programs. In addition, the schools run by the Bureau of Indian Affairs (BIA) are not part of the OE coding scheme. These cases had to receive unique, arbitrary codes, which were assigned to avoid any match with future OE codes.

The BEMIS project used the 1980 listing of school district codes from the National Center for Education Statistics (NCES) to prepare its files. These are updated OE codes and reflect the changes in districts in the period between 1976 and 1980. The special entities already described and the BIA schools still are not part of this coding scheme, so BEMIS assigned them an entirely different set of unique, arbitrary identification codes. Naturally, this made it difficult to match these entities across the two data bases. Luckily, there were only a few score of such places and they could be hand-matched to update the file.

Much of the information in the BEMIS file comes from records maintained by the Assistance Management and Procurement Services (AMPS). This system is designed to track all Department of Education grants to local entities (not states) from application to completion with some detail about dates of funding, funding levels, and actual expenditures. It would be useful to be able to merge AMPS information directly onto files containing other information about school districts that NCES gathers periodically (e.g., enrollments and financial data). AMPS, however, does not use OE codes to identify school districts; instead, it uses the Employer Identification Number (EIN) of the Internal Revenue Service. As far as can be determined, no concordance of OE numbers and EINs exists.

NCES has prepared a master file for 1979-1980 which is designed to list all regular elementary and secondary school districts in the United States. Basically, this utilized the same information used by BEMIS. As both the master file and AMPS records contain postal ZIP codes, I considered using these as the basis for a merger in this study. However, nearly one-third of the districts in the country share ZIP codes with others. One ZIP code is shared by 44 different districts!

The office for Civil Rights (OCR) data to be merged were taken from their 1980 sample survey. NCES was to provide census mapping data (1980 census data aggregated to the level of school district) for the project. Because this was late in preparation, the master file was used to prepare for the merger. About 20 percent of the records in the history file and BEMIS file did not match with the master file for reasons given earlier (BIA schools, special entities, districts that could not be identified accurately). In addition, 2 percent (or 124) of the OCR districts could not be matched to the master file, even though the OCR survey occured in the same school year the master file represents.

Specific points may be made about this example: (1) It would have been helpful if the staff preparing BEMIS had made use of the coding scheme for special entities developed by the group that prepared the history file; (2) it would be somewhat useful for NCES to prepare an automated translation from districts in the past to districts in the present (although it probably would be very expensive compared to its utility); and (3) a linkage between the EIN codes and the OE codes could be very helpful. More generally, the lessons to be learned are that even a master file may only cover a part of the universe of interest, and that dynamic entities are difficult to trace through time.

CONCLUSIONS

Random assignment is a major benefit of the true experiment, but knowing with certainty which cases got which treatments is an even greater benefit. The only way to attain the same certainty in a quasi-experiment is to have the researcher present at the time cases are allocated to treatments (whatever the basis of allocation) to record the result of that allocation process. Once the researcher had abdicated the responsibility for recording the treatment allocation, there is a strong likelihood that misclassification errors will arise which threaten the validity of the conclusions of the research.

But simply recording the treatment conditions allocated at the start of an intervention or evaluation does not guarantee the success of the evaluation. In the now classic case of the Emergency School Aid Act (ESAA) evaluation, in which schools within districts were assigned at random to treatment conditions (ESAA funding or no ESAA funding), some districts allocated other funds to make up the difference ESAA funding would have provided. (See the special issue of the *Journal of Educational Statistics* 3,1: 1978, devoted to this evaluation.)

Several suggestions can be made, drawing on the examples presented here.

(1) Archival records are only as good as motivated program administrators are willing to make them.

(2) Whenever possible, obtain a second indicator of the treatment allocated to each unit. Even asking the same person on a different form can provide a revealing check.

(3) Probe for full explanations of all information fields in a data base. Sometimes there are built-in checks or additional information about treatments that will modify the first opinion formulated from other indicators.

(4) Determine how records are updated and how often. Look for automated ways to transition from one updating to the next.

(5) Determine if there are special entities not routinely included in the data base.

(6) Be prepared for manual labor.

NOTE

1. Chapter 1 of the Education Consolidation and Improvement Act is the largest federally funded compensatory education program, with annual expenditures over $2.5 billion. It is the successor to Title I of the Elementary and Secondary Education Act.

REFERENCES

KEESLING, J. W. (1984) Differences Between Fall-to-Spring and Annual Gains in Evaluation of Chapter 1 Programs. Reston, VA: Advanced Technology: Education Analysis Center for State and Local Grants.

— — —and L. BURSTEIN (1976) Evaluation of the California Early Childhood Education Program, Volume II : An Audit Report on Early Childhood Education Program. Los Angeles: University of California, Center for the Study of Evaluation.

MCKAY M. and J. MICHIE (1982) Title I Services to Students Eligible for ESL/Bilingual or Special Education Programs. A Special Report from the Title I District Practices Study. McLean, VA: Advanced Technology, Inc.

USING LONGITUDINAL EARNINGS DATA FROM SOCIAL SECURITY RECORDS TO EVALUATE JOB-TRAINING PROGRAMS

Howard S. Bloom

This chapter illustrates procedures for using longitudinal earnings data from individual Social Security records to determine the impact of job-training programs on the future earnings of trainees. The basis for this discussion is a recent national evaluation of CETA programs for adults conducted for the Congressional Budget Office and the National Commission for Employment Policy. Because this chapter focuses primarily on data-related issues, many of the analytic issues and substantive findings from the original evaluation either are not discussed at all or are only referred to in passing. (For a more complete discussion of these issues, see Bloom and McLaughlin, 1982). This study examines the data and how they were obtained, a model for analyzing the data, a validation of the data, and an extension of the analysis using complementary data.

AUTHOR'S NOTE: This chapter draws largely from a report, *CETA Training Programs: Do They Work for Adults?*, prepared by myself and Maureen A. McLaughlin for the Congressional Budget Office and the National Commission for Employment Policy. All opinions expressed herein are my own and do not necessarily reflect the policies or official positions of either of the sponsoring organizations.

The analysis is based on data from the Continuous Longitudinal Manpower Survey (CLMS) funded by the U.S. Department of Labor, Employment and Training Administration and conducted jointly by the U.S. Census Bureau, the U.S. Social Security Administration, and Westat, Inc.[1] This large national data base cost millions of dollars to construct and took many years to complete. It was designed to serve two main purposes: (1) to provide CETA participant profiles on a regular ongoing basis, and (2) to provide data for a major national impact evaluation of the program.

The treatment group comprised a large national sample of participants from a variety of different CETA program activities (e.g., classroom training, on the job training, work experience, public service employment, summer youth programs, and direct job referrals). Data for this group described their demographic, social, and economic characteristics; their preprogram, inprogram, and postprogram labor market experience; the CETA services they received; and their attitudes toward the program. This information was compiled from local CETA program records, four participant surveys (at roughly two, nine, eighteen, and thirty-six months after entry to the program), and individual Social Security records. As will be discussed, Social Security records were the most important data source.

The present analysis only considers adults (persons over 24 years of age) who entered CETA classroom training, on the job training, or work experience between January 1975 and June 1976. Data for a sample of 1,615 women and 1,608 men from this entry cohort were available for the analysis. The comparison group was drawn from the March 1976 Current Population Survey (CPS) and comprised a sample of 21,096 women and 9,752 men.[2] The Current Population Survey is a large monthly national survey of U.S. households. It is the basis for much, if not most, of our national statistics on labor force characteristics and labor market conditions. In addition to the detailed information regularly collected by the CPS, complete Social Security earnings histories for each individual in the sample were added to the file. Merging this amount of data from so many different sources for so many individuals was a major undertaking requiring a high degree of cooperation among the organizations involved.

A MODEL FOR USING LONGITUDINAL EARNINGS DATA TO ESTIMATE PROGRAM IMPACTS

The effect of training was estimated as the average annual difference between participants' earnings during their first two to three years after leaving

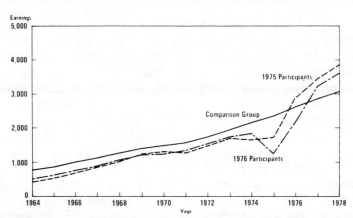

SOURCE: Bloom and McLaughlin (1982), estimated from the continuous Longitudinal Manpower Survey.

Figure 12.1   Average Annual Earnings for Female CETA Participants and Comparison Group Members from 1964 to 1978

the program and the best available estimates of what they would have earned if training had not been provided.

EARNINGS BEFORE AND AFTER TRAINING

Figures 12.1 through 12.6 illustrate the average annual earnings of the sample of CETA participants before and after training, plus corresponding earnings for the comparison group. Although the statistical analysis used to obtain final program impact estimates was more elaborate than the simple graphs in the figures (see Bloom and McLaughlin, 1982), these graphs tell almost all of the story conveyed by the longitudinal earnings data upon which the analysis was based.

Figure 12.1 illustrates that before training the long-term earnings profile of female participants was slightly below that of female comparison group members. Immediately after training, however, the average earnings of female participants jumped sharply above that of the comparison group and remained there for at least two to three years (the period for which data were available).

This pattern, which strongly suggests a pronounced and sustained program impact, was experienced both by women who entered CETA in 1975 and by women who entered in 1976.[3] In addition, it was experienced to a

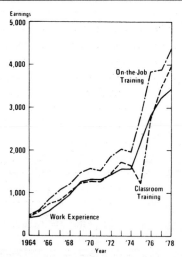

SOURCE: Bloom and McLaughlin (1982), estimated from the Continuous Longitudinal Manpower Survey

Figure 12.2 1975 Female CETA Participants' Average Annual Earnings from 1964 to 1978

SOURCE: Bloom and McLaughlin (1982), estimated from the Continuous Longitudinal Manpower Survey

Figure 12.3 1976 Female CETA Participants' Average Annual Earnings from 1964 to 1978

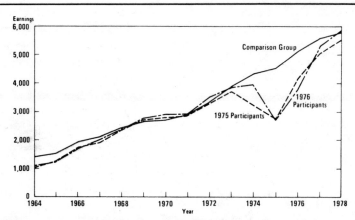

SOURCE: Bloom and McLaughlin (1982), estimated from the Continuous Longitudinal Manpower Survey.

Figure 12.4   Average Annual Earnings from Male CETA Participants and Comparison Group Members from 1964 to 1978

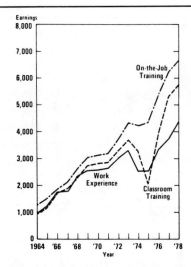

SOURCE: Bloom and McLaughlin (1982), estimated from the Continuous Longitudinal Manpower Survey.

Figure 12.5   1975 Male CETA Participants' Average Annual Earnings from 1964 to 1978

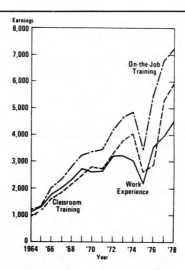

SOURCE: Bloom and McLaughlin (1982), estimated from the Continuous Longitudinal Manpower Survey.

Figure 12.6   1976 Male CETA Participants' Average Annual Earnings from 1964 to 1978

similar degree by women in classroom training, on the job training, and work experience (see Figures 12.2 and 12.3). Thus, it appears that the effects of these three CETA program activities were approximately the same.

The pattern experienced by male participants was entirely different (see Figures 12.4, 12.5, and 12.6). Their average long-term earnings profile before entering CETA was virtually the same as that of male comparison group members. But the year before entering the program male participants experienced a sharp drop in earnings. Nevertheless, soon after the program their earnings had returned to their preprogram trend.

The best available data indicate that the "pre-program dip" experienced by male participants (and to a lesser degree by female participants) was a temporary phenomenon that would have disappeared rapidly, even in the absence of training.[4]

For both *a priori* and empirical reasons, this phenomenon appears to be a regression artifact produced by the short-run earnings screen used to determine CETA eligibility. Appendix A briefly outlines the analysis of this issue. (For further details, see Bloom and McLaughlin, 1982: A15-A25.)

AN INTERRUPTED TIME-SERIES ANALYSIS OF
THE EARNINGS DATA

One simple way to use longitudinal earnings data to estimate job-training program impacts is to conduct an interrupted time-series analysis of the treatment and comparison groups' average annual earnings profiles (Figures 12.1-12.6). Perhaps the single greatest strength of this approach is that "what you see is what you get." In addition, as will be demonstrated below, this simple approach is algebraically equivalent to an extension of fixed effect covariance models for panel data.

An interrupted time-series analysis would proceed as follows: One would fit a trend line (a linear approximation is not bad, although nonlinear functions also could be used) through the treatment group preprogram earnings path; forecast postprogram earnings from this trend; and compute the deviation from trend for each postprogram year.

To control for shifting economic conditions during each postprogram year, one could repeat the process for the comparison group and estimate program impact as the difference between the treatment group and comparison group deviations from trend in each postprogram year. A regression specification for this aggregate estimation procedure is displayed below. It is an application of the classic comparison series design (see Campbell and Stanley, 1966) and can be estimated separately for each postprogram year t'.

$$Y_{kt} = \hat{a}_T \cdot T + \hat{b}_T \cdot T \cdot t + \hat{D}_{t'} \cdot T \cdot PP_{t'}$$

$$+ \hat{a}_c (1\text{-}T) + \hat{b}_c (1\text{-}T)t + \hat{e}_{t'} (PP_{t'}) + u_{kt} \qquad [1]$$

where:

Y_{kt}	= group k's mean earnings in year t;
T	= 1 for CETA trainees and 0 for comparison group members;
t	= a counter for time which increments by one for each year that elapses (it does not matter what value of t is used for the first year in the data-series);
$PP_{t'}$	= 1 for postprogram year t' and 0 otherwise;
$\hat{a}_t$ and $\hat{b}_t$	= the estimated mean intercept and slope of the trainee preprogram earnings trends;
$\hat{a}_c$ and $\hat{b}_c$	= the estimated mean intercept and slope of the comparison group preprogram earning trends;
$\hat{e}_t$	= the comparison group deviation from mean trend in postprogram year t';
$\hat{D}_{t'}$	= the difference between the trainee and comparison group deviations from mean trend in postprogram year t' (in other words, the estimated program effect);
u_{kt}	= group k's residual in year t.

AN EQUIVALENT MODEL FOR INDIVIDUAL
PANEL DATA

The interrupted time-series model described above (the difference between group deviations from mean trend) is deceptively simple. As demonstrated in Appendix B, this aggregate model produces program impact estimates that are identical to those that would be obtained from the following extension of fixed-effect covariance models for panel data.

$$Y_{it} = a_i + b_i \cdot t + D_{t'} \cdot T_{it'} + e_t = e_{it} \tag{2}$$

where:

Y_{it}	= person i's earnings in year t;
t	= a counter for time which increments by one for each year;
$T_{it'}$	= 1 for postprogram year t' for trainees and 0 otherwise;
$D_{t'}$	= the effect of the program on trainee earnings in postprogram year t';
a_i and b_i	= person i's preprogram intercept and slope;
e_t	= a year-specific error component reflecting prevailing economic conditions;
e_{it}	= person i's random individual error component in year t.

Standard fixed-effect models for panel data specify individual unobserved error components that are constant over time, representing fixed individual differences. Equation 2, on the other hand, specifies individual effects that vary over time according to individual-specific trends ($a_i + b_i \times t$). Thus, equation 2 is a time-varying, fixed-effect model.

Another way to express the difference between standard fixed-effect models and equation 2 is to note that standard models specify a separate intercept for each person, whereas equation 2 specifies both a separate intercept and a separate slope. Intuitively, equation 2 estimates program-induced earnings gains as follows. For any given postprogram year t, each individual's deviation from his or her preprogram trend is determined. Then program impact is estimated as the difference between the mean trainee deviation from trend and the corresponding mean comparison group deviation from trend. By computing each individual's deviation from his or her own trend, one controls explicitly for unobserved factors that determine long-term earnings.

Program impact estimates obtained from this model (equation 2) are algebraically equivalent to those obtained from the aggregate interrupted time-series model described earlier (equation 1) because of the particular way in

TABLE 12.1
Average Annual Postprogram Earnings Gains for
Adult CET Participants (in 1980 dollars)

Type of Training	For Women	For Men
All CETA training	$1300	$200
Classroom training	1400	300
On the job training	1100	300
Work experience	1300	−100

NOTE: All results for women are significant at the 0.01 level. No results for men are significant at the 0.05 level.

which the data were aggregated. This equivalence derives from the fact that the difference between the trainee and comparison group deviations from their mean trend ($d_{t'}$ in equation 1) equals the difference between the mean deviation from each individual trainee trend and the mean deviation from each individual comparison group member trend ($D_{t'}$ in equation 2). This equivalence is demonstrated in Appendix B.

EMPIRICAL RESULTS FOR ADULT CETA PARTICIPANTS

Table 12.1 presents estimated postprogram earnings gains obtained from the Continuous Longitudinal Manpower Survey using an extension of the estimation procedure described above. These extensions explicitly include in the analysis further controls for demographic characteristics, a serial correlation analysis of the preprogram dip and a conversion of all results to 1980 dollars (see Bloom and McLaughlin, 1982: A1-A13). Except for the final conversion to 1980 dollars, none of the extensions changed the results noticeably from those that would be obtained from the interrupted time-series analysis described above.

Consistent with Figures 12.1-12.6 presented earlier, the results in Table 12.1 indicate that women experienced large postprogram earnings gains, whereas men did not. To place these findings in perspective, it should be noted that even after training, women only earned about two-thirds as much as men, due primarily to differences between their hourly wage rates.

VALIDATING THE SOCIAL SECURITY EARNINGS DATA

Two potential problems with Social Security earnings data are frequently cited—changes over time in the coverage of certain occupations and truncation due to the upper bound for reported earnings. The following analysis indicates that these factors probably had a negligible effect on the CETA program impact estimates presented above.[5]

CHANGES IN SOCIAL SECURITY COVERAGE

Not all jobs are covered by Social Security and, thus, not all earnings are reported by Social Security records. Therefore, earnings reported by Social Security records could artificially change because of changes in coverage (due to the increase over time in occupations covered or due to individual shifts from covered to uncovered employment or vise versa). If this phenomenon occurred and if it affected CETA participants and comparison group members markedly differently, it could bias estimates of the effect of CETA training programs.

The likely magnitude of this potential bias was approximated by comparing Social Security earnings data for CETA participants with survey earnings data for the same group during the year before and the first year after training.[6] Comparable data for comparison group members were not available. Table 12.2 reports the ratio of mean earnings according to Social Security data relative to mean earnings according to survey data.[7] In almost all cases, this ratio was close to 1, indicating a high degree of consistency between the two independent sources of earnings data.[8]

More important, however, is the fact that this ratio changed very little over time. It was 1.05 for female CETA trainees in the year before training and 1.00 in the year after training, representing a 5 percentage point decrease (see Table 12.2). Corresponding results for male trainees were 0.97 and 0.93, or a 4 percentage point decrease. Roughly comparable changes were experienced by participants in each of the different types of training.

To estimate the likely bias due to the preceding decreases in Social Security earnings coverage requires an estimate of the corresponding shift in coverage for comparison group members. Direct information about this shift was not available. But because there was no change in the Social Security law affecting the occupations that were covered during the analysis period, there probably was no shift in coverage for the comparison group.

Thus, the maximum likely relative shift for participants (the difference between their shift and that of comparison group members) was a 5 percentage point decline for women and a 4 percentage point decline for men. Based on the average first postprogram-year earnings of $4300 and $6800 for female and male trainees, respectively, these declines imply maximum likely

TABLE 12.2
The Ratio of Social Security to Survey Based
Average Annual Trainee Earnings

	For Women			For Men		
	Year Before Training	Year After Training	Percentage of Change	Year Before Training	Year After Training	Percentage of Change
All CETA training	1.05	1.00	−5	0.97	0.93	−4
Classroom training	1.07	1.05	−2	1.07	0.99	−7
On the job training	1.00	0.89	−11	0.98	0.95	−3
Work experience	1.03	0.98	−5	0.85	0.82	−4

NOTE: Earnings from both data sources were expressed in 1980 dollars.

negative biases of roughly $200 and $300 in estimates of the impact of training—not enough to affect the conclusions of the evaluation.

Furthermore, this bias probably was even smaller, due to a potential shift in the coverage of earnings by the surveys. Preprogram earnings data were obtained from surveys administered while trainees were in the program. Thus, trainees may have understated their preprogram earnings to protect their eligibility for the program. This was less likely to be the case for the postprogram earnings data obtained from surveys administered after trainees had left the program. Thus, the ratio of Social Security to survey earnings may have overstated Social Security coverage during the preprogram year but not during the postprogram year. If this were the case, the previous estimate of the decline in trainees' Social Security coverage between these two years probably represents an upper bound.

THE SOCIAL SECURITY REPORTING MAXIMUM

Only earnings up to a specified limit are covered by Social Security taxes, so earnings are reported up to this limit.[9] If a substantial number of trainees or comparison group members reached this limit for a number of years, and this problem occurred more frequently during the preprogram period than it did during the postprogram period (or vice versa), and this disproportionate occurrence was more pronounced or entirely different for CETA trainees than it was for comparison group members, then program impact estimates might be biased.

But few CETA trainees or comparison group members ever reached the Social Security earnings maximum during the 1970-1978 analysis period

TABLE 12.3

Percentage of the Sample that Reached the Social Security Earnings
Maximum During the Analysis Period (1970 to 1978)

Percentage Who Reached Maximum	Women			Men		
	Once	Twice	More Times	Once	Twice	More Times
All CETA training	1	0	0	6	3	5
Classroom training	1	1	0	7	3	5
On the job training	2	0	0	7	4	9
Work experience	1	0	0	4	3	2
Comparison Group	0	0	0	3	1	0

NOTE: This maximum was $7600, $7800, $9000, $10,800, $13,200, $14,100, $15,300, $16,500, and $17,700 in 1970 to 1978, respectively. Percentages do not sum across different types of training because the base for each group was different.

TABLE 12.4

Percentage of Male CETA Trainees Who Reached the Social
Security Earnings Maximum Before and After Training

Number of Times Before Training	Number of Times After Training		
	0	1	2
0	86	1	0
1	5	0	0
2	3	0	0
3+	4	1	0

(see Table 12.3). This was especially true for female trainees and all comparison group members.

The 14 percent of the male trainees who ever reached the earnings maximum did so primarily during the preprogram period (see Table 12.4).[10] This probably produced a slight underestimate of postprogram earnings in the absence of training, which probably overestimated the effect of training for men slightly. But due to the small proportion of male trainees involved and the relatively infrequent occurrence of this phenomenon, its effect probably was negligible.

USING SURVEY DATA TO EXAMINE THE COMPOSITION OF POSTPROGRAM EARNINGS GAINS

The policy implications of program impact estimates for women in CETA depend on the composition of their earnings gains. To better understand these gains, it was important to decompose them into corresponding shifts in the amount of time worked (in hours per year) and the hourly wage rate (in constant 1980 dollars). This information is not available from Social Security records, so it was necessary to approximate it using survey data obtained for CETA trainees.

BASIC APPROACH

By definition, annual earnings can be decomposed as follows:

$$Y = H \times W \qquad [3]$$

where:

Y = annual earnings (in 1980 dollars);
H = the number of hours worked per year;
W = the average hourly wage rate (in 1980 dollars).

The proportional change in earnings, $\Delta Y/Y$, equals the sum of the proportional change in each of its components plus their interaction. In general, this interaction is so small that it can be ignored. Therefore, as a reasonable approximation,

$$\Delta Y/Y \approx \Delta H/H + \Delta W/W \qquad [4]$$

Therefore, the proportion of the change in earnings due to a change in hours worked can be approximated by the proportional change rate for hours worked divided by the sum of this rate and its counterpart for the hourly wage rate. The proportion of the change in earnings due to a change in hourly wage rates then simply equals 1 minus the result for hours worked. Note that this procedure implicitly allocates each component's contribution to the interaction in proportion to its contribution to the sum of the first-order effects.

DATA AND ANALYSIS

Complete earnings component survey data were available for CETA trainees for the year before and the year after they were in the program. Corresponding data were not available for the comparison group,[11] so it was necessary to infer the composition of postprogram earnings gains, using the observed composition of the gross change in participants' earnings from the year before to the year after training. This information is summarized in Table 12.5.

TABLE 12.5
The Components of Female CETA Trainee Earnings
in the Year Before and After Training

	Hours Worked Per Year	Hourly Wage Rate*
All female trainees		
Year before	543	$3.81
Year after	966	4.49
Classroom trainees		
Year before	520	3.77
Year after	866	4.65
On the job trainees		
Year before	643	3.99
Year after	1281	4.46
Work experience		
Year before	558	3.76
Year after	945	4.19

*In 1980 dollars.

TABLE 12.6
Composition of Female CETA Trainee Postprogram Earnings Gains

	Percentage Due to A Change in:	
	Hours Worked Per Year	Hourly Wage Rate*
All CETA Training	81%	19%
Classroom training	74	26
On the job training	89	11
Work experience	86	14

*In 1980 dollars.

Applying the computational procedure described above to the information in Table 12.5 produces the estimates of the composition of post program earnings gains displayed in Table 12.6.

INTERPRETATION OF THE FINDINGS

According to the findings in Table 12.6 the primary impact of all three types of CETA training for women was through increased hours worked rather than increased wage rates. For all CETA training, only 19 percent of this impact was due to increased wage rates and, for classroom training, on

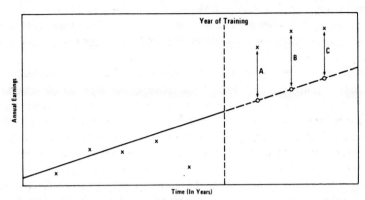

SOURCE: Bloom and McLaughlin (1982)
x = Actual annual earnings.
O = Predicted annual earnings without training.
A, B, and C = Difference between actual and predicted earnings.

Figure 12.7   Earnings After Training Relative to Past Long-Term Earnings Trend of a CETA Participant Who Experienced a Postprogram Earnings Gain

the job training, and work experience, only 26, 11, and 14 percent of this effect, respectively, was due to increased real wage rates.

This finding helps to explain why each of the three types of training had similar impacts, even though job training practitioners almost uniformly assume that on the job training is by far the best, followed by classroom training, which in turn is trailed at a considerable distance by work experience. If these programs perform mainly a placement and counselling function rather than increasing trainees' skills (which is likely given the fact that on average training only lasts for 20 weeks and costs about $2500 per trainee), it is entirely possible that they are equally effective in performing this limited (but potentially important) function.

LIMITATIONS OF THE FINDINGS

Several potential problems limit more precise interpretation of these results. First, gross earnings changes (upon which the earnings component analysis was based) do not overlap perfectly with postprogram earnings gains (to which the results of this analysis were inferred). Nevertheless, the average postprogram deviation from trend in the first year after training (Segment C in Figure 12.7), which largely determined the average postprogram earnings gain for women that year,[12] comprised about three-fifths of the average gross earnings change for female trainees (Segments A plus B plus C). Thus, there was a substantial overlap between the two measures of change in earnings.

A second potential problem stems from the fact that data for the components of earnings were obtained from retrospective surveys. Participants were asked on a quarter-by-quarter basis about the extent to which they sought employment, the percentage of time they were employed, their wages rates, and their total earnings. Undoubtedly, this produced numerous reporting errors. But individual reporting errors largely cancelled one another in the determination of the group averages upon which the present analysis was based. For example, as indicated earlier, average survey earnings data were generally within about 5 percent of average Social Security earnings data. Thus, it is unclear to what extent survey errors were a problem.

CONFIRMATION OF THE FINDINGS

Because of the potential limitations of the data discussed above, the results of the decomposition analysis were compared with a similar analysis based on an alternative source of data—the findings for AFDC recipients (all of whom were women) from the national Supported Work Demonstration (see MDRC, 1980). The Supported Work Demonstration was a large-scale national experimental to test the effectiveness of extensive and intensive work experience for four groups of hard-core unemployed persons: long-term AFDC recipients, exdrug addicts, exconvicts, and high school dropouts, half of whom had criminal records.

Because the demonstration was a randomized field experiment, its impact estimates are perhaps the most internally valid ones available. On the other hand, the major potential problem with using data from this study for the present analysis is limited external validity of inferences from the Supported Work population to CETA trainees.

Nevertheless, there are some striking similarities between the findings of both studies that serve to reinforce their interpretations. First, only women (the AFDC recipients) in the Supported Work Demonstration experienced substantial earnings gains (about $900 a year in 1980 dollars, see Appendix C for a discussion of how this finding was obtained). This is consistent with the findings presented above for adult CETA participants.

The second similarity between both studies is equally if not more striking: 74 percent of the estimated earnings gains for female AFDC recipients in Supported Work were due to increased hours worked (see Appendix C for a discussion of how this finding was obtained). Thus, only 26 percent of the earnings gain was due to increased real wage rates. This is consistent with the corresponding figure of 22 percent for all female CETA trainees and 16 percent for female CETA work experience participants. In both cases, it appears that the overwhelming majority of the impact of the program is due to increased hours worked.

CONCLUSIONS

Next to an experimental design, it appears that the use of longitudinal earnings data from individual Social Security records may be the most effective way to estimate the net earnings impact of job-training programs. The strengths of this approach include the following characteristics of the data:

(1) They are relatively inexpensive to obtain for large samples.
(2) They are consistent with corresponding information obtained from surveys.
(3) They can provide considerable statistical control for differences in individual earnings potential (by controlling for differences in individual preprogram trends).
(4) They can provide multiple years of follow-up information from which to examine the temporal pattern of postprogram earnings gains (and thus facilitate estimation of the present value of these gains for benefit-cost evaluations).
(5) They can preserve the confidentiality of the individuals involved.
(6) They can be analyzed quite simply using an aggregate interrupted time-series model with a direct graphical interpretation that is algebraically equivalent to estimates obtainable from a time-varying fixed-effect model of individual panel.
(7) Thus, they can facilitate metaanalysis of the results of job-training programs for different groups, in different locations, at different points in time, by providing a standard data-source and a standard methodology.

On the other hand, there are several major problems with the use of this information that must be overcome before its widespread application will be possible. The first such weakness is the long lead time and high degree of institutional cooperation necessary to obtain Social Security earnings files. Although data for past earnings currently exists in each individual's records, corresponding postprogram information takes considerable time to obtain. For example, earnings data for the first postprogram year may not be available until the end of the second postprogram year, making information unusable for ongoing program monitoring. Thus, it is only suitable for large-scale periodic impact evaluations.

Even periodic requests for these data with long lead times may be problematic, depending on the existing workload of the Social Security Administration and its prevailing policy on requests for this information. Not all requests are granted. At times, the policy of the Social Security Administration has been not to release this information to anyone outside the agency. Thus, a concerted effort to work with the Social Security Administration on this issue is clearly warranted.

A second problem to consider is the limitation of longitudinal earnings data for certain groups. In particular, it is clear that this information is not terribly useful for evaluations of youth employment programs.[13] Because youth have limited past labor market experience, these data will provide limited statistical control for their differences in earnings potential.

Furthermore, it is not clear that earnings should be the primary criterion for evaluating programs for youth. Other outcomes, such as increased school attendance and graduation rates, participation in the military, and reduced delinquency, are widely recognized as equally if not more important performance indicators.

Despite these shortcomings, the use of longitudinal Social Security earnings data contributes substantially to our ability to evaluate employment and training programs. This approach, therefore, deserves considerably more attention from the evaluation research community.

APPENDIX A

ANALYZING THE PREPROGRAM DIP

The following is a brief sketch of the analysis of the preprogram dip experienced by adult CETA trainees presented by Bloom and McLaughlin (1982: A15-A25).

ALTERNATIVE EXPLANATIONS OF THE PREPROGRAM DIP

The preprogram dip reflects a mix of two factors: (1) temporary forces that produce unusually low earnings the year before CETA trainees enter the program; and (2) permanent forces that would have persisted in the absence of training. The basic point at issue is the relative mix of these two factors.

A temporary preprogram dip of some magnitude almost certainly was produced by the fact that eligibility for CETA programs was based on earnings during the six months prior to the program. This phenomenon is a classic example of the statistical artifact generally referred to as regression to the mean. In the present context, this problem may arise because of idiosyncratic events, such as being fired because of a fight with the boss, having unusually good or bad luck finding a new job, or being laid off by a bankrupt employer. These events produce good years and bad years relative to one's long-run earnings potential.

Basing CETA eligibility only on recent experience results in overrepresenting persons having just experienced an unusually bad year. It does so because it eliminates persons having just experienced good luck (whose current earnings thus are above the eligibility threshold), it makes it possible for persons with normally higher earnings who recently experienced a temporary economic setback to qualify for the program, and it is likely that among all persons eligible for CETA, those who just experienced an unusually bad year are more highly motivated to apply than those having just experienced a better than average year who still fall within the eligibility limits.

All of these factors would lead to a sample of CETA trainees whose recent earnings are temporarily below that of their long-term trend. In other words, for the year before training, the trainee sample would overrepresent negative transient error components. In future years, as random idiosyncratic events produce equal proportions of positive and negative individual temporary earnings components, overall average earnings for this group will increase back to "normal" in the absence of training. Thus, without training this group would regress back to its underlying mean (its preprogram trend).

On the other hand, it might be argued that persons who recently experienced a permanent decline in their future earnings recognize the permanence of this change and apply for CETA training. This would produce a preprogram dip that would not disappear in the absence of training. This explanation characterizes the experience of dislocated workers who have lost specialized, well-paying, stable jobs in declining regions or industries and have little prospect of regaining their former economic status.

But CETA participants generally are disadvantaged individuals with little previous work experience or with a history of low-paying, unstable jobs. Indeed, it is the instability of these jobs that is often considered the root of their employment problem (see Doeringer and Piore, 1971). Thus, the typical jobs held recently by CETA participants were unlikely to be any more diffi-cult to replace than other jobs they had held in the past. Furthermore, given the instability of their past employment experience, it is highly unlikely that CETA participants could distinguish between temporary economic setbacks (about which they need do little to overcome) and permanent setbacks (for which they need programmatic assistance). Therefore, on a priori grounds it is most plausible that the preprogram dip reflects a temporary rather than a permanent economic setback.

OUTLINE OF THE EMPIRICAL EVIDENCE

Ideally, to measure the rate at which the preprogram dip would have dis-appeared in the absence of training, one must observe what happened to per-sons who were identical to the CETA trainees, but who did not enter the program. Unfortunately, without a true experiment based on random assign-ment of applicants to training and a control group, this was not possible.

Nevertheless, there were two independent sources of information from which to approximate the decay rate for the preprogram dip: (1) the past ex-perience of trainees and (2) the experience of comparison group members during the pre-to-post program period. For both groups, yearly fluctuations in earnings disappeared quickly.

CETA participants (especially men) experienced large, unrelated year-to-year fluctuations in earnings for a number of years before they entered the program. During this period, they both recovered rapidly from unusually bad years and failed to maintain the levels they reached during unusually good years.

Similarly, there was little relationship between the relative performance of comparison group members during the preprogram year (1974 and 1975) and the postprogram years (1976-1978). Persons doing unusually poorly or unusually well during the preprogram year were back on their trends by the postprogram period.

These findings were based on estimates of the correlation between devia-tions from trend in one year and subsequent deviations from trend in later years. A strong positive correlation would indicate that such deviations dis-appeared slowly, whereas a weak positive correlation would indicate a quick disappearance. A negative correlation (which was unlikely and did not oc-cur) would indicate a systematic pattern of good years followed by bad years and vice versa. Weak positive correlations (that is, deviations that disap-peared rapidly) were observed for all groups.

Judged by the past ability of male CETA participants to recover from unusually bad years, virtually none of their $1200 preprogram dip would have remained during the postprogram period, even in the absence of CETA. Judged by corresponding results for comparison group members, roughly 11 percent (or $130) would have remained during the first postprogram year, 4 percent (or $50) would have remained during the second postprogram year, and 1 percent (or $10) would have remained during the third postprogram year. Similar results were obtained for women, based on their much smaller preprogram dip ($400).

APPENDIX B

THE EQUIVALENCE BETWEEN AGGREGATE INTERRUPTED TIME-SERIES ANALYSIS AND THE TIME-VARYING FIXED EFFECT MODEL FOR INDIVIDUAL PANEL DATA

The time-varying, fixed-effect model of individual panel data described in the text can be represented as follows:

$$Y_{it} = a_i + b_i \cdot t + D_{t'} \cdot T_{it'} + e_t + e_{it} \qquad [B1]$$

where

Y_{it}	= person i's earnings in year t;
t	= a counter for time which increments by 1 for each year;
$T_{it'}$	= 1 for postprogram year t' for trainees and 0 otherwise;
$D_{t'}$	= the effect of the program on trainee earnings in postprogram year t';
a_i and b	= person i's preprogram intercept and slope;
e_t	= a year-specific error component reflecting prevailing economic = conditions;
e_{it}	= person i's random individual error component in year t.

This model specifies separate underlying earnings trends for each individual in the sample. These trends reflect all unobserved factors that determine individual differences in earnings potential. To estimate program-induced earnings gains from this model for postprogram year t′ we compute individual deviations from trend in year t′, compute the mean trainee and the mean comparison group deviation from trend in year t′, and take the difference between these two mean deviations from trend.

To derive the aggregate interrupted time-series model from equation B1, first take its mean for the comparison group:

$$Y_{ct} = a_c + b_c \cdot t + e_t + e_{ct} \qquad [B2]$$

Y_{et} = mean comparison group earnings in year t;
a_c and b_c = the mean intercept and slope of comparison group members' preprogram trends;
e_t = the effect of economic conditions in year t;
e_{it} = the mean comparison group random error term in year t.

Equation B2 can be estimated from mean annual comparison group earnings data for the preprogram period and postprogram year t' as follows:

$$Y_{ct} = \hat{a}_c + \hat{b}_c \cdot t + \hat{e}_{t'} + (PP_{t'}) + u_{ct} \qquad [B3]$$

where:

$PP_{t'}$ = 1 for postprogram year t′ and 0 otherwise;
$\hat{a}_c$ and $\hat{b}_c$ = the intercept and slope of the comparison group preprogram
trend;
$\hat{e}_{t'}$ = the comparison group deviation from trend in postprogram year
t′;
u_{ct} = the residual term for each year.

Equation B3 fits a line through the comparison group preprogram trend and measures the group's deviation in postprogram year t′ from this trend. The deviation ($e_{t'}$) reflects economic conditions in year t′ and is identical to corresponding estimates of the mean deviation from each individual comparison group member's deviation from his or her own trend (obtained from the time-varying fixed-effect model, equation B1). This equivalence arises because of the manner in which the data were aggregated.

Aggregate and disaggregate parameter estimates are identical whenever each independent variable in the model is constant across individuals within each aggregate unit of observation (see Kmenta, 1971: 322-335). To see that this condition is met in the present case, note that the only independent variables in the aggregate model (equation B3) are t (a counter for time) and $PP_{t'}$ (a dummy variable for the postprogram year). Both variables are constant across individual comparison group members for any given aggregate unit of observation (a specific year).

Next take the trainee mean for equation Bl:

$$Y_{Tt} = a_T + b_T \cdot t + D_{t'}(PP_{t'}) + e_t + e_{Tt} \quad [B4]$$

which can be estimated from mean annual trainee earnings data for the preprogram period and postprogram year t' as:

$$Y_{Tt} = \hat{a}_T + \hat{b}_T \cdot t + (\hat{D}_{t'} + \hat{e}_{t'})PP_{t'} + u_{Tt} \quad [B5]$$

The coefficient for $PP_{t'}$ ($D_{t'} + e_{t'}$) is the trainee group deviation in postprogram year t' from its mean preprogram trend. As was true for comparison group members, this aggregate result is identical to that which could be obtained directly from the panel data for individual trainees.

To estimate the effect of training on earnings in postprogram year t', we can now take the difference between the trainee and comparison group deviations from their respective trends. One simple way to do this is to pool the aggregate data for trainees and comparison group members and estimate:

$$Y_{kt} = \hat{a}_T \cdot T + \hat{b}_T \cdot T \cdot t + \hat{D}_{t'} \cdot T \cdot PP_{t'} + \hat{a}_c(1-T)$$
$$+ \hat{b}_c(1-T)t + \hat{e}_{t'}(PP_{t'}) + u_{kt} \quad [B6]$$

where:

Y_{kt}	= group k's mean earnings in year t;
T	= 1 for trainees observations and 0 for comparison group observations;
u_{kt}	= group k's residual in year t; and all other terms as defined above.

Equation B6 specifies separate average trainee and comparison group preprogram trends, a comparison group mean deviation from trend, and a difference between the trainee and comparison group mean deviations from trend ($D_{t'}$).

APPENDIX C

DECOMPOSITION OF THE SUPPORTED WORK
EARNINGS GAINS FOR AFDC RECIPIENTS

The following is a description of how the results for AFDC recipients who participated in the National Supported Work Demonstration program were used to examine the components of their earnings gains in order to compare the composition of these gains with the composition of postprogram earnings gains experienced by adult female CETA trainees.

ESTIMATING ANNUAL POSTPROGRAM
EARNINGS GAINS

As indicated in the chapter, of the four groups served by the Supported Work Demonstration—AFDC recipients (all of whom were female), former drug addicts, exconvicts, and high school dropouts (almost all of whom were

TABLE C1

Supported Work AFDC Experimental Versus Control Group
Differences in Postprogram Monthly Earnings, Hours Worked
Per Month, and Hourly Wage Rates*

Months After Entry	Experimental Versus Control Group					
	After Monthly Earnings		Hours Worked Per Month		Hourly Wage Rate	
	Difference	Control Group	Difference	Control Group	Difference	Control Group
16-18	$48	$191	5.3	46.0	$0.52	$4.15
19-21	70	194	12.9	42.9	0.20	4.52
22-24	90	200	14.2	46.0	0.48	4.34
25-27	97	202	15.9	45.9	0.42	4.39
Average for entire period	76	197	12.1	45.2	0.41	4.35

SOURCE: MDRC (1980: Tables 4-3, 4-2, and 4-4).
*In 1980 dollars.

male)—only AFDC recipients experienced substantial postprogram earnings gains. This result is consistent with the finding that adult female CETA trainees experienced substantial postprogram earnings gains whereas adult males in the program did not.

To compute the average annual postprogram earnings gains for AFDC recipients in Supported Work, figures from Table 4-3 in MDRC (1980) were obtained which gave the average monthly difference between experimental and control group earnings for each of the sixth through ninth quarters after assignment to the program (or control group). By this time, virtually all Supported Work participants had left the program. Thus, their earnings did not reflect inprogram wages.

These earnings gains (transformed into 1980 dollars) are listed in Table C1. Their average is listed at the bottom of the table. Multiplying this average by 12 yields an estimated $900 annual postprogram earnings gain.

DECOMPOSING ANNUAL POSTPROGRAM EARNINGS GAINS

Next, the experimental versus control group differences in hours worked per month and average hourly wage rates (transformed into 1980 dollars) for the sixth through ninth follow-up quarters were obtained (see MDRC, 1980: Tables 4-2 and 4-4). These findings, plus corresponding base values for the control group, are listed in Table C1.

The proportional differential was then computed for each factor by dividing each difference by its corresponding base rate. The proportional differential in hours worked per week was 0.268 and the proportional differential in hourly wage rates was 0.094, producing a total differential of 0.362. The change in hours worked constituted 74 percent of this total and the change in the hourly wage rate constituted 26 percent. Note that as discussed in the chapter, the interaction between hours worked and hourly wage rates thus was implicitly divided in the same proportions.

NOTES

1. See Westat Inc. (1980).

2. The comparison group included all persons from the March 1976 Current Population Survey who earned less than the maximum earnings reported by Social Security records in every year between 1970 and 1975, who were between 25 and 60 years old, and who were members of families with incomes of less than $30,000 in 1975.

3. To minimize distortions due to timing mismatches, the 1975 CETA entry cohort included all adults who entered the program between January and August, 1975; and the 1976 cohort included all adults who entered the program between September, 1975 and July, 1976.

4. Thus, one should not include earnings during the year before entering CETA in the preprogram trend.

5. The truncation problem examined here only concerns measurement error in the dependent variable. It does not include the statistical problem of truncated samples.

6. Second postprogram-year survey earnings data also were available for trainees, but only for a portion of the sample.

7. Earnings were expressed in constant dollars to control for the slight timing mismatch between the Social Security and survey earnings data.

8. Both Social Security and survey earnings data contain random measurement error and, thus, are not as consistent for each individual as they are for group averages. These individual errors cancel each other and do not affect group averages appreciably. Because estimates of the effect of training are based on group averages, they are not biased by individual random measurement error in the dependent variable.

9. This limit was $7,800, $7,800, $9,000, $10,800, $13,200, $14,100, $15,300, $16,500, and $17,700 during 1970 to 1978, respectively.

10. From 5 to 9 percent of the male trainees reached the earnings maximum in any given year during this period.

11. Earnings component data for the comparison group were only available for one year. Thus, an analysis of the change in these components was not possible.

12. Postprogram earnings gains actually represent the average of segments A, B, and C in Figure 12. 7 minus their comparison group counterparts (which were quite small) plus a serial correlation adjustment for the preprogram dip (which also was small).

13. To a certain extent, this problem also applies to women, many of whom were out of the labor force before entering CETA. This issue is examined by Bloom and McLaughlin (1982: A45-A50).

REFERENCES

BLOOM, H. S. and M. A. MCLAUGHLIN (1982) CETA Training Programs—Do They Work for Adults? Washington, DC: Congressional Budget Office and National Commission for Employment Policy.

CAMPBELL, D. T. and J. C. STANLEY (1966) Experimental and Quasi-Experimental Design for Research. Chicago: Rand McNally.

DOERINGER, P. B. and M. J. PIORE (1971) Internal Labor Markets and Manpower Analysis. Lexington, MA: D. C. Heath.

KMENTA, J. (1971) Elements of Econometrics. New York: Macmillan.

Manpower Demonstration Research Corporation (MDRC) (1980) Summary and Findings of the National Supported Work Demonstration. Cambridge, MA: Ballinger.

Westat, Inc. (1980) Continuous Longitudinal Manpower Survey: Handbook for Public Use Tapes. Washington, DC: U.S. Department of Labor.

AN INFORMATION SYSTEM FOR PLANNING AND EVALUATING GERIATRIC CARE: THE DUKE OLDER AMERICANS RESOURCES AND SERVICES PROGRAM

George L. Maddox

Evaluation research has increasingly become an area of special expertise with its own special subcultural artifacts, language, values, rules, and roles. Handbooks, journals, textbooks, careers, business organizations, and professional societies are dedicated to evaluation research. Evaluation scientists tend to develop their own professional enclaves. Academic scientists frequently note these developments, usually from a safe distance, without indicating a desire to become deeply involved personally or to train their students to be interested in and good at evaluation research. Some of the reasons for the detachment of academics have become clearer to me over the decade since I was asked by a federal agency to consider answering an alarmingly comprehensive program evaluation question: Are there effective and efficient alternatives to the long-term institutionalization of impaired older adults?

AUTHOR'S NOTE: Preparation for this chapter was supported in part by the Sandoz Foundation (U.S.).

Innocence and naiveté largely account for my initial interest in and optimism about responding to this question. Experience dissipated these characteristics rather quickly as the problems of conceptualizing and implementing answers emerged. The natural history of the Older Americans Resources and Services (OARS) Project summarized below will help explain why. The problems of conceptualization, measurement, sampling, data acquisition, data analysis, and interpretation encountered would now be obvious to and expected by experienced evaluation research analysts. The problems were not so obvious initially.

Before details are reviewed, it will help to note some problems which arise in gathering data for evaluation research on the effects of alternative geriatric care. While "good" data are the *sine qua non* of adequate evaluation research, good data can be trivial and/or irrelevant in the absence of both strong theory and attention to the sociopolitical aspects of evaluation research. Technically "bad" data can be the product of scientific ignorance and poor execution of standard procedures. These sources of difficulty can be attacked by promoting better research training. This chapter will stress, however, factors other than ignorance and poor execution that affect both data quality and data utilization in evaluation research. These other factors are concomitants of the embeddedness of evaluation research in sociopolitical contexts that affect the probability of securing and using effectively good data. Teaching evaluation scientists techniques of research design, sampling, and measurement seems considerably easier than teaching them how to manage the practical politics of implementing what they know about research.

DISTINCTIVE ISSUES IN EVALUATION RESEARCH

Thomas Kuhn (1970) suggested that, in theory, evaluation research is "essentially normal science," and as such poses basic scientific problems of articulating theory, methods, and appropriate data sets. All scientists are exhorted to use conventional canons of research practice. But in practice, evaluation research poses some distinctive problems that are more likely to be political than technical. Personal experience suggests, for example, several distinctive sociopolitical problems that have a bearing on the quality of data researchers collect and use in evaluation research.

First, the questions presented for evaluation research usually are questions posed *for* and not *by* scientists. The questions posed *for* scientists frequently are not puzzles they would ordinarily chose to solve or puzzles that appear to be solvable with their existing theory, methods, or data sets. Evaluation questions are likely to have an *ad hoc* urgent quality that reflects the immediate concerns of nonscientists. Providing timely answers to *ad hoc* problems is fundamentally at odds with the circumspect approach to problems most scientists are taught to value. Although working on unfamiliar puzzles may be intellectually stimulating, the novelty of a puzzle may require novel responses. Futhermore, attempts to respond to urgent needs for information to solve more puzzles surely underlie the temptation to take and justify short cuts in the implementation of evaluation research. Pragmatic attempts "to do the best one can under the circumstances" can be distinguished from scientific ignorance and recognizably bad research practice.

Second, the situation of practitioners in and consumers of evaluation research is different from the situation of those working on conventional disciplinary scientific problems. Significant problems for evaluators rarely are reducible to the domain of any single discipline. This fact ensures that most evaluation research will be multidisciplinary and generate a distinctive set of problems that are more practical than scientific but that affect the quality and performance of research. Public policy analysts, resource allocators, and program managers, for example, typically do not have the same passion for sampling and the validity/reliability of data as those who identify themselves primarily as scientists. Among scientists, training in different disciplines produces, not only different preferences for methodology and styles of communication, but also differential interest in data about individuals (e.g., clinicians) in contrast to data about aggregates (e.g., epidemiologists, economists, and systems analysts). An enormous amount of energy in evaluation research goes into assembling and maintaining an appropriately trained staff who can, want to, and will work together. Some of the compromises in research design and implementation that occur to placate staff members with different views of what constitutes adequate science accounts for some of the inadequacies of evaluation research data.

Third, the stakes for evaluators and other scientists are different. For academic scientists, the personal stakes in whether they do good science may be high, but the social stakes usually are not very high or at least are not always obvious. For scientists concentrating on evaluation research, the social stakes are not always perceived to be high, but they can be. Any scientist who proposes seriously that information about an organization's efficiency, an implemented policy's effectiveness, or a program's desirability is the basis for a definitive summary judgment, and who suggests that this judgment is the basis for allocating or reallocating resources, is making a political statement and is playing for high social stakes. Typically, concern about the scientific adequacy of evaluation data becomes critical precisely and only when the social stakes are perceived to be high. Information intended to lead to consequential recommendations about the future allocation of resources gets attention. Scientists, particularly the academic variety, are a rare breed for whom the proof or disproof of a proposition—or demonstrating the effectiveness or ineffectiveness of a policy or program—is equally valuable. This fact encourages them either to be relatively indifferent to or to misread the social stakes involved in evaluation research. Much evaluation research, whether technically good or bad, is ignored as trivial or irrelevant because there is no expectation that it will be used.

Fourth, good science is costly. Bad science ultimately may be even more costly; but scientists, by and large, are not trained to think about or do cost-benefit analysis on their research. Academic scientists usually attempt to select problems for which relevant data are available or attainable. Scientists pursuing evaluation research typically find that the data they need and/or want are not the data which are conveniently available. This leads one to suspect in the absence of proof that adequate evaluation research is relatively costly and that its costs will tend to be underestimated because the contingencies in implementing evaluation studies cannot be estimated precisely. Estimating the cost of a conventional sample survey is much easier than estimating the cost of a program evaluation study, in part because the contingencies are easier to estimate for a sample survey.

Fifth, the *ad hoc*, urgent, specific concerns of a great deal of evaluation research has at least two unfortunate effects on data gathering and data quality. One is that we do not expect that findings from evaluation research will be generalizable. Findings often are generated from evaluation research, whereas principles of interventions and their effects are not. Evaluators also tend to settle for identifying the immediate effects of interventions of programs rather than their long-range consequences. Sometimes it appears that the questions evaluation scientists ask are irrelevant by the time they have any answers or perhaps irrelevant by the time they are asked. Such perceptions do not encourage concern about data quality. As a matter of strategy, evaluation scientists might profitably concentrate relatively less on the questions they are asked initially and more on the next questions most likely to be asked. This would require thinking of evaluation research as a continuing process rather than an *ad hoc* activity.

Finally, evaluation research involving older populations presents some special if not unique challenges. It has been typical for social surveys and until recently for the Census to have been satisfied with the identification of a

GEORGE L. MADDOX 251

demographic category "65 years of age and older." One consequence of treating older adults as an undifferentiated category is that the available information on later life has masked substantial differences among older populations—for example, cohort differences and age-related differences in functional impairment. The problem is compounded frequently by the use of very small samples of older adults. Lack of information about or lack of awareness of relevant differentiations in older populations makes it difficult to specify a proper sampling frame.

Furthermore, the age-related impairments and dependency of older populations ensures a high probability of exposure to multiple interventions; this makes the identification of the effects of any particular intervention particularly problematic. The high cost of gathering information makes the use of relatively low-cost self-reported or interview information attractive. Although scientists should worry more than they do about the reliability and validity of self-reports and interview data, such information from older populations is especially problematic. An estimated 8 to 10 percent of older adults living in the community are not cognitively intact enough to supply reliable, valid information about themselves. An investigator who does not screen for cognitive impairment of older respondents risks distorting the data. And, quite apart from the issue of memory, because older adults are subjected to a large number of planned and incidental interventions, they have a lot to remember. Exposure to multiple interventions ensures that the identification of effects of a particular intervention will be expecially difficult.

Age is predictably related to increasingly impaired functioning. Evaluation research designed to demonstrate the beneficial effects of interventions faces a special problem of interpretation. The "success" of an intervention in late life often may be conceptualized more appropriately as "modifying the rate of decline" than as "improvement in functioning."

In sum, there are situational determinants of technically inadequate data. Confronting and dealing effectively with these situational factors is more likely than exhortations to produce the "good data" needed for adequate evaluations.

The data problems distinctively illustrated by the Duke project are not the kind attributable to ignorance about or poor execution of good research procedures regarding sampling and measurement. Nor are they attributable to the chance factors we might call bad luck (e.g., unexpected changes in staff or unanticipated inaccessibility of necessary information). The problems involved proved to be (1) negotiating evaluation questions that our client wanted answered and we believed we could answer, (2) specifying a model that might provide the answers, and (3) interpreting the findings.

HISTORY OF THE DUKE OARS INFORMATION SYSTEM

The Duke OARS project is not presented as exemplary evaluation research that consistently produced high quality data. But the project does not provide an example of Murphy's Law, either, which predicts that if research can go sour, it will, and that what is most likely to go sour will produce maximally bad effects. Several factors made an important difference in how the project was conducted.

First, the academic multidisciplinary project team was developed from staff already at the Duke center. Early in the project, the team realized the importance they attached to the problem to be studied and understood their shared passion for securing quality data.

A second difference that influenced the way the project was conducted was the fact that the initial finding agency proved to be remarkably flexible in negotiating the project desired. The goal agreed upon was primarily identifying satisfactory ways to answer policy questions about the effects of alternative geriatric services, rather than identifying a single best way to organize these services.

Third, an alliance between Duke and the U.S. General Accounting Office (GAO) introduced new financial and political resources at a critical time in the project. This association with the GAO provided simultaneous access to relevant data from both private service organizations of the the study community and federal records not ordinarily available to nonfederal personnel. The collegial relationships developed between investigators at Duke and the GAO were perceived as so productive and professionally satisfying that work related to the project has continued (now for six years) beyond the end of federal funding through the assistance of a variety of private sources. We learned at least as much about our problem after the official end of the project as we did during the project. We recognize our position as privileged and have no defense for any inadequacies in our data gathering.

The Duke Older Americans Resources and Services Program began with a telephone call from a federal agency to myself. I was, at the time (1972), the director of the Duke Center for the Study of Aging and Human Development. The question posed to Duke had been posed to the agency by Congress. Are there viable, economic alternatives to long-term institutionalization of impaired older adults? This remarkably broad question, which may appear tiresome currently, was relatively novel in 1972. As we understood the question, its answer would require multidisciplinary research using a quasi-experimental design that would provide simultaneous longitudinal information about the characteristics of a defined older population, about alternative geriatric service "treatments," and about the effects of alternative treatments on individuals with known characteristics in the defined population.

Furthermore, we perceived immediately that any conclusions reached and recommended by such a study would be politically consequential. We therefore attempted to anticipate the probable different interests of clinicians (particularly physicians), resource allocators, scientists, and consumers in the outcomes. We did not have in mind tailoring conclusions and recommendations to please specific target audiences but, rather, concentrated on effective communication with different audiences (Maddox, 1972). This initial political sensitivity had beneficial effects in the long run (Yin and Heinsohn, 1980). Over the past decade we have had productive and continuing interaction with hundreds of scientists, program managers, and evaluation specialists about the OARS methodology, its findings, and the limitations as well as the potential applications of the OARS information system.

The Duke project leadership was able to convince the sponsoring federal agency that, in the absence of appropriate existing data, concentrating on how to answer the important questions posed should take precedence over reaching conclusions prematurely. With the concurrence of the agency, Duke designed a study with three major components: (1) multidimensional functional assessment of older adults, (2) characterization of the geriatric service production system, and (3) a matrix in which the functional characteristics of older individuals exposed to different service treatments could be followed over time.

COMPONENTS OF THE DESIGN

The conceptualization and instrumentation are described in detail elsewhere (Maddox and Dellinger, 1978; Duke Center, 1978; Maddox et al., 1984). However, the essence of each component in the proposed information system can be summarized briefly here.

Functional Assessment

At the risk of alienating medical colleagues, the study focused on impairment in the functional capacity of individuals to meet personally and socially appropriate levels of role performances rather than on disease and pathological states. In deference to clinicians, however, information was gathered on disease states, but the concentration was on characterizing individuals in terms of functioning that clinicians would recognize and not reject out of hand as trivial. In fact, a great deal of attention was paid to a variety of characteristics suggested by both the literature and clinical experience as important in understanding the behavior of older adults.

Five reasonably orthogonal dimensions of functioning were identified and measured: social, economic, mental health, physical health, and activities of daily living (ADL or self-care capacity). The acronym for the dimensions became SEMPA. Respondents were located on a 6-point summary scale of impaired functioning for each SEMPA dimension based on a total of 69 items in a multidimensional functional assessment questionnaire (MFAQ). Insofar as possible, these items were derived from widely used, published measures.

The reliability and validity of the MFAQ summary scales have been studied extensively (Fillenbaum and Smyer, 1981; George et al., 1982) and found to be satisfactory and appropriately sensitive to change in functioning when administered by both lay and professional interviewers. Reliable, valid machine-scoring procedures for locating individuals on the 5 functional dimensions have been demonstrated (George et al., 1982).

The 69 MFAQ items related to functional status require 30-45 minutes to be administered by an interviewer with at least a high school education trained for one and a half days. Therefore, it is possible to use the instrument in social surveys as well as in clinical settings. As cognitive intactness is a critical issue, a 10-item "present state" scale initiates the interview and, on indication of cognitive impairment, the MFAQ identifies information to be sought from a knowledgeable person if available.

There have been hundreds of users of the MFAQ, most often in community needs surveys or for clinical screening instruments. There have been 10 extensive applications involving cumulatively over 6000 subjects in a wide variety of settings and involving individuals in various socioeconomic conditions (rural/urban, American Indians, Non-English-speaking ethnics, SSI recipients). The MFAQ has been translated formally into two Spanish versions and has been administered in 13 different languages. Duke OARS has been used with institutionalized, highly impaired elderly, but we are not confident that the instrument is appropriate for such settings. In such settings the incidence of cognitive impairment is high, homogeneity of economic and social resources increases, and the medical differentiations become too crude.

Service System Characterization

Conceptualization of our problem in terms of person/service system interaction led from locating individuals in social space, with emphasis on functional capacity, to characterizing the service system which generates packages of services or treatments. One of the reasons intervention studies so frequently produce evidence of no effect or ambiguous effect surely lies in an inadequate specification of treatments. Organizations, we found, typically record client contacts only or specify poorly who provides what, in what amounts, and at what unit cost.

Proper specification of service packages and not the type of service agency was, in our view, the heart of the alternative issues. The alternatives were not the physical location (institution or community) of an older adult, but the packaging of services delivered. Our response was to develop, with the assistance of experienced service providers, a list of 24 generic types of services commonly provided for older adults, defined in terms of who provided which type of services, in what unit, in what quantity, at what cost. This procedure for disaggregation of generic service components was tested in a wide variety of service organizations and found to be relatively unproblematic in interpretation and use. Additional attention needs to be given to the specification of treatment packages and to the reliability and validity of the classifications used.

The same disaggregation procedure in simplified form appears as a special section of the MFAQ. In this case respondents indicate generic services which they currently use and in what quantity; they also indicate services they use but perceive they "want" in greater quantity, and those they do not use but want or perceive they need. In the MFAQ, the specification of who provides a particular service is particularly important. As will be noted below, a large majority of services used by older adults living in the community reportedly are supplied by informal care givers (family and friends), not formal organizations. The probability that this is the case increases with degree of functional impairment. A substantial minority of very impaired older adults in the community receive services, the total real cost of which far exceed the cost of institutionalization. The disaggregation and utilization of generic services has facilitated analysis of cost of different service packages identified empirically.

The Transition Matrix

At least two types of exercises were implied in assessing transitions in functional status which might be attributable to service interventions. One was to follow functional status over time to illustrate "normal" transition in functional status in a defined older population without regard to specific service interventions. This was intended to provide a baseline against which to

compare transitions illustrating stability or change in functional status related to exposure to specific service packages. The first task was pursued
with relative ease using conventional social survey procedures with provision of longitudinal follow-up of subsamples (see, for example, Maddox et
al., 1979). The second task, requiring simultaneous longitudinal information about both individuals and service system exposure proved to be complex and initially impossible for political rather than scientific reasons. In
the early 1970s, the nation was preoccupied with a debate on privacy and the
ethics of research. Experience indicated that service organizations would be
unwilling and/or legally unable to match service records with trained individuals. Our initial plan to establish our own experimental service system
proved to be ill-advised. It would have been too costly and, in any case, established service agencies were outraged by the prospect of a service system
that would "experiment" with patients or clients. We had designed an information system that appeared to have no practical application.

THE DISTINCTIVE ROLE OF THE GAO

In a development only indirectly related to the Duke project the GAO was
asked by Congress to address a comparably immodest question. As federal
legislation had created and funded many special programs intended to improve the well-being of older adults, what was the evidence that these investments had had beneficial effects? The GAO staff designated to answer this
question had concluded that creating federal programs did not ensure exposure to these programs and that exposure without specifying "exposure to
what?" was not likely to be useful. They anticipated that the next implicit
question could be, which programs make a difference or which programs
have relatively more effect?

As it turned out, the GAO staff had decided independently that a quasi-
experimental design of the kind being developed at Duke provided their best
opportunity to provide useful answers to the questions asked. They anticipated that, although concentration on a defined population in a bounded service system probably was necessary initially, eventually there would be a
problem of generalizing any findings based on the experience of a particular
population exposed to a particular service agency.

The GAO and Duke staffs came into contact through ordinary professional communication channels and, in 1974, agreed to join forces. The
GAO had the resources to implement the Duke Information System design
and instruments in a single community. They also had two other critical
characteristics of immediate importance. They had the authority at the time

to access federal records related to Social Security, Medicare, Medicaid, and the Veterans' Administration. They also were astute in the practical politics of organizational relationships in the community chosen to implement the study. The GAO assured access to the detailed service records of 121 private service agencies serving older adults in Cleveland, Ohio.

Of long-range importance was the fact that, with encouragement from Duke, the GAO placed the data produced by their application of the Duke OARS Information System in the public domain. This had two implications: First, experience with the project would be widely presented in professional societies and publications as issues and findings emerged; this issue was important to the Duke academics and increased the likelihood of useful scientific criticism. Second, the documented data set would be developed with the intention that it would be declared public data at the earliest possible time. In our view, the understanding that the information would be in the public domain enhanced the care with which data were collected and stored. This information has come to be called the Cleveland OARS data set and has been available to the public for a number of years. Its availability has permitted continuing work by a broad range of investigators on a number of basic problems that were raised but not resolved in the initial joint Duke and GAO project.

ILLUSTRATIONS OF DATA ISSUES IN EVALUATION RESEARCH

The Cleveland OARS study is the single application of the complete Duke Information System and will be the focus of the discussion that follows. It is relevant to note, however, that an additional 9 relatively large data sets in which the Duke MFAQ has been used are available in the Duke Center's Data Archive and Related Social Science Laboratory. The 10 studies cumulatively involve more than 6000 older subjects representing samples of older adults as various as American Indians, states, congregate housing units for the elderly, and the total case loads of large service agencies. The pooled samples have provided a laboratory for extensive studies of machine assignment of functional status, quasi-normative distributions of the SEMPA classification of functional states, the development of alternative classifications of functional status that supplement the relatively simplistic SEMPA classifications, and further explorations of the complex ways in which geriatric care is packaged by service agencies (see, for example, George et al., 1982).

The Cleveland OARS study proved to be remarkably free of ordinary data quality problems about which we are warned by textbooks and experience. The study was able to begin with a well-explicated design, extensively pretested instruments for which reliability and validity were known, and relatively free access to service agency records.

SAMPLING AND FIELD EXPERIENCE

In implementing the Cleveland study, the GAO had the best advice available in the sample design and implementation which produced a 2 percent area probability sample of persons 65 years of age and older in the target county ($N = 1609$) and an oversample of older SSI recipients ($N = 225$). The refusal rate was less than 20 percent, which is very good for samples of older persons. Training of interviewers and surveillance of field interviewing were carefully done. There was no evidence of special problems in data acquisition, storage, or retrieval. Missing data are minimal.

The relative absence of common data acquisition problems permitted the project leadership to concentrate appropriately on the practical politics of access to private agency data about services provided and access to federal data sets in which named individuals could be matched to service records. For each individual in the initial sample there is in the project data tape a merged record of the total range and quantity of services received during the year between the first and second observation.

Of the initial Cleveland OARS panel, 82 percent completed a second MFAQ interview one year later. Data from this second interview are in the merged file. A third observation of this panel was scheduled for 1984.

SAMPLING BIAS

There are at least two basic issues to consider. One is the generalizability of the sample to the population from which it was drawn. No indications of special problems are apparent here. The sampling procedure was sound on design and implementation. All routine checks indicate the sample is representative of the locale. Participation bias was minimal. Participants were screened for cognitive status. An approximation of the universe of information on services was achieved.

The second issue is the generalizability of the sample to an implied national population of older adults. Having chosen for good reason to use a design focused on a defined population in a bounded service system, the Cleveland project paid the obvious price of being unable to generalize its findings with confidence. Our GAO colleagues in responding to their Congressional mandate have been tempted to play the what if game (i.e., what if the Cleveland sample and their experiences were generalizable?) in modeling some stochastic processes representing the effects of different service packages on individuals in various functional status categories. It is reassuring to note that they have been appropriately cautious and uncomfortable about such exercises.

The availability of 9 other samples on which MFAQ data and data on self-reported service utilization has permitted some exploration of generalizability. In controlled comparisons of functional status distributions in which gender, socioeconomic status, education, rural/urban residence, and ethnicity are considered, the Cleveland SEMPA distributions match reasonably well the distributions in other samples. In controlled comparisons of service packaging reported by individuals in the special section of the MFAQ, local variations in typical packaging of services have been found to vary significantly. How Cleveland packages geriatric services clearly does not generalize. This fact, however, is important and anticipating that this might be the case underlies our initial interest in relating individuals to a specific bounded service system.

Our experience in Cleveland has not led us to argue for parallel sample surveys of individuals and service systems but, rather, has led us to argue for additional "model reporting sites" in which appropriate variations in and interactions between populations and local service systems could be explored. We continue to believe that this is the strategy of choice in understanding the effects of alternative geriatric care programs.

PROBLEMS OF SPECIFICATION

This suggests that, in a broad sense, the general model is adequately specified, that is, as adequately as is possible. We are less confident that we have adequately handled the related specification of the three major components of our system—functional status, service packaging, and transitions in functionl status. The 5 SEMPA scales, each with 6 subclassifications, generate 7776 states. This procedure generates a large number of empty cells (only 577 of the possible 7776 states have entries); the 10 most common states account for only 23 percent of the sample (332 individuals are in unique states). Although this is interesting in itself, it is unwieldly. We initially settled for 5 dimensions, dichotomized as impaired/unimpaired to generate 32 discrete states. This produces no empty cells and the assignments are reliably achieved both by machine and clinical assignment. It is not clear whether this compression of empirically observed collectivity is achieved at an acceptable cost in the analysis. Currently, we are exploring substitution of 11 more focused classifications of functional states that are known to increase the reliability of subject classification.

Our experience with service system classification has been particularly perplexing. It is estimated that there potentially are 131 billion service package combinations. The most common 153 packages observed account for only 26 percent of the Cleveland sample's experience. Some simplifying assumptions clearly are required and the problem is still being explored (Maddox et al., 1984; George et al., 1982).

The transition matrix still needs a great deal of work. For example, our picture of normative transitions in functioning without regard to specific service interventions remains sketchy. There is no sound basis for estimating normative age-related transitions in functioning against which to compare transitions modified by service interventions. Furthermore, it has not been possible to generate from expert testimony or from observation what constitutes "best professional practice" in designing effective interventions for older individuals in various states of functional impairment. Improvement and decline in functioning in older adults have been observed but our models to date have not proved very helpful in explaining definitively either of these transitions.

These difficulties in appropriate specification do not seem to arise from a methodological problem. Our studies are identifying symptoms of the real complexity of human functional impairments and of service system organization and management. If empirical reality is as complex as it appears, evaluation scientists may have a basis for appreciating what their clinical colleagues have been maintaining all along: There is a jungle out there.

Several practical implications follow from this observation. Simple generalizable models of effective intervention with older populations at this point are unlikely to be persuasive or useful. This may not be a desirable conclusion, but it is the conclusion that these studies suggest. This does not provide practitioners or planners with very useful advice about ways knowledge of functional status can be translated effectively into prescriptions of effective service packages. In the long run, a variety of service packages may prove equally effective in responding to persons in the same functional status classifications.

CONCLUSIONS

The probability of getting good data is partly a function of mastering the sociopolitical environment in which the data are gathered and not just a function of the scientific sophistication of investigators. Even technically good data do not ensure sufficient information for answering reasonable and important evaluation questions definitively.

One of the roles of the evaluation scientists may be to scale down the questions they are asked in order to make them more answerable. This is, as Thomas Kuhn suggests, what scientists do typically. In choosing their puzzles, scientists prefer and handle best the puzzles they think they can manage. This is one of the bases of tension between scientists and policy analysts, managers, or resource allocators. Real public problems outrun the scientists' capacity to respond, no matter how clever they are.

The Duke OARS experience does not necessarily lead to a counsel of despair. The project contributes to our understanding of how complex important policy questions can be. And, though the OARS and GAO projects could not answer the questions as originally posed—and did not pretend to—the project design, measurements, implementation, analytic strategies, and findings have made useful contributions. We know more than we did about the distribution of functional impairment in older populations and about the complex ways that service organizations package their services. Data on the distribution of impairments in a defined population and their utilization of services permits the following: (1) assessment of some basic epidemiologic and planning questions regarding the capabilities that service systems require; (2) the identification of served and underserved categories of older adults; and (3) the performance of the service system for patients or clients who do make contact (Blazer and Maddox, 1982). Understanding the effects of service interventions requires information based on defined populations in bounded systems. This is necessary not so much because the distributions of impairment vary among particular subpopulations of older adults, but because the service systems available to these subpopulations differ substantially in organization and service packaging.

For subpopulations requiring multiple services, attempts to demonstrate the effects of particular interventions are not practical and, more importantly, probably are not a useful exercise. How multiple services are packaged is the critical issue.

Taking a long-range view of the objectives of policy-relevant research increases the potential of making useful contributions. There is particular significance in developing and assessing evaluation research strategies and instruments that have broad application, and in the possibility of using public use data sets generated by such research for training.

REFERENCES

BLAZER, D. and G. MADDOX (1982) "Using epidemiologic survey data to plan geriatric mental health services." Hospital and Community Psychiatry 33, 1: 43-45.

Duke Center (1978) Multidimensional Functional Assessment: The OARS Methodology—A Manual. Durham, NC: Duke University, Center for the Study of Aging and Human Development.

FILLENBAUM, G. and M. SMYER (1981) "The development, validity, and reliability of the OARS multidimensional functional assessment questionnaire." Journal of Gerontology 36: 428-434.

GEORGE, L. R. LANDERMAN, and G. FILLENBAUM (1982) Developing Measures of Functional Status and Service Utilization: Refining and Extending the OARS Methodology. Working paper. Durham, NC: Duke University, Center for the Study of Aging and Human Development.

KUHN, T. S. (1970) The Structure of Scientific Revolutions. Chicago: University of Chicago Press.

MADDOX, G. (1972) "Interventions and outcomes: notes on designing and implementing an experiment in health care." International Journal of Epidemiology 1, 4: 339-345.

— — — and D. DELLINGER (1978) "Assessment of functional status in a program evaluation and resource allocation model." Annals of the American Academy of Political and Social Sciences 438: 59-70.

MADDOX, G., G. FILLENBAUM, and L. GEORGE (1979) "Extending the uses of the LRHS data set." Public Data Use 7, 3/4: 57-62.

MADDOX, G., D. DELLINGER, W. AMMANN, and W. LAURIE (1984) "The Duke OARS Information System: objectives and design, service delivery, use of feedback, and a national perspective," in C. Tilquin (ed.) Proceedings of the International Congress in Systems Science in Health-Social Services for the Elderly and Disabled. Montreal: International Institute for Systems Science in Health Care.

YIN, R. and I. HEINSOHN (1980) The Use of Research Sponsored by the Administration on Aging, Case Study 2: Older Americans' Resources and Services. Washington, DC: American Institute for Research.

FROM SCIENCE TO TECHNOLOGY: REDUCING PROBLEMS IN MENTAL HEALTH EVALUATION BY PARADIGM SHIFT

William D. Neigher
Daniel B. Fishman

In the years between 1965 and 1980, many new federal social welfare programs were developed and implemented, mostly in the form of categorical grants. Many of these programs in turn grew to enormous proportions, attracting supporters and detractors, champions and reformers. Some programs were steeped in theory and grounded in supporting research; others were conceived amid political turmoil and quick-fix efforts for traditionally intractable social problems. Others had manageable goals and definable target populations, whereas still others had mere good intentions broadly aimed at a host of economic and social ills. In a telling chapter subheading, Peter Rossi (1978) summed up the problem: "vague goals, great expectations, weak effects."

Making generalizations about the programs as a whole, as we have just done, risks perpetuating the myth of program homogeneity—a range of program delivery sites, like chains of McDonald's restaurants, all serving up the same quality product, with uniform ingredients and quality assurance "at a price you can afford." They did not and do not fulfill that promise as one might reasonably expect. They varied in the degree to which they were implemented as planned, staffed, and funded. One variable they shared, how-

AUTHORS' NOTE: The authors contributed equally to the preparation of this chapter. Our thanks to Charles Windle and Gerald Leventhal for their helpful comments and suggestions.

ever, was that they came under increasing pressures for "accountability," and became, themselves, a target group for evaluation.

There are almost as many reasons for this evaluative scrutiny as there were reasons for the programs themselves. Chelimsky (1981) reviewed 14 of the major complaints about categorical grant performance: (1) they were ineffective in achieving their goals; (2) they were inefficient in program operations; (3) they were excessively centralized and controlled at the national level, thus decreasing local input and accountability; (4) federal requirements for planning, local matching funds, and increasing dependence on federal support distorted state and local priorities; (5) overlapping programs and agencies caused fragmentation and even contradictions in requirements; (6) programs were underfunded; (7) they were inequitable, in that targeted program recipients benefited less than the bureaucracy; (8) they expanded the public sector contribution to economic productivity at the expense of the private sector; (9) they produced exaggerated expectations for success; (10) they singled out for special reward individuals because they belonged to a disadvantaged race, creed, or sex as opposed to merit and, thus, were value-eroding; (11) they were bureaucratizing; (12) they were difficult to control and difficult to terminate; (13) they were wasteful; and (14) they rewarded the self-interests of program staff ahead of program recipients.

The programs fell far short of promised expectations. Ten years later, the government's interpretation of "entitlements" and the consolidation in 1981 of more than 50 categorical grants and two already existing block grants into nine new block grant programs (PL 97-35) may well shape programs for the next ten years. What role can evaluation play, now that it, too, is decentralized? To search for an answer, we will examine some past and present evaluation experiences.

This chapter consists of four sections. The first reviews the nature of these problematic results of evaluation, with a particular emphasis on issues of data unreliability in community mental health evaluation. The second section proposes a causal explanation of these problems by analyzing evaluation projects in terms of two different paradigms, science (Cartesian model) versus technology (Baconian model), which can underlie an evaluation project. An argument is set forth that a basic cause of unreliability in evaluative data is adherence to the science rather than to the technology paradigm.

The third section presents two case examples—one from Colorado and one from New Jersey—to illustrate the causal analysis in the previous section. The Colorado example describes the increase in data reliability that accompanied the move from a science to a technology paradigm in the statewide evaluation of community mental health. The New Jersey example describes a similar process, together with an empirical study of the type of perceptual distortions that play a major role in generating unreliability in data. Building on lessons learned in the prior sections, the final portion of the chapter outlines an action plan for increasing data reliability in community mental health.

SOCIAL PROGRAM EVALUATION:
SPIRALING COSTS, NEGLIGIBLE UTILIZATION

Chelimsky (1983) points out that the demand for evaluation has been related to cycles of political reforms, the most recent beginning with Johnson's War on Poverty (1961-1968) and ending with the exit of the Carter administration in 1980. During this period, the federal government's sponsorship of social program evaluations went from almost nothing in 1960 to approximately $180 million in 1980. Although these are some of the evaluation costs, an estimate of the benefits is much more elusive. Although the Institute for Program Evaluation in the General Accounting Office (GAO) currently is developing a general strategy for promoting the cost-effectiveness of its evaluations, problems of definition, criteria, time frame, shifting values, and cost accounting leave the issue largely unaddressed (e.g., Alkin and Solmon, 1983). Many commentators have offered highly critical assessments of the evaluation track record to date. Wholey et al. (1970:40) concluded that "the recent literature is unanimous in announcing the general failure of evaluation to affect decision-making in a significant way." Cohen and Garet (1975:19) found that "there is little evidence to indicate that government planning offices have succeeded in linking social research and decision-making." Deitchman (1976:390) concluded that the "impact of the research on the most important affairs of state was, with few exceptions, nil." Finally, Carol Weiss (1972:10-11) viewed underutilization as one of the foremost problems in evaluation research: "Evaluation research is meant for immediate and direct use in improving the quality of social programming. Yet a review of evaluation experience suggests that evaluation results have not exerted significant influence on program decisions."

WHY SOCIAL PROGRAM EVALUATIONS FAIL

Much of the difficulty with data collection in our efforts for program evaluation in federal action social programs begins with the legislative authority itself. Because these programs often are aimed at diverse target populations and multiple problem areas, the enabling legislation often is by choice overly broad in scope to allow flexibility in services delivery. Not surprisingly, however, when the legislative goals are ambiguous or frequently change in scope over time, the evaluative authority for those programs is similarly vague. This problem is evident in the legislative authorities for evaluation in such major Department of Health and Human Services programs as the Education of the Handicapped Act (PL 89-650), the Elementary and Secondary Education Act of 1965 (PL 93-380), Head Start (PL 93-644), the Juvenile Delinquency Prevention and Control Act of 1968 (PL 90-445), the Mental Retardation Facilities and Community Health Center's Construction Act of 1963 (PL 90-170), the Older Americans' Act of 1965 (PL 93-29), the Rehabilitation Act of 1973 (PL 93-516), and Title V of the Social Security Act, the Maternal and Child Health and Crippled Children's Services Section.

Although the language authorizing program evaluation in these acts is similar, two sets of statements are most consistent. These excerpts from the evaluation authority for Head Start illustrate:

> The Secretary shall provide, directly or through grants or contracts, for the continuing evaluation of programs under this part, including evaluations that measure and evaluate the impact of programs authorized by this part, in order to determine their effectiveness in achieving stated goals, their impact on related programs, and their structure and mechanisms for delivery of services, including, where appropriate, comparisons with appropriate control groups composed of persons who have not participated in such programs. Evaluations shall be conducted by persons not directly involved in the administration of the program or project evaluation (sec. 521 a).

> In carrying out evaluations under this part, the Secretary shall, whenever feasible, arrange to obtain the specific views of persons participating in and served by programs and projects assisted under this part about such programs and projects (sec. 521 d).

Neigher and Schulberg (1982) point out that although some legislation alludes to the comparison of served and unserved groups, most statutes only state that impact is to be evaluated; specific evaluation guidelines are left to program staff. The Elementary and Secondary Education Act, for example, calls for the executive branch to develop objective criteria, techniques, and methods that are comparable on a statewide and nationwide basis. The Head Start program similarly requires that general standards for evaluation be developed to measure project effectiveness and that they be used in future funding decisions. In the late 1970s, secretaries of the Department of Health, Education, and Welfare (now Health and Human Services) urged that more objective criteria be included in the evaluation regulations and guidelines of approximately 133 health and human service programs. However, little progress is evident. Examples of evaluation authority from cabinet departments other than DHHS (Departments of Agriculture, Energy, Housing and Urban Development, Interior, Labor, Transportation, Treasury, and Veterans Administration) also are cited by Chelimsky (1981: 57-63). Similar to examples from Health and Human Services, evaluation authority often is lacking in specificity and measurement criteria, and consequently diminishes both the responsiveness and utilization of the evaluation efforts that follow.

What we have described is a major threat to the internal validity of program evaluation data within programs. The question of precisely what is being evaluated in any specific program becomes compromised when the overall mission, goals, objectives, and evaluation criteria are purposely vague and subjective. Obviously, there are different intentions and purposes for program evaluation. Similarly, there are different audiences, users, and perspectives surrounding program evaluation data that affect both the validity and reliability of the data itself and, in addition, its utilization in the decision-making process. Many federal categorical grant programs had local matching requirements as prerequisites. Thus, local program delivery sites had at least several masters: the mission of the federal program for which they accepted funding as well as the rules and regulations guiding local matching funds often contributed by state and regional funding authorities. Further revenue support often was obtained through localities and municipalities, which further specified program direction in terms of local needs of service populations. We suggest that these two factors—multiple purposes and perspectives for mandated program evaluation efforts— resulted in a largely unresolved conflict for program evaluators, which in turn compromised the validity and reliability of the evaluation data base. These problems became most acute when conflicting or incompatible evaluation models were applied concurrently by regulatory agencies and local program delivery sites. These two variables merit a more detailed examination.

CONFLICTING EVALUATION MODELS
AND PERSPECTIVES

Windle and Neigher (1978) identified four purposes for program evaluation. The first, amelioration, views program evaluation as generating better information for decision makers. In this view, the information produced increases the ability of staff to comprehend what they are doing, make more effective use of resources, and feel more comfortable in decision making. The second purpose is accountability. Assuming that a program should be evaluated by the public or those who fund and support it, this model focuses on public data disclosure and citizen participation in the evaluation process. The third purpose, advocacy, considers program evaluation as a strategy used by organizations to advance their interests when vying for resources. In contrast to traditional conceptions of accountability, this evaluation purpose adapts itself to adversarial proceedings and assumes that selective information sharing is one of the mechanisms legitimately utilized in the competition for funding. The fourth purpose is evaluation research which applies scientific methods to establish causal linkages between interventions and their outcomes. All have been used to some extent to meet program evaluation requirements.

Similarly, data from human service settings can be interpreted from several perspectives, which also can be in conflict (e.g., Fishman, 1981; House and Mathison, 1983; Strupp and Hadley, 1977). They include (1) the funder or sponsor of human service programs, such as federal or state government, private foundations, or special categorical funding programs; (2) the provider, such as a school system, community mental health center, juvenile first-offender program, or income maintenance project; (3) the recipients of human services, the clients, patients, students, or other service users; and (d) the public taxpayers in the case of publicly financed programs or other constituencies who have supported services through contributions of time and money. Each perspective utilizes different types of data in judging a program's value. For example, group homes for the retarded may be clinically more effective and more cost-efficient than institutional care according to criteria selected by professional staff and funding agencies. Community residents, however, may consider different criteria in determining a program's worth. On the basis of such indicators as property values, homeowners may reach different conclusions about whether to support the group home's continued existence. Thus, it is important, even vital, to identify program performance criteria that are specific to each perspective, and to assess the pros and cons of including them in program performance indicator systems (Neigher, 1979).

Earlier we described how local agencies had to serve a number of masters in terms of program goals, objectives, target groups, and desired outcomes. Similarly, federal-level funding, regulatory authorities, and many local service agencies shared program evaluation requirements. At times, these were consistent program evaluation missions; in other examples, however, evaluation efforts were concurrent, sequential, or even independent or duplicative efforts. Neigher et al. (1983) described an example of a multifocus evaluation effort and its consequences on data collection from the federal Community Mental Health Centers (CMHC) program (PL 94-63). The CMHC program, from 1963 to 1981, was heralded as a revolution in mental health care. From its inception in 1963 (PL 88-164) to its final year of categorical funding in 1981 (PL 97-35), it was considered landmark legislation that helped change the country's mental health care system. By October of 1980, 789 centers received federal funding from the National Institute of Mental Health (NIMH) and their programs covered 53 percent of U.S. mental health service areas. Championed by many and severely criticized by others, the actual impact of the program on the nation's mental health remains unclear. The authorization to evaluate the CMHC program originally came from congressional legislation (PL 90-174) and later from the policies and regulations of NIMH under a series of federal laws, notably PL 94-63. From 1976 to 1980, two dominant evaluation strategies were prevalent: funds expended by NIMH each year for studies of CMHC services or programwide evaluations and a much larger expenditure by CMHC to conduct their own independent evaluations following federal guidelines (PL 94-63).

In 1968, PL 90-174 set aside 1 percent of the funding appropriated under the CMHC Act to be used to support a wide variety of NIMH studies of CMHC services. These focused on process studies from individual programs, methodology development, evaluability assessment, data collection, management information systems development, and projects intended to evaluate the program as a whole. In 1975, Congress passed a series of amendments to the CMHC program in part to counter administration opposition to the program. Beginning in 1976, each center was to spend 2 percent of its operating costs in service to NIMH evaluation guidelines which required annual efforts to evaluate the center's performance in such areas as cost of operations, service utilization, availability, accessibility and acceptability of services, and CMHC impact on service area residents. The overwhelming majority of the evaluation funding effort was spent on the 2 percent local evaluation requirement.

Paradigm Lost?

There was little coordination between the central 1 percent NIMH evaluation set aside and the 2 percent CMHC self-evaluation requirements. As Neigher et al. (1983: 299) explain, the results were as follows:

> Opportunities were lost for natural or controlled experiments with different centers collecting data on the same instruments, and studying comparable client populations. Studies of treatment outcome were conducted. . . but valid and reliable measures are just now reaching psychometric maturity. Thus, even if a coordinated effort had been developed during the formative years of the CMHC program, evaluation technology and staff resources were not ready to support it.

Not surprisingly, both efforts seemed to fall short on their own regard. Charles Windle (1983: 298), who worked on the NIMH central evaluation effort, summarized his experiences as follows:

> NIMH's 1% evaluation studies which focused on what was occurring within the program were too narrowly conceived. They did not test the program's

assumptions or alternative theories of what constitutes effective treatment. They did not compare CMHCs with other ways of organizing systems of care. And they did not examine community systems of care, including the integration of CMHCs with other service systems. Again the CMHC Program ended with little information to permit wiser decisions in the future.

Similarly, Flaherty and Olsen (1978: 289) in an NIMH-funded 1978 study of the impact of the 2 percent evaluation requirement on CMHCs, concluded as follows:

> The new requirements were perceived as reflecting not the centers' needs, but the federal government's needs for more data; there was much doubt about the utility of this data to the federal government as well. As a result, centers tend to "work around" the requirements, conducting minimal studies in most of the required areas, studies which consume resources and produce data useless to the center.

In this evaluation effort, the whole appears to have been less than the sum of its parts, and even the individual parts themselves appear to have been insufficiently supported to make an independent contribution.

FROM SCIENCE TO TECHNOLOGY:
A DIFFERENT PARADIGM

In the previous section we outlined a variety of interrelated problems that have plagued program evaluation generally, and the evaluation of community mental health programs specifically—problems such as vague goals in the legislation that defines the programs themselves, vague evaluative authority in the legislation mandating evaluation, conflicting evaluation models, and conflicting evaluation perspectives.

We turn now to a consideration of the underlying causes of these problems. We begin with the particular manifestation of these problems which is the focus of this chapter, namely, problems in data reliability. In a recent paper, Burstein et al. (forthcoming) catalogue a variety of technical faults in the data collection involved with social program evaluation. Examples include "variations in rewards and gratifications provided for respondent cooperation," "inconsistent training of data collectors," "burdensome volume, duration, or frequency of data collection," and "failure to verify that the data were collected, and in the ways prescribed." Burstein et al. conclude that "the consequence of [such] defective data collection, to a large extent, can eviscerate the refinements in evaluation technology that have occurred in recent years."

What causes the kind of technical faults in data collection that Burstein et al. describe? In our view, one of the major causes is the lack of consistent, positive motivational incentives for reliable and accurate data collection in those individuals who are involved in the data collection process. These individuals, whom we will call data collectors, include the evaluators who design a study and link it, where appropriate, with policy; the individuals who actually collect the data; and those who collate and organize the data into information systems for later analysis. As has been documented widely in the organizational behavior literature (e.g., Frederiksen, 1982; O'Brien et al., 1982), without proper environmental incentives, individuals who function in roles such as data collector will not develop and implement the quality control mechanisms needed to ensure that consistency and accuracy are maintained in their work.

We contend that there are two basic incentive conditions that typically must be present in order for a study's data collectors to be properly motivated to work toward data reliability. First, there must be "data importance," that is, the stated purpose of the study must be viewed as personally and/or professionally valuable by a substantial number of the data collectors, and especially by the study's designers. Moreover, the data involved must be viewed as truly important to the purpose of the study. Otherwise, there is not strong enough motivation to devote the extra effort required, as the collection of reliable data demands more effort than that of unreliable data.

Second, assuming that there is data importance, there must be strong incentives to prevent the participants from introducing bias into the data collected. This second condition, which we call "incentive against bias," typically is necessary. If data are important, there are likely to be interest groups who hope the data will suit their own particular purposes and who may try to influence the results of evaluations. Without explicit incentives to counteract these biasing factors, objectively accurate data are unlikely.

These two motivating conditions, data importance and incentive against bias, can influence a study in different ways, depending on the general stated purpose of the evaluative project. These purposes can be separated into two major types, based on two different philosophy of science "paradigms" (Kuhn, 1962) that underlie most social evaluation studies. These are a "science" paradigm, which involves data for the purpose of theory building, and a "technology" paradigm, which involves data for the purpose of managerial decision making. Bevan (1980) describes the individualistic, esoteric, "dogma eat dogma" nature of the Cartesian view of research associated with the scientific paradigm. For the Cartesian investigator, "doing science is like running a race, and one's colleagues in the field can therefore only be viewed as strong competitors. . . . The public is perceived as having only one role, that of patron" (Bevan, 1980: 790). In contrast, the Baconian view, which is

TABLE 14.1
Contrasting Characteristics of Science and Technology

Science (Basic Research)	Technology (Applied Research)
1. *Cartesian view* (Bevan, 1980) of research as an individualistic, competitive, esoteric, intrinsically satisfying activity.	1. *Baconian view* (Bevan, 1980) of research as a social, collaborative means for contributing to the general public welfare.
2. *Tradition of academic freedom:* The individual researcher follows his/her own interests in deciding on what is to be studied.	2. *Tradition of mission orientation:* The area of study is determined by program needs.
3. Emphasis on knowledge relating to *controlled, laboratory conditions.*	3. Emphasis on knowledge relating to *actual program conditions "in the field," "in the real world."*
4. Emphasis on *hypothesis-testing:* Findings of "no difference" are discouraged.	4. Emphasis on the *systematic, standardized observation and classification of natural phenomena,* of conditions as they exist "in the real world."
5. Emphasis on *theoretical payoff:* The goal is theory-based knowledge.	5. Emphasis on *pragmatic payoff:* The goal is to reduce high-priority social and psychological problems in the most cost-effective and ethical manner.
6. Emphasis on *publication in esoteric, highly technical journals.*	6. Emphasis on *communication with lay decision-makers* concerning programs and policies.
7. Emphasis on deriving *general statements* about human behavior.	7. Emphasis on deriving *particular evaluations of specific* programs.
8. Emphasis on conceptual and methodological *innovation.*	8. Emphasis on *maintaining* proven programs and *replicating* them in new situations.

SOURCE: Reprinted from *American Psychologist,* Vol. 37, No. 5, May 1982. Copyright 1982 by the American Psychological Association. Reprinted by permission.

associated with the technological paradigm, stresses that research is "a cooperative activity within a professional community marked by a clear-cut division of labor but bound by a single shared altruistic commitment to the promotion of human welfare" (Bevan, 1980: 780-781). In an earlier paper (Fishman and Neigher, 1982), we described the differences between these two paradigms, which are summarized in Table 14.1. As can be seen from the table, theory-oriented, "basic" research involves individualistic investigators who employ controlled, laboratory-like conditions to derive general laws and theories about human behavior. Technological, "applied" research, on the other hand, involves mission-oriented groups of investigators who employ "real world," field conditions to derive particular, decisionfocused knowledge about specific programs.

TABLE 14.2
Conditions Determining Data Reliability in Various Types of Program Evaluation Studies

A. Stated Purpose of the Data	Motivating Conditions for Reliable Data		D. Probability of Data Reliability	E. Type of Evaluation
	B. Actual Importance of Data to the Study's Purpose	C. Incentive Against Bias in Data Collection		
Managerial decision-making (technology paradigm)	High	High	High	(1) Amelioration*
	High	High	High	(2) Accountability*
	High	Low	Low	(3) Advocacy*
	Low	–	Low	(4) Data as ritual
Scientific understanding (science paradigm)	High	High	High	(5) Ideal social science
	High	Low	Low	(6) Actual social science, type X
	Low	–	Low	(7) Actual social science, type Y

*Amelioration and Accountability Evaluation are differentiated by their organizational focus. Amelioration Evaluation, which has an internal organizational focus, is directed toward the improvement of functioning within a program. Accountability Evaluation has an external focus, involving both the program itself and its outside constituencies. It is directed toward an objective assessment of the program in order to inform choices about continuing support for the program by the outside constituencies. For a detailed discussion contrasting Amelioration, Accountability, and Advocacy Evaluation, see Windle and Neigher (1978).

Retaining the paradigm distinctions, Table 14.2 outlines how the motivating conditions of data importance and incentive against bias determine data reliability in various types of program evaluation studies. Column A in the table lists the two paradigms, managerial decision making and scientific understanding. Column B lists high versus low values for the actual importance of study data to the stated purpose of the study. When data importance is high, pressures toward biasing typically develop. Column C lists two possible conditions in response to these pressures—high incentive against bias in data collection versus low. Column D presents the probability of data reliability based on the conditions in columns B and C. As can be seen, only when data importance and incentive against bias are both high is data reliability viewed as being highly probable. Finally, Column E labels seven types of evaluation that are differentiated by columns A-D. These types, which are an expansion of those by Windle and Neigher (1978), are summarized below. In orienting the reader to Table 14.2, it is important to emphasize that these are "pure" types and that, in actual practice, most studies involve a mixture of different types. Moreover, the categorizations of "high" versus "low" in columns B-D are relative and, in practice, they define anchoring points on continuous variables.

TECHNOLOGICAL, MANAGEMENT-FOCUSED TYPES OF EVALUATION

Amelioration Evaluation (E1 in Table 14.2) refers to studies conducted within an organization in order to improve its internal efficiency and effectiveness. Such studies do not directly affect how outside constituencies view the agency. An Amelioration Evaluation is taken seriously by the organization's administration. Data objectivity is important and, thus, antibias mechanisms are built in to assure data reliability.

Accountability Evaluation (E2 in Table 14.2) is conducted by outside constituencies to assess in an objective fashion the performance of a service program. The data are important in key real-world decisions, for instance, in program funding, but there is a commitment to objectivity demonstrated by active efforts to reduce bias.

Advocacy Evaluation (E3 in Table 14.2) takes place in a context in which the evaluation data are important to administrative decisions, but antibias mechanisms are not in place. Thus, the evaluation data collection process becomes politicized and is at the mercy of whichever advocacy group can gain ascendance (Cronbach et al., 1980).

Finally, Data as Ritual Evaluation (E4 in Table 14.2) describes the situation in which evaluative process is mainly lip service and the resultant data do not affect administrative decisions:

Some evaluations are "shows" set in motion to make the sponsoring agency or elected official look good or to discomfit an opponent (Cronbach et al., 1980: 47).

Despite no existence in this situation of an incentive for bias, such low data importance leads to a lack of incentive for data reliability.

SCIENTIFIC, THEORY-FOCUSED TYPES OF EVALUATION

Ideal Social Science Evaluation (E5 in Table 14.2) refers to the type of study in social science that parallels the best models from the biological and physical sciences: a controlled, laboratory-like evaluation that tests hypotheses derived from abstract psychological and social theory in a methodologically rigorous manner that controls for possible bias (Fishman and Neigher, 1982). Thus, Ideal Social Science involved data that clearly are related to important theories and basic principles and that are collected in an accurate nonbiased manner.

As we and others have argued (see Fishman and Neigher, 1982; Gergen, 1982), Ideal Social Science is rarely attained. Rather, most studies are not able to achieve both data importance and incentive against bias and, thus, we have labeled such studies Actual Social Science Evaluation. For example, in Actual Social Science Evaluation there are negative incentives for replication, which is an important method for determining data reliability; a bias toward producing data that reject the null hypothesis; little encouragement of data that have ecological, pragmatic importance; and a general refusal both to describe data collection procedures in detail and to share raw data with other investigators, thus increasing the chance for inadvertent or deliberate bias and error (Burstein et al., forthcoming; Ceci and Walker, 1983; Fishman and Neigher, 1982).

As seen in Table 14.2, there are two types of science-oriented evaluation that spawn unreliable data: Type X (E6 in Table 14.2) produces data that are biased and Type Y (E7 in Table 14.2) produces data that are not important in more than a ritualistic way to the major purposes of the study. An example of Type X data, which is the more rare, is Cyril Burt's infamous work on the genetic nature of intelligence (Kamin, 1974). Examples of the ritualistic use of data (Type Y) are pervasive because of the nature of the data incentives in Actual Social Science Evaluation mentioned above. Thus, if data were important in more than a ritualistic way, there would be a primary emphasis on replication of studies; an interest in all reliable data, whether or not it rejected the null hypothesis; and a general practice of investigators carefully examining one anothers' data.

While there is question about the extent to which ideal Social Science Evaluation has been successfully implemented with high data reliability, there are numerous examples of technological evaluations that achieve high data reliability—for example, national economic indicators, the U.S. Census, sports statistics, political polls, life insurance actuarial statistics, accounting data in large corporations and banks, and inventory control systems. We contend that one way to achieve increased data reliability in evaluation studies is to more closely align these studies with the technological/managerial decision-making paradigm rather than with the scientific understanding paradigm.

Table 14.3 specifically applies the contrasting characteristics of present, actual practice of the science and technology paradigms to data collection in evaluation studies. What emerges are clusters of interrelated differences. The first two columns of Table 14.3 contrast these differences and the third column summarizes why the management paradigm tends to create a higher incentive for reliable data collection.

Tables 14.2 and 14.3 can be used to guide future practice. Historically, contemporary evaluation was, in a sense, born out of a marriage among social science research, data-based management, and policy formation as it takes place in real-world politics. However, we contend that the social science research component in that mix has tended to predominate, leading to two types of problems in evaluation studies: the types of data unreliability problems associated with Actual Social Science, discussed above, and the poor utilization of study results, which is due to the low degree to which studies are embedded in the managerial and political policy context of program planning and monitoring.

Cronbach et al. (1980) set forth similar arguments. They point out that, until recently, "highly controlled summative studies" have tended to be the ideal type of evaluation. They conclude that it has not been until the mid-and late 1970s that there

> has been full recognition that politics and science are both integral aspects of evaluation. . . . Evaluators who see themselves as fearless seekers after truth come to feel that they have been assigned walk-on parts in a political pageant. . . . The evaluator venturing into the political arena can no longer be guided solely by the habits of thought of the scientist (Frankel, 1976). The political sensitivity he acquires ought to be used in addition to, and not in place of, his training in impartiality (Cronbach et al., 1980: 35, 47, 71).

Tables 14.2 and 14.3 are designed to clarify to the evaluator the paradigmatic options and related conditions determining reliability that are open to him or her. A basic guiding principle that emerges from the tables is that an evaluation study has the best chance of yielding reliable, useful, and utilized

TABLE 14.3

Contrasting Characteristics of Theory-Based Research and Management, as Actually Practiced

Data Collection in the Service of Theory-Based Research (Science)	Data Collection in the Service of Management (Technology)	Why the Management Paradigm Tends to create a Higher Incentive for Reliable Data Collection
1. *Data as a means:* emphasis upon data as a vehicle for defending a theory.	1. *Data as an end in itself:* emphasis on data for its descriptive value per se.	1-4. Data as an end in itself for real-world description creates a higher incentive for reliability than when the data is only a means for the testing of abstract, theoretical hypotheses.
2. *Goal of theory confirmation:* most important goal is for the data to confirm the theory and its hypotheses being tested.	2. *Goal of real-world description:* most important goal is for the data to measure accurately the real events being directly assessed.	
3. *Data collected in artificial settings:* the ideal setting for hypothesis-based research is the controlled laboratory environment, which is artificial by design.	3. *Data collected in natural settings:* data typically are collected in real settings about real events.	
4. *Exemplars:* psychological experiments, e.g., experiments that support theories about the psychological mechanisms in attitude change.	4. *Exemplars:* sports statistics, economic indicators, political polls, life insurance actuarial statistics, accounting data, inventory control systems, and the U.S. Census.	
5. Emphasis is on the *derivation of general knowledge,* i.e., on the development of general psychological laws.	5. Emphasis on the *derivation of situation-specific knowledge,* e.g., on the evaluation of a specific program in a particular organization.	5. Focus on situation-specific knowledge increases the salience for the specifics of the data than does focus on deriving general psychological laws.
6. Data-collector is held *externally accountable for summary statistics only* (e.g., Ceci and Walker).	6. Data-collector is held *externally accountable for raw data,* e.g., the outside CPA's examination of a business's "audit trail" in evaluating its accounting activities.	6. There is a higher incentive for reliable raw data when that data itself is under direct accountability, as opposed to accountability only for summaries of data.

(continued)

TABLE 14.3 Continued

Data Collection in the Service of Theory-Based Research (Science)	Data Collection in the Service of Management (Technology)	Why the Management Paradigm Tends to create a Higher Incentive for Reliable Data Collection
7. Emphasis on *nonstandardized operational definitions*, which are individually tailored to the hypotheses being investigated in the particular study.	7. Emphasis on *standardized operational definitions* and comparability of data, e.g., the Federal Bureau of Labor Statistics.	7-9. Standardized operational definitions used over long periods of time are employed by more individuals in more situations, and, thus, the collective effort that goes into creating and clarifying these tends to be greater than that for nonstandardized definitions.
8. *Short-term focus on data collection:* data typically is collected in the context of "one shot" hypothesis-testing studies.	8. *Long-term focus on data collection:* data typically is collected in the context of ongoing monitoring and evaluation for operational management.	
9. *Innovation emphasis:* stress on the generation of new theory-embedded knowledge.	9. *Replication emphasis:* stress on the ongoing repetition and standardized replication of established administrative procedures and programs.	
10. Emphasis on *conclusions and implications* that can be drawn from the data. Primary mission is for *data to generate knowledge.*	10. Emphasis on *practical decisions and applications* that can be drawn from the data. Primary mission is for *data to generate action.*	10-11. Data directly connected to decisions for action have more concrete impact that data connected primarily to knowledge creation. Thus, unreliability in the former would tend to generate more concern and corrective response than unreliability in the latter.
11. *Evaluator's reward: publication based on peer review.*	11. *Evaluator's reward: to contribute to the successful management of a particular program.*	
12. *Data are indirectly tied to dollars:* when summarized, data can support hypotheses leading to publication and the subsequent payment of researchers.	12. *Data are directly tied to dollars:* financial decisions are based directly on data.	12. Money is a powerful incentive. Other factors being equal, the more directly data is tied to financial contingencies, the more incentive there is for attention to data reliability.
13. As focus of data is short term, *limited incentive for the development of formal data-base systems with quality control mechanisms.*	13. As focus of data is long term, *strong incentive for the development of formal data-base systems* with quality control mechanisms.	13. Unreliability of data collection can be viewed as a "natural," baseline condition. Therefore, specific quality control mechanisms have to be instituted to combat it.

data only if it is significantly tied into the Amelioration or Accountability Evaluation model—that is, only if the study data are clearly linked to important managerial decisions, either inside or outside the program—and only if formal mechanisms are built into the study to create explicit incentives against bias in data collection. It is important to emphasize here that we are not calling for an abandonment of the methods and theories of traditional social science research. However, we are arguing that use of such research methods and theories must be tempered by and integrated with a managerial decision-making mind-set, including both the decisions associated with politically developed policies and the decisions associated with the administration of social programs.

The two case studies in the following section illustrate this theme. The Colorado example describes the increase in data reliability and utilization that accompanied the move from a science to a technology paradigm in the statewide evaluation of community mental health agencies. Specifically, the science model involved the placing of in-house evaluators in each agency to bring a scientific objective perspective to the running of the agency, whereas the technology model directly linked evaluative data into the statewide management system for allocating funds to each agency. The New Jersey example describes a similar process, together with an empirical study of the type of perceptual ambiguity that plays a major role in generating unreliability in data.

CASE STUDIES

PERFORMANCE CONTRACTING IN COLORADO

As described above, the federal Community Mental Health Center (CMHC) program began in 1963 and, through categorical grants and required local matching funds, it stimulated the growth of CMHC's across the country. This growth is exemplified in Colorado, which expanded from few community mental health services in 1960 to statewide service provision by the early 1970s through a network of 20 regional CMHCs.

Also as described above, federal funds stimulated two types of evaluation of the CMHC agencies: (1) NIMH contract evaluation, which involved evaluation studies initiated and managed by NIMH and primarily financed by a 1 percent "set-aside" from the funding appropriated by the federal CMHC legislation; and (2) agency self-evaluation, which generally consisted of a research and evaluation (R&E) department in each center, the directors of which were at least partially financed by NIMH. (After 1976, a minimum required level of agency self-evaluation was set by NIMH at 2 percent of a CMHC's operating budget.) By hiring a staff with a background and title in research and evaluation, agency self-evaluation was created to introduce a more objective, rational, scientific perspective into the planning and administration of the centers, and to gather scientifically valid information about the needs of the agency catchment areas and about the costs, accessibility, and impact of the agencies' services (Cook and Shadish, 1982).

In Colorado the requirement for agency self-evaluation was successful in bringing to the agencies, both as R&E directors and as consultants to those directors, a knowledgeable, able, and committed group of evaluators. A number of these individuals developed positive national reputations through attaining and then carrying out a variety of cost-effectiveness-oriented NIMH contract evaluations in the early 1970s (e.g., see Binner, 1975; Ciarlo, 1977; Fishman, 1978, 1981; Sorensen and Phipps, 1972).

In spite of these scattered individual successes in technology development in the early 1970s, evaluation had relatively little impact on the information base about the Colorado CMHC program. Although there was an increase in the quality of information about selected centers, there continued to be poor standardization of basic definitions and data unreliability across centers as a whole. Generally, the dynamics that were present nationally in the agency self-evaluation program (Cook and Shadish, 1982) were at work in Colorado. In many instances, no one really was interested in the substance of the data generated. Rather, the evaluation consumers were only concerned that the evaluation process took place and was visible, implicitly following the Data as Ritual or Type Y Actual Social Science models in Table 14.2. In those instances in which evaluation consumers were interested, they usually were agency directors and the basis of their interest typically was public relations, to generate support for their center, adhering to the advocacy model in Table 14.2.

Such evaluation had no direct impact on funding, so there was little incentive to evaluate programs in a careful, reliable, and standardized manner across all centers. Rather, the major funders of the CMHCs—NIMH and state government—both made their funding decisions on the basis of pre-established grant levels of federal grant dollars together with a formula that determined state dollars to meet the required local match.

Participants in the NIMH Contract Evaluation program testify that this work was carried out under carefully planned and documented contracts that demanded specific evaluation products that were carefully monitored by NIMH evaluation officers. The fruits of these efforts were the development and pilot testing of sophisticated cost-effectiveness methodologies that were linked in concept to models of decision making about mental health planning and evaluation. However, though the content of these projects was technological and management-oriented, their context was more individualistic,

Cartesian science. They had no direct impact on the funding process and other centers, therefore, had relatively little incentive to adopt them.

Though the centers generally were willing to continue the formula arrangement of the early 1970s indefinitely, the Joint Budget Committee (JBC) of the Colorado State Legislature, the most powerful force in the governmental budgeting process, clearly was not. Rather, the JBC was moving from "line item" budgeting to "performance budgeting" which falls under the model of Accountability in Table 14.2. In the words of Joe Shoemaker (1977: 9, 45), a lawyer by training and a dominant figure on the JBC from 1969 to 1977:

> The JBC began using "line items" in the late 1960's to tell administrators specifically how certain appropriated dollars were to be used. For a line-item example, one read: "$2,000 of this operating expense appropriation ($257,000) shall be used to purchase books for the prison library." A performance budget goes several steps beyond such one-liners. It requires . . . a dollar's worth of governmental performance for every tax dollar granted to their agencies through the budgetary process.

As an example of this approach, Shoemaker cites the JBC's reaction to years of confusing, unclear, unreliable data about who was receiving services from the Rehabilitation Division of the State's Department of Social Services:

> Setting out to use our purse strings to try solving this administrative nightmare, we funded the Division for only the first nine months of the year, with the final three months left contingent on the following criteria: (1) A goal of 70% of all clients who are classified as rehabilitated must be employed by a private or public employer for a minimum of 4 months in a job directly related to the services provided by the Division, and (2) At least 75% of all clients accepted for service must have physical or emotional disabilities which materially limit their capabilities to work (Shoemaker, 1977: 46-47).

In the context of this working philosophy, the JBC began requesting and later demanding performance budgets from the CMHCs in the early 1970s. The agencies resisted, citing the complexity of what they were doing and methodological problems in its measurement. Finally, in the spring of 1975, the JBC despaired and assigned its own budget analyst, John Bliss, to develop a performance and need-based, unit-cost reimbursment system for the budget year 1975-1976. Not only did the budget analyst come up with such a system, but the application of that system resulted in a projected reduction of the CMHC budget from the roughly $10 million the agencies had been expecting in 1975-1976 to $8 million. Needless to say, the "Bliss formula" did not live up to its name in the effect it had on the agencies!

In fact, the Bliss formula was a methodological nightmare. It used a grossly oversimplified, arbitrary method to convert different kinds of service units—inpatient, outpatient, etc.—into a single kind of standardized unit. Moreover, it treated the unreliable workload data and the unstandardized and incomparable financial data submitted by the agencies to the state as valid information. Finally, its definition of "need" was arbitrary and unfair.

However, the reality of the impending Bliss formula provided a major incentive for the agencies to take seriously the reliability, standardization, and comparability of their data and to come up with some way of coping with the threatened reduction of $2 million in funding. This political situation allowed a small group of R&E directors to act as mediators between the JBC and the agencies. The plan worked out was this: The agencies would have 6 months to come up with an alternative unit-cost budgeting formula, based on the relative needs of each catchment area and a unit-cost reimbursement system for services actually delivered. If such a formula was not forthcoming, the Bliss formula would be implemented.

This plan had major advantages for each side. The JBC was open to an alternative to the Bliss formula, as long as the system used was need and unit-cost based. However, the JBC was unwilling to allow the agencies the indefinite delay of which they had taken advantage in the past, so it required the 6 month deadline. From the agencies' perspective, it gave them a reprieve of 6 months and a course of action that, although somewhat unpalatable, promised to restore the lost $2 million. Moreover, the agencies decided that if the JBC was mandating performance-based budgeting, the agencies wanted to be the ones to define performance criteria.

As the plan contained positive incentives for each side, it was accepted. The threat of the Bliss formula became a strong enough motivator to overcome the agencies' traditional political rivalries and competitiveness, so that they came together with a relatively high degree of mutual trust and good will. The situation then allowed the R&E directors to work together and take advantage of the unit-cost and cost-effectiveness models of budgeting and evaluation that they had each been developing in a separate and uncoordinated context.

The result of all these efforts was an alternative to the Bliss formula that involved separate calculations of unit-cost for inpatient, outpatient, and other types of service units. The formula was accepted by the JBC and the $2 million restored. Now that funds really were going to be based on data, both workload and financial, the agencies were mobilized into action to finally create a reliable, standardized statistical and financial data base.

A technical assistance grant was obtained from NIMH, which allowed James Sorensen, a national expert on unit-cost accounting in mental health, to develop standardized forms and procedures for computing the unit-costs at each agency. When Sorensen actually reviewed each agency's data in detail, he was struck by the degree to which, for both workload and financial data, standardized definitions were lacking, data were unreliable and/or unclear, and data were not comparable.

It is not surprising, then, that when Sorensen employed his standardized forms to agency data for the 1974-1975 fiscal year, there was great variability in the cost per unit he obtained across the agencies: Outpatient care varied from $15 to $37; consultation and education, from $7 to $36; inpatient care, from $64 to $162; partial hospitalization care, from $4 to $65; and "other" care, from $13 to $155. In short, he found the unit costs to vary across the agencies by a factor of from 2 to 16 times! It is important to note that such results are not unique to Colorado. In another case study, similar results were found:

> The cost of a single program in a CMHC was derived by using various methods currently employed by CMHCs. Seventeen cost figures were calculated, the highest being 184% of the lowest. Any of the 17 costs could legitimately be reported as the unit cost of the program (Zelman et al., 1982:40).

Sorensen's efforts resulted in a preliminary set of accounting and auditing guidelines that, in effect, created the standardized system that should have existed in the first place. The initial wild variation in unit costs came down into a manageable range quickly once the agencies received feedback on and technical assistance about the problem, together with a clear commitment from the state that unit-cost reimbursement would continue to be directly related to funding.

Once the performance-based, unit-cost system was begun, the JBC would not let it go. As of 1978-1979, state of the art performance contracting became a fact of life in Colorado's CMHC program, with formal built-in mechanisms for data quality control—a true example of the Accountability model in Table 14.2. For example, the 1978-1979 contract includes the requirement that agencies meet such requirements as "an independent fiscal audit, according to strict, well-developed guidelines," and "a certification by the auditors of the numbers of clients served and that clients received the services reported" (Miller and Wilson, 1981).

PERFORMANCE MEASUREMENT IN NEW JERSEY

New Jersey, similar to Colorado, needed a way to measure and control the costs of its share of the publicly supported mental health system. Funding for mental health in New Jersey is, by statute, per capita based, allocating dollars on the number of people who live in each service area. In order to develop specific criteria for data reporting, normative measures for subsequent funding decisions were developed through a collaborative effort between state government and provider agencies. Because of the recent changes in federal funding, the importance of the new data base to both parties became critical.

Under the new block grant formulas (PL 97-35) and diminished government support for human services, both state funding and regulatory agencies as well as providers themselves face difficult questions on resource allocation. For the states, they are faced with giving away less money in times of generally greater need. At the same time, Neigher and Stone (1984) suggest that not only are local provider agencies faced with tough internal program decisions, but choices about how they relate through competition, cooperation, or coalignment with their sister agencies are becoming more critical. If providers adopt a business and industry orientation, they will need to make major changes in their operation.

At the other extreme is a model of integrated human service, with agencies reducing duplication of effort, pooling resources, and moving in parallel or coordinated directions (e.g., Broskowski et al., 1982). While agencies remain client-directed, they are nonetheless sensitive to one anothers' financial and programatic needs. For example, if a regional social detoxification center for alcoholism treatment requires a 60 percent occupancy rate to stay in operation, referring agencies recognize that they must refer people if they are to have that facility continuously available.

Between these extremes are models in which interagency and provider-funder relationships are less structured, less clear, and more informal. Competition or cooperation also may be unintentional consequences of poor planning, or even misconceptions on the part of provider agencies about future clients, funding, or regulation. Thus, the importance and accuracy of data become imperative to organizational survival. Having to share agency data even for purposes of accountability can create bias toward an advocacy model.

Public sector program evaluation, once the purview of federal regulations, is now the primary responsibility of the states. A recent GAO study (1982) has suggested that evaluation efforts are likely to vary among the states because of differential emphases on program accountability and the fact that funding problems associated with federal cutbacks in aid may curtail state evaluation efforts. Nonetheless, attempts at systems-level program evaluation, usually in the form of program performance measurement systems (PMS), are under way in a number of states (see Neigher and Schulberg, 1982). These systems typically include indicators of an agency's financial viability (e.g., cost per care episode), accessibility (e.g., rate per thousand of target populations in active caseload), staff productivity (e.g., face-to-face contact hours), and measures of effectiveness (e.g., changes in clients' levels of functioning).

The current environment for this kind of evaluation data collection has changed dramatically for public programs. Under the federal categorical funding model of a few years ago, program data collection was required and mandatory. Currently, federal data collection efforts are voluntary for the most part, with little uniformity for similar programs across states. How can state funders, who pay only a part of an agency's operation, deal with the issues of data bias and incentive that we described earlier?

There are various possible roles for evaluation data under PMS. From a funder perspective, program performance measurement systems should not be viewed as ends unto themselves, but as means to achieve one or a number of policy goals. As data collection systems, PMS may be more efficient and focused ways of collecting data from program delivery sites in the absence of formal federal data collection responsibility. They also may be seen as vehicles for states to provide a comparative data base to view agency performance, to initiate reforms on new scales of economy, to enhance cooperation or competition between agencies, to facilitate movement toward integration of human services, or to cut through traditional turf issues such as professional guilds. The extent to which agencies cooperate in providing fully reliable and valid data into PMS systems depends to a large extent on the good will between funder and contract agency, on the consonance of a mission and values between them, on the degree of accuracy of mutual expectation, and, finally, on the perception of awards and consequences—the incentives and disincentives associated with PMS data collection systems.

A number of these issues can be illustrated by New Jersey's experience with the development of PMS effort for its mental health delivery system. The state of New Jersey has funded community mental health services through performance contracts since 1975. In 1982, public mental health agencies, counties, the state's Division of Mental Health and Hospitals and the state's program evaluation association formed a coalition to establish PMS as a basis for future mental health service contracting. In 1981, all community mental health funding sources were consolidated into annual level-of-service contracts. In 1982, selected performance indicators were incorporated into a need-based plan for federal block grant funding. The effort to develop a system of performance indicators began in 1981 and 1982 and two statewide joint conferences led to the formation of a task force to design and implement the PMS plan (Waizer and Kamis-Gould, 1983).

New Jersey's plans for the phased development of the PMS effort are presented in Figure 14.1. In four phases—quality control, piloting and valida-

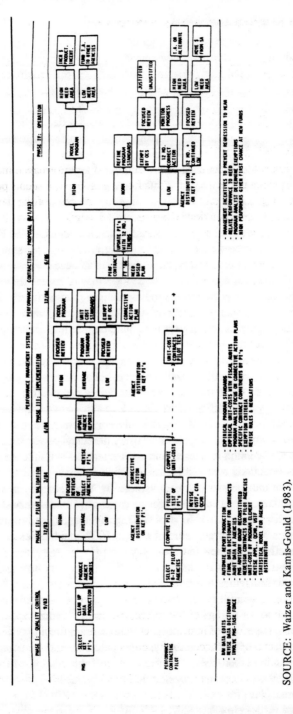

SOURCE: Waizer and Kamis-Gould (1983).

Figure 14.1 Implementation Plan: New Jersey Mental Health Performance Indicator System

tion, implementation, and operation—the implementation plan attempts to enhance the quality of the data, shake out problems in field trials with pilot agencies, turn around data, and take a series of action steps based on the findings. Funding allocation changes in response to PMS data are an integral part of the fully operational plan.

Provider Agencies' Responses

If one perceived consequence of low scores on a performance indicator suggests to a program that it will have its funding reduced, it seems possible that agencies would be likely to compromise the integrity of the data base rather than risk discontinuation of a program's funding. This would introduce data bias. Furthermore, because legitimate philosophical and conceptual differences exist between agencies as what constitutes good practice of community mental health, and because there is a disparity between need, demand, and resources within service localities to deliver services, specific and objective program performance indicators may contrast with what are competing overall agency goals that must take in the perspectives of a number of funding sources, target groups, and community constituencies (Neigher, 1979). To the extent that problematic program indicators prospectively could be identified, the integrity of the data base could be enhanced from the beginning of the PMS development effort.

To this end, Neigher and Stone (1984) conducted two questionnaire surveys among program participants to the statewide PMS conferences. A questionnaire on the importance of 22 performance indicators was distributed. The differential attribution of importance for each of the performance indicators was rated by both provider agency representatives and funding agency representatives as their own judgments and as they would perceive the importance of the indicators would be evaluated by the other group. Results computed between mean ratings of importance to providers and funders showed significant differences on 16 of the 22 indicators. Most of the indicators were perceived as more important to the state, but indicators of quality assurance, staff productivity and cost containment were rated significantly more important to service providers.

There were similarities, however, in the way in which the issues were associated by both groups of raters. Factor analytic pattern matrices were generated for each set of ratings of the indicators, and six factors appeared to represent the same group of indicators: chronic care, indirect services, cost containment, target group accessibility, client outcome, and temporal availability. The results of this analysis are presented in Table 14.4. To differentiate factor differences between providers and funders, sets of factors for each were generated. The primary difference between the two solutions was in the percentage of variance explained by each factor; for example, chronic care

TABLE 14.4
New Jersey Program Performance Indicators: Differential Attribution of Importance

Performance Indicator Factor Scale	$\bar{X}$ Important to Providers				$\bar{X}$ Important to State			
	Variance[1]	Rater[2] Provider	State	t	Variance	Rater[2] Provider	State	t
Chronic care	44.2	5.97	5.80	NS	16.5	5.90	5.75	NS
Indirect services	19.6	4.69	5.04	NS	7.5	4.00	4.52	-1.99*
Cost containment	14.2	5.78	5.84	NS	44.4	5.54	5.67	NS
Target group accessibility	9.7	4.89	3.97	3.91***	14.5	5.71	5.13	2.64**
Outcome	7.0	4.93	4.75	NS	11.7	5.35	5.48	NS
Temporal accessibility	5.3	5.64	5.47	NS	5.3	5.07	5.17	NS

1. Rotated factor weights > .40.
2. 1.0 = of no importance; 7.0 = of critical importance; NS = nonsignificant.
*p < .05
**p < .01
***p < .001

explained 44 percent of the variance in the ratings of importance to agencies, but only 17 percent of the importance to state personnel.

Table 14.4 shows that some performance indicators clearly were identified as more important to funder or provider. For example, representatives of the state significantly underestimated the importance of serving high priority target groups to the agencies, whereas service providers overestimated the importance of these services to the state. In a second example, provider agencies significantly underestimated the importance of indirect services (e.g., prevention, consultation) to state officials. A study in progress is monitoring the reliability and validity of these performance indicators to see if perceptual congruence between funder and provider is directly associated with poor quality data.

On two important policy dimensions for mental health service delivery, target group services for the chronically mental ill and the importance of preventively oriented services to the public, both funders and providers expressed inaccurate perceptions of how the others viewed the relative importance of the indicators. It would not be unreasonable to assume in addition that expectations for the use of data linked to these indicators also could be inaccurate. This potential source of bias in the validity of program performance indicators on these two dimensions, however, probably could be reduced if both provider and funder agencies were given the opportunity to clarify their respective positions, and have providers' questions about the consequence of indicator scores in these areas clarified by the funding agency with regard to program consequences.

Returning to Figure 14.1, it is evident that planning for evaluation data quality assurance has been built into the PMS Implementation Plan. With a little additional effort, however, areas of disagreement or confusion on the meaning or perception of key indicators could be clarified. The mechanism could simply be direct contact between program managers and evaluators of both funder and provider agencies. An agenda would not require agreement or even concensus as a prerequisite; rather, the parties would have the opportunity to define accurately their perceptions and intended use of the data, for purposes of both accountability and ameliorative program internal use.

AN ACTION PLAN FOR DATA RELIABILITY

A seven-step plan of action is suggested for increasing the reliability of evaluation data: (1) changing the role and responsibility of individual evaluators; (2) creating a national open data bank; (3) certifying public evaluators; (4) shifting paradigms; (5) conducting no-fault program evaluation; (6) requiring public review of public programs; and (7) building evaluability into program legislation.

CHANGING THE ROLE AND RESPONSIBILITY OF INDIVIDUAL EVALUATORS

Reluctance of professionals to adequately police their own memberships is well known. Professionals historically have been opposed to a continuum of regulatory or monitoring activities that have ranged from opposition to advertising to PSROs. The fact that incidents of fraud in research in general have been increasing (e.g., Rensberger, 1977) further points to the need for identifiable and uniform standards for the professions that practice evaluation research. Evaluation research in particular involves the need to design, implement, and report data with an emphasis on utilization by decision makers in both the private and public sectors. Additionally, the multidisciplinary nature of its practice cuts across ethical standards of such professions as psychology, medicine, social work, education, and sociology. However, there are a number of specific ethical issues involved in program evaluation research that lie outside most generic professional ethical standards (see Windle and Neigher, 1978).

Recently developed standards by the Joint Committee on Standards for Education Evaluation (1980), the U.S. General Accounting Office (1978), and the Evaluation Research Society (1980) have taken an important direction in addressing both the ethical concerns of program evaluation and issues related to methodology and utility. Although there is the risk that any minimum set of standards tends to become, in practice, maximum standards and that some standards may inhibit methodological creativity and slow the advancement of the field (e.g., Berk, 1982; Cronbach, 1982), standards nonetheless provide the bench mark by which those outside the profession can judge the adequacy of evaluation efforts.

We need, however, to go beyond the mere promulgation of standards to several additional steps. First would be the adoption of sanctions for their violation, together with professional peer support to help evaluators maintain individual integrity when there is political pressure to compromise. Unethical or incompetent behavior on the part of professionals in most of the disciplines within health, human services, and education can be brought to the appropriate professional review boards for hearing and potential disciplinary action. There also is the opportunity for arbitration, providing a forum to clear individuals of inappropriate charges or claims against them. Violations of evaluation research standards similarly could be brought to the attention of an individual's professional ethics committee for review and consideration.

In this way program evaluators could be held individually responsible for the serious compromise of evaluation research integrity, in terms of both methodological design and the accuracy of data collection effort. Without the liability running to the individual professional, there is a diffusion of responsibility within organizations and often undue organizational pressure on internal program evaluation staff to make methodological or data interpretive compromise. In this way the standards and their consequences for violation would help support evaluation researchers in resisting outside political pressures. Although there always is an inherently political nature to the evaluation enterprise itself (Berk and Rossi, 1976), internal program evaluators working in publicly supported social action programs often feel isolated and confronted with inconsistent expectations for their evaluation efforts. Evaluation standards, such as those cited earlier, provide specific criteria that evaluators and their employees can stand for and stand by.

A NATIONAL OPEN DATA BANK

A second approach to strengthening evaluators' individual responsibility is to increase accountability in the data collection process that they use. One method for doing this is to open up the data collection process, including raw data, to the public and investigators. Ceci and Walker (1983) address this by raising the issue of the ownership of data supported by tax dollars. They point out the legal, ethical, and pragmatic reasons given for refusing to share the raw data of one's federally sponsored research with others. Arguing for a Baconian rather than a Cartesian view of research (see Table 14.1 and Bevan, 1980), Ceci and Walker set forth a proposal to mandate data sharing as follows:

> It is proposed that in the long term, a national data bank be created or extant operations at some agency already versed in the problems of archiving large amounts of data in easily accessible form (e.g., the Census Bureau, the Library of Congress, or the National Archives' Division of Machine-Readable Data) be expanded to accommodate the routine cataloguing and dissemination of raw data from all publicly sponsored investigations. This would encompass all research grants, federal cooperative arrangements, decennial censuses, and contracts in which the classification of data is not clearly in the interest of national security or the protection of human subjects.

> Because this ambitious proposal is unlikely to be implemented in the near future, we propose as a short-term solution that each federal funding agency encourage data sharing by its recipients. Guidelines governing the dissemination of one's data should be negotiated at the time of an award to clarify possible exemptions for reasons such as breach of confidentiality or national security (Ceci and Walker, 1983:418).

As these authors suggest, there is strong reason to predict enormous resistance to such a proposal by researchers. In fact, a controversial change in the editorial policies of the *Journal of Personality and Social Psychology* required authors to submit copies of data analysis, summary tables, detail for the conduct of an exact replication, and assurance that raw data would be available to other investigators for at least five years after publication (Greenwald, 1976). This policy shift brought a drop in the number of articles submitted, a drop in subscription rates, and the consequent abandonment of the new editorial policies. To successfully accomplish the implementation of an open evaluation data base probably will require legislative initiative, public support, and the cooperation of the evaluation community.

Burstein et al. (forthcoming) recently reviewed a number of evaluation studies to assess the extent to which data collection problems created unreliable data. Their conclusion was that researchers simply do not describe their procedures in sufficient detail to make this assessment. The Ceci and Walker proposal, like the *Journal of Personality and Social Psychology* requirement, would mandate such descriptions, thus allowing a continuous monitoring of data quality assurance. It also would allow other investigators to conduct exact procedural replications or to make methodological improvements.

CERTIFIED PUBLIC EVALUATORS

It would be necessary to institute organizational changes in the incentive structures within which evaluation researchers function. One approach would adopt the model used to ensure the reliability of financial data. Thus, as there is the certified public accountant (CPA), there could be an analogous certified public evaluator (CPE). Three aspects of the CPA model are particularly noteworthy. First, there is a formal, competency based certification process that specifies minimum standards for accounting professionals and accesses individual skill. Second, objective criteria for the practice of accounting, both ethical and methodological, have been identified by their professional association (the American Institute of Certified Public Accountants). Finally, CPAs have strong and explicit sanctions and incentives to remain independent of their clients and to guard against conflicts of interest.

Assuming that evaluation standards such as those developed by ERS would be acceptable, the issue of licensure or certification remains. Many evaluators currently are certified or licensed in their professional disciplines; the extent to which additional certifications are helpful must be carefully examined. Prerequisites, including levels of experience and specialized training, also are important issues. The functional role of the CPE, however, would be a formal integration of themes we have described: individual accountability, objective standards, ethical guidelines, explicit incentives against conflicts of interest, and a formal mechanism for arbitration, peer review, and support.

SHIFTING PARADIGMS

One of the major causes of unreliability in evaluation data is the lack of positive motivational incentives for accuracy for those individuals who are involved in all phases of the data collection process—study design and linkage with policy, research methodology, data collection, and data interpretation. We have argued that a significant determinant of this incentive deficit is the underlying paradigm within which an evaluation study is conducted. Two such paradigms have been contrasted: theory-based scientific understanding (science), which has been predominant in evaluation, and managerial decision making (technology). As actually practiced, the technological, management paradigm tends to create a higher incentive for reliable data collection (see Table 14.3).

Consequently, we call first for an increased awareness on the part of evaluators to paradigm options and their implications for data reliability and usefulness. The science paradigm need not automatically be adopted. Second, we call for a general shift within the evaluation discipline to view the technological paradigm as comparable in desirability and status to the science paradigm.

NO-FAULT PROGRAM EVALUATION

The aphorism "no risk, no medal" implies the vulnerability of efforts that ultimately achieve great success. The risks involved in agency program self-evaluation carry a negative effect as well, including program sanctions, funding cuts, public embarrassment, and civil and criminal liability in extreme cases. If a reconciliation period were allowed for service agencies by their monitoring sites to remediate deficiencies identified either by the agencies or by site visit, deficiencies could be adequately addressed and sanctions made unnecessary. Many of the negative consequences of disclosing negative program evaluation findings thus could be diminished. This no-fault concept of program evaluation would seem to serve both program managers and accountability agencies if guidelines for such a procedure were clearly accepted by both sides in a shift from an adversarial to a collaborative focus. Such an agreement could shift prospective problem identification from the perception of a serious potential liability to an advantage of reducing the organization's vulnerability.

This evaluation approach obviously is enhanced if there are positive incentives for self-evaluation and corrective action. Possible incentives should go beyond the mere escape from the usual negative reinforcement that characterize compliance sanctions. They could include a sharing of savings from increased cost-effectiveness or additional funding to help correct serious program staffing or operating deficiencies. This approach would only make public uncorrected deficiencies, which has its advantages and disadvantages, reflecting both the strengths and weaknesses of the model.

PUBLIC REVIEW OF PUBLIC PROGRAMS

Windle and Neigher (1978) have pointed out that not only does the accountability model lack internal institutional support, but for the advocacy model of evaluation to function within the perspective of an adversarial system, there must be strengthened consumer representation. Olander and Lindhoff (1975) point out that the public typically is underrepresented in the market place for most goods and services, mainly being represented by public interest advocates and media investigative reporting. The current adversarial system is overbalanced by advocates of service programs; the public in most cases has little access to evaluation data and even less ability to validate the information it does receive.

If steps are taken to ensure that publicly supported or publicly accountable social program evaluation research is routinely subject to public scrutiny, evaluators will know their work will be accountable and verifiable. Government has a special responsibility for helping to ensure this kind of citizen participation in the evaluation process. One example of a formal citizen role in program evaluation came from the Community Mental Health Centers amendments of 1975 (PL 94-63), which required CMHCs to disclose and review evaluative statistics with residents of the catchment area (Windle and Ochberg, 1975). The NIMH program evaluation guidelines that implemented the legislation also at one time required program managers to document administrative action taken (or not taken) on recommendations from the evaluation studies, and make the information public. In addition, NIMH attempted to help educate citizens in their new participant roles in evaluation through publications and training activities (e.g., MacMurray et al., 1976).

The actual impact that citizen review of program evaluation efforts had is less than clear. Professionals, in general, are reluctant to involve citizen advisory boards in their efforts, and lay board members do not feel competent in challenging professionals in program areas of which they have little knowledge, and often do not fully understand data analysis and findings (e.g., Dinkel et al., 1982). Some efforts have been successful, for example, giving citizen patient ombudsmen responsibility for collecting and disseminating client satisfaction data from service programs.

BUILDING EVALUABILITY INTO
PROGRAM LEGISLATION

As we indicated in the chapter's first section, broad program missions and vague specification of program affect doom evaluations from the start. Each of the four evaluation perspectives identified (funder, provider, consumer, and the public) views the accomplishments of social programs through its own eyes. As Bruner and Postman (1947) have experimentally validated, perception is a form of adaptive behavior, reflecting the dominant needs, attitudes, and values of the observer. Perception is selective; certain key elements are accentuated at the expense of others and are influenced by past perceptual responses.

This inherent and natural source of bias will always exist. It can be reduced as a source of variance and systematic error in program evaluation design, interpretation, and utilization, however, with some concerted government effort. Public agencies responsible for implementing evaluation policy and guidelines must work with legislators to draft clear, measurable statements about program goals, objectives, and performance criteria. These guidelines and performance measures then would form the superstructure from which those who would evaluate these programs can build a framework.

CONCLUSIONS

The results of evaluation in community mental health over the past two decades have been disappointing. Paralleling the results of social program evaluation in general, unreliable data and little impact have been the watch words. Underlying many of the complex and interrelated symptoms of these problems has been a misplaced overcommittment by evaluators and policy makers to a theory-focused science paradigm, at the expense of undercommittment to a management-focused technology paradigm. These dynamics are illustrated in the evolution of statewide performance contracting in Colorado and New Jersey. To address evaluation's problems prospectively, we have proposed a number of concrete action steps for building into the practice of evaluation an increased number of positive incentives for both data importance and data reliability.

REFERENCES

ALKIN, N. C. and L. C. SOLMON (eds.) (1983) The Costs of Evaluation. Beverly Hills, CA; Sage.

BERK, R. A. (1982) "Where angels fear to tread and why," pp. 59-66 in P. H. Rossi (ed.) Standards for Evaluation Practice. San Francisco: Jossey-Bass.

——— and P. H. ROSSI (1976) "Doing good or worse: evaluation research politically reexamined." Social Problems: 337-349.

BEVAN, W. (1980) "On getting in bed with a lion." American Psychologist 35: 779-789.

——— (1976) "The sound of the wind that's blowing." American Psychologist 31: 481-489.

BINNER, P. R. (1975) "Outcome value analysis: an overview," in B. Willer et al. (eds.) Proceedings of IF Conference, York University, Toronto, November, 1974. Toronto: York University.

BROSKOWSKI, A., G. O'BRIEN, and J. A. PREVOST (1982) "Interorganizational strategies for survival: looking ahead to 1990." Administration in Mental Health 9: 198-210.

BRUNNER, J. S. and E. L. POSTMAN (1947) "Tension and tension-release as organizing factors in perception." Journal of Personality 15: 300-308.

BURSTEIN, L., H. E. FREEMAN, K. A. SIROTNIK, G. DELANDSHERE, and M. HOLLIS (forthcoming) "Data collection: the Achilles heel of evaluation research." Sociological Methods and Research.

CECI, S. J. and E. WALKER (1983) "Private archives and public needs." American Psychologist 38: 414-423.

CHELIMSKY, E. (1983) "Improving the cost-effectiveness of evaluation, " pp. 149-170 in M. C. Alkin and L.C. Solmon (eds.) The Cost of Evaluation. Beverly Hills, CA: Sage.

— — — (1981) "Making block grants accountable," pp. 89-120 in L. Datta (ed.) Evaluation in Change. Beverly Hills, CA: Sage.

CIARLO, J. A. (1977) "Monitoring and analysis of mental health program outcome data," pp. 647-656 in M. Guttentag (ed.) Evaluation Studies Review Annual, Vol. 2. Beverly Hills, CA: Sage.

COHEN, D. K. and M. S. GARET (1975) "Reforming educational policy with applied social research." Harvard Educational Review 45 (February): 17-41.

COOK, T. D. and W. R. SHADISH (1982) "Metaevaluation: an assessment of the congressionally mandated evaluation system for community mental health centers," pp. 221-253 in G. J. Stahler and W. R. Tash (eds.) Innovative Approaches to Mental Health Evaluation. New York: Academic.

CRONBACH, L. J. (1982) "In praise of uncertainty," pp. 49-58 in P. H. Rossi (ed.) Standards for Evaluation Research Practice. San Francisco: Jossey-Bass.

— — — J. B. AMBRON, S. M. DORNBUSCH, R. D. HESS, R. C. HORNIK, D. C. PHILLIPS, D. F. WALKER, and S. S. WEINER (1980) Toward Reform of Program Evaluation. San Francisco: Jossey-Bass.

DEITCHMAN, S. (1976) The Best-Layed Schemes: A Tale of Social Research and Bureaucracy. Cambridge, MA: MIT Press.

DINKEL, N. R., C. WINDLE, and J. W. ZINOBER (1982) "Community participation in evaluation," pp. 163-192 in G. J. Stahler and W. R. Tash (eds.) Innovative Approaches to Mental Health Evaluation. New York: Academic.

Evaluation Research Society (1980) Exposure Draft: Standards for Program Evaluation. Potomac, MD: Evaluation Research Society.

FISHMAN, D. B. (1981) A Cost-Effectiveness Methodology for Community Mental Health Centers: Development and Pilot Test. DHHS Publication ADM-81-767. Washington, DC: Government Printing Office.

— — — (1978) "A computerized cost-effectiveness methodology for community mental health centers," pp. 43-63 in J. Johnson et al. (eds.) Technology in Mental Health Care Delivery Systems. Hillsdale, NJ: Lawrence Erlbaum.

— — — and W. D. NEIGHER (1982) "American psychology in the eighties: who will buy?" American Psychologist 37: 533-546.

FLAHERTY, E. W. and K. OLSEN (1978) An Assessment of the Utility of Federally Required Program Evaluation in Community Mental Health Centers. Contract Report by the Philadelphia Health Management Corporation to the National Institute of Mental Health. Acquisition PB80207327. Springfield, VA: National Technical Information Service.

FRANKEL, C. (ed.) (1976) Controversies and Decisions: The Social Sciences and Public Policy. New York: Russell Sage.

FREDERIKSEN, L. W. (ed.) (1982) Handbook of Organizational Management. New York: John Wiley.

GERGEN, K. J. (1982) Towards Transformation in Social Knowledge. New York: Springer-Verlag.

GREENWALD, A. G. (1976) "An editorial." Journal of Personality and Social Psychology 33, 1: 1-7.

HOUSE, E. R. and S. MATHISON (1983) "Educational intervention," pp. 323-338 in E. Seidman (ed.) Handbook of Social Intervention. Beverly Hills, CA: Sage.

Joint Committee on Standards for Educational Evaluation (1980) Standards for Evaluation of Educational Programs, Projects, and Materials. New York: McGraw-Hill.

KAMIN, L. J. (1974) The Science and Politics of I.Q. Hillsdale, NJ: Lawrence Erlbaum.

KUHN, T. S. (1962) The Structure of Scientific Revolutions. Chicago: University of Chicago Press.

MACMURRAY, V. D., P. H. CUNNINGHAM, P. B. KATER, N. SWENSON, and S. S. BELLIN (1976) Citizen Evaluation of Mental Health Services: A Guidebook for Accountability. New York: Human Sciences Press.

MILLER, S. and N. WILSON (1981) "The case for performance contracting." Administration in Mental Health 8: 185-193.

NEIGHER, W. D. (1979) "A multiple focus approach to community mental health needs assessment," pp. 42-44 in G. Landsberg et al. (eds.) Evaluation in Practice: A Sourcebook of Program Evaluation Studies from Mental Health Care Systems in the United States. DHEW Publication (ADM) 78-763. Washington, DC: Government Printing Office.

— — — and H. C. SCHULBERG (1982) "Evaluating the outcomes of human service programs: a reassessment." Evaluation Review 6: 731-752.

NEIGHER, W. D. and J. STONE (1984) "Valuating performance indicators: necessary conditions." Denville, NJ: St. Clare's Hospital. (unpublished)

NEIGHER, W. D., J. CIARLO, C. HOVEN, K. KIRKHART, G. LANDSBERG, E. LIGHT, F. NEWMAN, E. L. STRUENING, L. WILLIAMS, C. WINDLE, and J. R. WOY (1983) "Evaluation in the community mental health center program: a bold new reproach?" Evaluation and Program Planning 5, 4: 283-311.

O'BRIEN, R. M., A. M. DICKINSON, and M. P. ROSNOW (1982) Industrial Behavior Modification: A Management Handbook. New York: Pergamon.

OLANDER, F. and H. LINDHOFF (1975) "Consumer action research: a review of the consumerism literature and suggestions for a new direction in research." Social Science Information 14: 147-184.

RENSBERGER, B. (1977) "Fraud in research is a rising problem in science." New York Times (January 23).

ROSSI, P. H. (1978) "Issues in the evaluation of human services delivery." Evaluation Quarterly 2: 573-599.

SHOEMAKER, J. (1977) Budgeting Is the Answer: A Story of a Unique Committee. Cleveland, OH: World Press.

SORENSON, J. E. and D. W. PHIPPS (1972) Cost-Finding and Rate-Setting for Community Mental Health Centers. NIMH Mental Health Statistics, Series C, No. 6. Rockville, MD: National Institute of Mental Health.

STRUPP, H. H. and S. W. HADLEY (1977) "A tripartite model of mental health and therapeutic outcomes: with special reference to negative effects in psychotherapy." American Psychologist 32: 187-196.

U.S. General Accounting Office (1982) A Profile of Federal Program Evaluation Activities. Washington, DC: author.

— — — (1978) Assessing Social Program Impact Evaluations: A Checklist Approach. Washington, DC: author.

WAIZER, J. and E. KAMIS-GOULD (1983) The Performance Management System: Performance Contracting for Mental Health Services in New Jersey. Implementation Plan. Trenton: New Jersey Department of Human Services, Division of Mental Health and Hospitals.

WEISS, C. H. (ed.) (1972) Evaluating Social Action Programs. Boston: Allyn and Bacon.

WHOLEY, J. S., J. W. SCANLON, H. G. DUFFY, J. S. FUKUMOTU, and L. M. VOGT (1970) Federal Evaluation Policy: Analyzing the Effects of Public Programs. Washington, DC: Urban Institute.

WINDLE, C. (1983) "Limited and limiting perspectives," pp. 296-298 in W. D. Neigher et al. "Evaluation in the community mental health centers program: a bold new reproach?" Evaluation and Program Planning 5: 283-311.

— — — and NEIGHER (1978) "Ethical problems in program evaluations: advice for trapped evaluators." Evaluation and Program Planning 1: 97-108.

WINDLE, C. and F. M. OCHBERG (1975) "Evaluation overview: enhancing program evaluation in the community mental health centers program." Evaluation 2: 31-36.

ZELMAN, W. N., A. V. STONE, and B. A. DAVENPORT (1982) "Factors contributing to artifactual differences in reported mental health costs." Administration in Mental Health 10: 40-53.

Reprise

DATA QUALITY ISSUES IN EVALUATION RESEARCH: SUMMARY COMMENTS

Peter H. Rossi

In contrast to similar meetings of social scientists drawn from several disciplines, the conference that was the source of this book was marked by two special qualities: First, despite the fact that the persons involved were not selected for their conviviality (nor was the opposite principle used), an air of mutual good will and understanding soon developed among the participants. It may have been due to the late March snowstorm that made it impossible to leave the inn at which the conference was held, but more likely the congeniality developed because all participants quickly realized that the problems aired around the conference table were *shared* problems. Common adversities apparently make for mutual understanding and solidarity. Second, although almost all the social science disciplines that deal with applied issues were represented by one or more conferees, disciplinary lines rarely developed in any of the discussions. The experiences of conducting evaluations usually within multi-disciplinary organizations, apparently had more or less homogeneized participants' ways of thinking so that it was difficult, if not impossible, to distinguish easily on the basis of the content of a discussion whether a particular speaker was an economist, psychologist, educational researcher, or sociologist. The roles in evaluations that participants had played over the years apparently had overridden their disciplinary identifications to produce a more or less common subculture. The purpose of this chapter is to summarize from the papers and the conference discussion com-

mon themes surrounding data collection. The fact that some of these issues
have been discussed in the Burstein and Freeman introduction to this volume
points to their centrality for the editors and the conference participants as
well. I am not sure that there was complete consensus in the group over the
issue of whether evaluation research is unique in the kinds of problems that
data collection presents; certainly, most of the problems enumerated below
can occur in almost any context. But there was agreement that these problems occur more frequently in the conduct of evaluations than in "basic science" research.

THE POLITICAL CONTEXT OF EVALUATION

Commentators on evaluation research (Cronbach, 1983; Weiss, 1972;
Rossi and Freeman, 1982) have emphasized the fact that evaluations are part
of the political process. The implications of this condition for data quality
were illustrated by the accounts; Andersen et al.'s chapter provides an instance of one type of impact stemming from the political context of evaluation research. In this case, the "client," a well-respected, private foundation,
imposed political considerations on the sampling plan. Foundation officials,
certain that some specific sites were likely to be successful, were sampling
only those sites. As a consequence, the potential of the evaluation was reduced. Parenthetically, it should be noted that the foundation officials were
not accurate in their predictions.

Although this instance is one in which political considerations and client
control over the research undermined the quality of the data collected, political pressures may well operate in the opposite direction, improving data
quality. An example of the latter process was the NBC-sponsored evaluation
of the impact of viewing TV programs that contained violence on the aggressiveness of young school children, as described in the conference paper by
Kessler et al. The sponsor of the evaluation insisted that the results had to be
as "clean" as possible in order to counter the discounting of study results
because of the strong stake-holder position of the sponsor. Any research that
a network sponsored would be subject to a large discount because of the stake
that the networks had in maintaining their freedom to decide which programs
were to be aired. The extreme care shown by Kessler and his associates in
measuring the critical independent and dependent variables was supported
by the interests of their client in establishing credibility with a highly critical
audience.

An insightful and useful discussion of the contrasts between disciplinary and evaluation research is provided in the chapter by Neigher and Fishman. Their chapter contrasts the research styles of Descarte and Bacon and draws out the implications of those contrasts for data quality, showing that the motivational structures of participants in programs and of program operators have to be taken into account whenever persons in those roles are to be involved in the data collection process. The Cartesian view of science emphasizes the pursuit of generalized knowledge that is sought irrespective of its application to practical affairs. In contrast, the Baconian view emphasizes technological applications. Clearly, evaluation, along with other applied research fields, is in the Baconian rather than the Cartesian tradition.

The political context of evaluation research is directly addressed by Chelimsky in her chapter assessing the implications for data quality of the current presidential administration. Despite the fact that basic data collection activities presumably are neutral with respect to social programs of all sorts, the Reagan administration's cost-cutting measures seriously threaten the quality of long-standing data collection. Indeed, there were some intransigent optimists among evaluation researchers who saw as important a role for evaluation research in an era of budget cutbacks as in an era of expansion of social programs, reasoning that if programs were to be cut, those that proved to be ineffective should be the likely candidates to fall under the axe. Hence, the administration would have an interest in funding evaluations to establish the ineffectiveness of the disliked social programs.

In fact, the optimists turned out to be wrong in their predictions. The Reagan administration's redlining extended to research and evaluations as well as to social programs. Indeed, generalized social research programs were cut even when their connections with social programs were tenuous. For example, budget cuts have set back the Census's publications schedule, effectively delaying publication of some 1980 Census monographs by several years. Other data collection activities have been hampered by the reduction of sample sizes or shifting to biannual from yearly schedules (e.g., the National Housing Survey). The overall consequence was to lower the utility of federal data collection activities and to deteriorate the quality of many data series.

Here, too, the issue can be raised whether the actions of the current administration are the proper exercise of managerial responsibility for the reduction of the federal deficit or whether the cuts were foolish in light of the information needs of a complex society. Researchers and evaluators tend to believe that the information needs of a society are large and pressing, whereas managers often are perplexed as to why data are being collected to be used by very diffuse audiences. For example, few members of the criminal justice industry, other than social researchers interested in crime and related topics, are direct and consistent consumers of the results of the National Victimization Surveys. Quite likely, police chiefs, criminal lawyers, criminal court judges, and district attorneys all would agree that, although interesting, the victimization surveys have no direct relevance for their operations.

The fact that these surveys have changed our ways of looking at crime and its incidence may someday change the functioning of the front line agencies, but the path will be an indirect one. In short, from a narrow time frame, the victimization surveys may appear to be a large-scale benefit only to criminologists and an appropriate candidate for budget reduction.

However, there is another element to the current regime's willingness to cut social research budgets. At least in the first year of the Reagan administration, there was considerable animus directed at social scientists, who were grouped together with "liberal" social critics and reformers. Although it appears that the administration has become more sophisticated, there still is the lingering fear among social researchers that the administration is trying to get "those pinkos."

Of course, it is difficult to draw a clear line between "undue" interference in professional and technical issues and the appropriate exercise of managerial obligations. On one hand, evaluation researchers tend to enlarge the definition of what is appropriately left to the professional researchers to handle; on the other hand, clients tend to expand what is appropriate managerial oversight. The resulting tension results in a chronic malaise in the relations between researchers and clients.

EVALUATING FUTURE PROGRAMS AND ONGOING PROGRAMS

Although the technical problems encountered in evaluating ongoing programs are, in almost all respects, identical to those encountered in the evaluation of "prospective" programs (i.e., those that have not yet been enacted and are to be tested before enactment), there are considerable differences in the degrees of freedom allowed to the evaluator. First, the evaluator of a prospective program often is in the position of having to set up her or his own implementing organization to run the prospective program (or, more likely, some small-scale version thereof), or at least have a strong say in it. Considerably greater control over implementation is thereby ensured, a critical issue in many evaluations as an understanding of the program "as delivered" is essential to the interpretation of findings. This point is highlighted by Berk and Sherman's prospective evaluation of a police effort to reduce domestic violence. Per force, its implementation had to be given to the police department, with consequent loss of some degree of control over the administration of the treatments being assessed.

Second, time schedules tend to be more generous in the evaluation of prospective social programs. The Rand Health Insurance Experiment, as described by Rogers and Newhouse, ended up as an effort lasting a decade. An equally generous time schedule was enjoyed by the Supported Work Experiment (Mallar and Piliavin). An important side benefit of generous time schedules is an increased ability to undertake careful technical research, as described by Rogers and Newhouse and Berk and Sherman.

Finally, prospective evaluations afford opportunities to use the more powerful research designs. Randomized field experiments are not often, if ever, used to evaluate ongoing programs, the exceptions being possible variations on such programs. Indeed, the major applications of randomized field experiments have been to prospective social programs such as income maintenance, housing allowances, supported work, and so on.

VULNERABILITIES IN DATA QUALITY

Much of the conference discussion centered on fairly specific issues in data quality maintenance in evaluation research. Most of the problems mentioned are general ones, common to all social research, but most also arise with particular force in evaluations either because of the ways in which evaluations ordinarily are designed or because of the enhanced requirements for accurate data in evaluations.

MOTIVATING THE DATA COLLECTION SYSTEM

Social science data, whatever their source, always are vulnerable to a variety of forms of corruption of quality. If nothing else, there always remains a large stochastic error component in most social science data, arising at least in part from the inherent instability of the objects being measured. But, in addition, social science data collection is, at least for the foreseeable future, a highly labor-intensive activity. People are needed in two roles in data collection, as data recorders and as data sources. The reliable collection of valid data requires that both data sources and data collectors be adequately motivated to perform the necessary tasks.

In four of the chapters—Sechrest, Berk and Sherman, Neigher and Fishman, and Berry—issues of data collector motivation loom large. One of Sechrest's case studies of evaluations emphasized how difficult it was to motivate observers of emergency medical technicians to perform their tasks well. Here, the primary issue was how to motivate the observers to show up consistently for their tours of duty. In his other case, police were being asked to fill out short questionnaires on certain incidents, a data collection activity that had to be shortened from one year to six months because of a catastrophic fall-off in consistency.

Berk and Sherman relied heavily on volunteer policemen to randomly administer one of three treatments to family violence incidents. Imperfect fulfillment of their experimental plans by the volunteer patrolmen threatened the validity of the experiment. Berk and Sherman found considerable evidence that the volunteer policemen experimenters frequently departed from the randomization scheme, forcing the authors to perform sophisticated tests of the extent to which such departures vitiated the experimental design.

Berry and her colleagues enlisted pharmacists to carry out the details of an experiment in providing information on drug properties to persons receiving prescriptions containing those drugs. Pharmacists were asked to enroll participants and to enclose in a systematic random fashion different printed forms containing information on the drugs with the prescriptions. The pharmacists tended to interpose their own judgments in deciding whether or not eligible subjects were to receive one of the packets containing experimental simuli materials.

Neigher and Fishman reported on an attempt to collect detailed information from operating personnel on services delivered in Colorado community mental health centers. Although the initial quality of the data so obtained was poor, a change in administrative regulations that tied reimbursement to the contents of operator reports improved data quality considerably.

In all of these illustrations, difficulties were experienced in motivating persons who were supposed to collect data and/or administer treatments to perform their tasks in a consistent and conscientious fashion. In many of the illustrative cases, the personnel involved were not employed by the evaluators but were volunteers. The risks borne by reliance on volunteers for data collection are known to every experienced social researcher who has tried to use students, or tried to help out the local Chamber of Commerce or League

of Women Voters using volunteers from those groups to collect data: However willing and eager volunteers may be at the outset, sustained effort rarely
can be maintained long enough to fulfill adequately any reasonably sophisticated research design.

Part-time paid data collection personnel also present problems, as Sechrest relates. Part-time paid observers may be willing to spend some of their
weekends accompanying ambulance drivers and emergency medical technicians for a few months, but a whole year of weekend duty tours are more than
the pay apparently justifies.

Of course, there are many circumstances under which volunteers and
part-time workers cannot be avoided. In the Berk and Sherman experiment,
no one but the police could be used, as obviously no one else could administer arrest as a treatment in family violence cases. Similarly, in Berry's Rand
experiment, it would have been difficult to imagine another way of delivering
drug information to prescription drug users other than through dispensing
pharmacists. In both these cases, it clearly would have been sensible to work
out some scheme of rewards that would supplement sheer good will on the
part of the volunteers. Perhaps Berk and Sherman might have compensated
the volunteer police officers for the "extra" time they had to devote to the
paper work involved. [1]

The general point to be drawn from this discussion is that consistent and
valid data collection requires that persons relied upon for carrying out the
task of obtaining basic data must be motivated sufficiently to accomplish the
tasks involved. The half life of attempts to persuade persons to carry out sustained data collection usually is short, shorter than needed to carry out the
usual evaluation research project.

HAZARDS OF ADMINISTRATIVE RECORDS

There must be hundreds of evaluation researchers who have been lulled
into a sense of false security that their data needs would be fulfilled by existing administrative records after being reassured by some administrator that
the records kept under his or her jurisdiction were full and complete. Indeed,
even an old-hand with several decades of experience can be gulled; I assumed when the director of the Georgia criminal justice system assured me
that that state's computerized arrest records were complete and accurate that
such would be the case. It was only after arrests for quite serious crimes—for
example, attempted murder—were reported by our respondents in interviews and could not be found in the criminal justice arrest tapes, that we

began to question the accuracy of his assessment. The consequence was that we were forced to do a handcheck of the arrests in each of the major police jurisdictions of Georgia in an effort to get valid readings of the postrelease criminal justice encounters of the exfelons in our study (Rossi et al., 1980).

Similar experiences were related in Keesling's chapter. An assurance from the State Department of Education about the records kept in local school districts—after all, the maintenance of those records were required under administrative regulations—simply were inaccurate to a large degree. Bloom's chapter relates a parallel experience with other types of records, this time those supposedly maintained by CETA prime contractors on CETA participants. Neigher and Fishman also relate the sad state of administrative record keeping in Colorado community mental health centers.

These three examples, of course, do not pronounce the death sentence on the use of official administrative records. Some records are relatively complete, especially when they are produced as a by-product of the main tasks of the agency in question. Thus, my colleagues and I could find only minor discrepancies between Employment Security agency records of payments of unemployment benefits to released felons (Rossi et al., 1980) and interview reported payments—such records are generated automatically as checks are cut on the computer. But when the record keeping is an add-on activity to main activities, as was the case for schools responsible for filing achievement test results, the fidelity of record keeping tends to deteriorate. Even when records may be needed to validate claims for reimbursement, the probability of actually being asked to produce such validation is so low that agencies may safely ignore the potential sanctions for not keeping the records.

The main reason for the poor state of administrative record keeping is simply a special case of the volunteer motivational gap described above. The incentives for keeping good records are not strong, and usually are the threat of negative sanctions invoked for noncompliance, when detected often takes the form of rather gentle admonitions to reform one's ways. I doubt whether any local or state agency has ever been removed from the roles of a federal program for improper maintenance of nonfiscal administrative records. That adequate records are kept at all in agencies is often due to the devotion to record keeping on the part of a particular administrator or sometimes even a devoted clerk.

Two kinds of solutions to the problem of poor administrative records were suggested at the conference. Neigher and Fishman go the route of increasing the motivation of record keepers, showing that when the records were closely related to the scheme used to reimburse mental health centers, the quality of administrative record keeping improved dramatically. Of course, this sort of motivational change is not one that ordinarily is available to the evaluation researcher: To use it requires being closely connected to the administrative machinery of the agency in question. In contrast, Bloom moves in the direction of devising ingenious technical devices for fixing the defects in the administrative data with which he had to deal.

There are at least three lessons that can be drawn from the examples of administrative data use in the conference papers: First, evaluation researchers should not assume that any administrative records are of adequate quality without thorough checking of completeness and accuracy. Second, it is possible to improve the quality of administrative records by providing positive incentives to operating personnel for accurate and complete recording. Third, under some circumstances it is possible to compensate for the known and estimated deficiencies of administrative data.

TREATMENT DESCRIPTION

In the early years of evaluation research, it appeared that one of the most attractive features of the randomized controlled experiment was that it was not necessary to know what the treatment was or whether the treatment made any sense theoretically. Perhaps the best example of this stance was the elaborate and lengthy experiment undertaken by Kassebaum and Ward (1971) on the rehabilitative effectiveness of group therapy for prisoners. There was little a priori reason to believe that group therapy administered within prisons to prisoners with untrained guards acting as group therapy leaders was going to be effective. Nor was there any theoretical ground to expect that the "causes" of criminality lay in affective disorders that could be ameliorated through group therapy. In short, there was little reason to conduct an evaluation of this program except for the fact that this sort of group therapy was California state prison policy at the time.

Nevertheless, a seven-year effort went into a rigorously designed and controlled experiment that essentially regarded the treatment as a "black box" and found it to be ineffective in changing the postprison levels of criminal behavior among released prisoners. It seems doubtful that anyone today would conduct an expensive randomized controlled experiment of that sort. (The experiment cost more than $5 million in 1984 dollars.) Rather, considerably more effort would have gone into attempting to construct a theoretical model of the treatment, into devising valid measures of the treatment and of the extent to which the treatment was delivered to inmates. The main problem with a black box experiment is that its results sustain only the conclusion that the treatment was successful or that it was not successful. We learn little about why it failed: Was the theoretical underpinning of the treatment defective? Was the delivery of the treatment defective in some way? Did the treatment interact with some element in the experimental situation so as to defeat the treatment's positive effects? All these are questions that are essential to answer before one can benefit maximally from a set of findings.

Indeed, especially when it comes to human services as a class of treatments, it is especially important that the treatment *as delivered* be described in great detail. Even more important, the treatment as delivered to specific clients needs to be measured in order that more precise estimates of treatment effects can be constructed. Thus, a community mental health center may be delivering, say, several types of treatments to its clients, but to disentangle the effects of one from the other, we need to know to which individual clients treatments of various sorts, in various combinations, and with what degree of intensity were delivered to clients. The great merit of Maddox's information system is that the full richness of the services (read "treatments") available to the old was extensively described. Indeed, it appears from a reading of his paper,[2] that various kinds of available services and their combinations number in the thousands. To ask the question whether the services available to the aged in Cuyahoga County are effective is to ask an almost meaningless question as the services offered are so diverse, varying according to the problems manifested by aged persons presenting different problems and the agencies with which aged persons made contact.

A similar diversity in community mental health services is described by Neigher and Fishman in their chapter. Although funding sources may impose a standard terminology on every local agency, the corresponding operational forms may differ widely.

TESTING FOR VALIDITY

An alternate name for the problem of data quality is "validity." To what degree are the measurements of treatments and outcomes "valid" measures? It is customary to place the term within quotation marks because it is not at all clear whether the issue of validity can ever be properly addressed in the social sciences. To assess the validity of a measure means to assess the extent to which that measure actually taps the characteristics it is supposed to be measuring. As many social science concepts cannot be transformed into "the" indicator that every or even a majority of social scientists would agree measures that concept, the best one can usually do is to demonstrate that a given measure has two characteristics: First, the measure should be consonant with the definitions commonly held among social scientists who are concerned with the domain in question. Thus, a measure of aggressiveness should not contain measures of hair color, as all would agree that aggressiveness does not cover that attribute. Second, the measure should be consistent with other measures of the same concept that qualify under the first criterion. Thus, my measure of aggressiveness should be consistent with yours, if most social scientists agree that, on the face of it, both measures appear to be part of the same domain.

The issue of validity arose with particular force in Kessler et al.'s chapter. Especially important were the issues of validity surrounding the measurement of aggressiveness in children and the measurement of their viewing behavior. The measurement of aggressiveness was solved in an ingenious way by having schoolmates identify one another as aggressive. If anyone is to know whether an eight-year-old is aggressive, it will be his or her class and age mates who are the likely targets of such behavior. Aggressiveness ratings also were obtained from teachers, who were in a good position to observe and note aggressiveness in the children under their charge. Both measures have a high degree of face validity, and it must have been a comfort to the researchers to find that they were highly consistent with each other.

Much more problematic was the measurement of TV program viewing. In principle, of course, it is possible to measure viewing with complete accuracy by observing each child throughout his or her waking hours. No one would suggest this as a practical measure as it is highly intrusive and, even more important, extremely expensive. Instead, the researchers were forced to rely on various forms of self-reporting. Were ordinary forms of self-reports the only measures of TV viewing used, Kessler and his colleagues would have been vulnerable indeed. In order to assess the accuracy of the self-reports, Kessler et al. ingeniously included several dummy (or false) programs among the programs included on a checklist. The extent that a child claimed to view those dummy programs (or claimed that he or she saw both of two programs that were aired at the same time) then became a measure of that child's "accuracy" in reporting TV exposure. As a check on the extent to which poor self-reporting may have obscured findings, the researchers ran separate analyses with and without poor reporters, showing that the analyses agreed.

Similar concern with the issue of validity in measurement was shown in the Mallar and Piliavin chapter. In this case, it was critical that some measure be obtained of the postprogram criminal behavior of those who participated in the Supported Work Experiment. Although official arrest and court records would provide a measure of that criminal behavior that came to the attention of the police and the courts, the authors were convinced that these records could not be inclusive enough, as a great deal of crime is not followed by arrests. Indeed, there is even a nontrivial argument that arrests reflect to some significant degree competence in the commission of crimes; a person who is good at crime does not get caught. Partially to correct this possible bias in official arrest records, the researchers asked for self-reports of crime and found those to reveal a greater extent of criminality and higher rates of crime commission; but they also found that self-reports produced more understandable findings when compared to official arrest records.

It is worth noting that attention to issues of validity appeared primarily to be a concern for those evaluations that were of prospective social policies. These apparently are the circumstances under which the researchers have sufficient time to pay careful attention to these issues.

ARE EVALUATIONS DISTINCTIVE
IN DATA COLLECTION PROBLEMS?

At the outset of the conference, the convenors raised the question of the distinctiveness of data collection problems in evaluation research. The issue as put was whether such problems were qualitatively different from similar problems encountered in other kinds of social research: That is, did such problems simply differ in degree, or were they identical in kind and degree to those encountered in all social science research? The answer to this question turned out to be more complex than the question allowed. There was agreement that, in some respects, evaluation research was distinctively different, but that, in other respects, the data collection problems differed mainly in degree.

Distinctive to evaluation research were those data collection problems that stem from the political context of evaluation work. Especially in the evaluation of ongoing programs, in which many stake holders impose tight time schedules on the research, data collection procedures often may have to be compromised. Particularly important in this respect was insufficient time allowed for the development of research designs and instruments that were sensitive to the diverse range of specific programs that typically grow up under the aegis of a national social program. Almost equal in importance is the often encountered interference by a client or other stake holder in a program in the exercise of professional judgment by a researcher. Of course, it is important to bear in mind that what an evaluation researcher may consider "interference," a client may deem to be good management, or a stake holder may believe to be simply correcting the "mistakes" of researchers. Whether interference or the proper exercise of oversight, the intervention of nonresearchers into the research process is a distinctive feature of evaluation research when compared to typical disciplinary research.

The other threats to data quality arising out of data collection problems are as typical of academic research. But often such problems arise with particular force in the conduct of evaluation research. Precisely because an evaluation might become the center of attention for a highly motivated set of stake holders, issues of validity and completeness of data collection coverage may arise with particular force. The research reported by Kessler et al. is an interesting case in point, although on the surface that research does not appear to be highly politicized. However, it was precisely because NBC believed that the research would come under fierce attack as partisan that scrupulous care was taken to make sure that the researchers were free to pursue their work as if they were doing academic research.

In some ways this conclusion of this conference is much like the interpreted findings of many evaluations. To the question, "Does X-program work?" the researcher usually gives the equivocal reply, "In some ways, yes and in some ways, no." Like other evaluation researchers, we too are skilled in equivocation: In some ways, evaluation research poses special problems of data quality and in other ways, it does not.

NOTES

1. Of course, the evaluators in question may have considered extra compensation to the policemen and rejected that move for good reasons.

2. Unfortunately, the same snow storm that fostered solidarity among conference participants prevented Maddox from attending the conference. Thus, his paper could not be discussed in detail.

REFERENCES

CRONBACH, L. (1982) Designing Evaluations of Educational and Social Programs. San Francisco: Jossey-Bass.

KASSEBAUM, G., D. WARD, and D. WILNER (1971) Prison Treatment and Parole Survival. New York: John Wiley.

ROSSI, P. H. and H. E. FREEMAN (1982) Evaluation: A Systematic Approach. Beverly Hills, CA: Sage.

ROSSI, P. H., R. A. BERK, and K. LENIHAN (1980) Money, Work and Crime. New York: Academic.

WEISS, C. J. (1972) Evaluating Social Programs. Boston: Allyn & Bacon.

SUBJECT INDEX

Aggressive behavior, 22-23, 36-44, 67-85

Capture-recapture models, 24, 164-169
Community health program, see Health care
Compensatory Education, 207-219
Criminal behavior, 24, 138-141, 161-175, 302-303

Data collection problems
    complexity of, 23-24, 116-118;
    data sensitivity, 21-23, 51;
    minimizing, 19-20, 201-204, see also Evaluation activities, improvements in;
    quality control, 62-65, 73-74, 109-118, 191-196;
    record information, 25-27; 110-113;
    see also Observation studies, Records, Surveys,
Data quality, see Data collection problems, quality control; Validity

Evaluation activities
    conditions for undertaking, 18, 196-202, 263-270, 274;
    costs of, 54-55, 261;
    improvements in, 44-47, 82-85, 102-105, 118, 132-133, 145, 172-175, 201-204, 236-237, 250, 284-287, 289-295;
    perspectives on, 16-17;
    political contexts of, 16-17, 54, 264-267, 294-295, 301-303;
    secondary data, 196-200;
    social science research, 16-19, 248-251, 261, 270-274; 280-281, 301-302, 311-312;

    stakeholders of, 17-18, 93-94, 249-250, 265-269;
    as treatment, 45-46;
    types and models of, 267-270-274-279
Evaluation designs
    and data collection, 19;
    experimental, 15, 36-40, 46-47, 113-114, 116-117, 122-128, 235-236, 305-306;
    panel, 22, 26, 28, 68, 141-144, 169-175, 227-231;
    populations studied, 18-19
    practical considerations in, 17-20, 31, 54, 56, 78-82; 93-94, 283-287;
    pre-post, 91-92;
    quasi-experimental, 91-92, 256-257, 259-260;
    statistical procedures for, 19-20, 28-29, 79-80, 128-130, 144-145, 147-159, 232-235, 238-246, 259-260;
    see also Observation studies
Emergency medicine, 21, 51-66
Experimental designs, see Evaluation designs

Federal data collection, 25-26, 162, 181-203, 256-257, see also Time series
Field studies, see Data collection problems
Forms, see Observation studies; Surveys

Headstart, 17
Health care, 17-18, 24, 89-106, 121-133

Information systems, 26-27, 29, 199-200, 247, 252-261, 279-289

Longitudinal designs, see Evaluation designs, panel

Mental health, 26-27, 279-289
Monitoring, see Treatment
Municipal hospital program, see Health care

Observation studies, 21, 49-66, 76
Older persons, 26, 247-262
Outcome measurement, 30, 40-43, 122-128, 253-254

Population processes, 25, 169-175

Randomization, see Evaluation designs, experimental
Records, 25-27, 40-42, 110-113, 124-133, 162, 207-219, 220-246, 252-262, 306-308
Reliability, 18, 289-296, see also Outcome measurement, Treatment, measurement of, Validity

Sampling, 23, 27-29, 92-93, 107-108, 110-116, 124-128, 142, 258-260, see also Population processing
Self-reports, 18, 24, 41-44, 51, 61-12, 70-72, 83-84, 92-93, 122-133, 162-164
Spousal violence, 135-148, 172-175
Surveys
    of aggressive behavior, 22-23, 36-44, 67-80, 83-85;
    of criminal behavior, 24, 30, 138-141, 162-163;
    of earnings, 229-232;
    of medical, care 30, 92-99, 111-113, 122-128;
    of older persons, 26, 253-260;
    of performance indicators, 287-289;
    of school information, 212;
    telephone, 92-93

Target populations, 18-19, 23, 28, see also Treatment, implementation of
Target selection, see Sampling
Treatment
    costs of, 252-253, 284-287;
    implementation of, 19, 22, 29-30, 36-40, 141-144, 218-219, 264, 304;
    measurement of, 38-40, 49-51, 54-62, 69-85, 124-128, 141-144, 207-219, 254-255, 279-289, 308-309;
    observation of, 53-65
Television violence, 67-68
Time series 181-206
    and program evaluation, 196-200, 220-246;
    purposes of, 183-188, 194-195;
    technical adequacy of, 192-196

Validity, 74-95, 99-105, 138-141, 192-194, 253-256, 267, 304-306, 309-311, see also Treatment, measurement of

Work programs, 24, 146-160, 220-246

NAME INDEX

Aday, L. A., 90-93, 98, 99
Alkin, N.C., 265
Ambron, J. B., 274-276
Ammann, W., 253, 260
Andersen, R. M., 90-93, 95, 98-99
Anderson, D. R., 165
Andrews, L. T., 52
Antilla, I., 162

Balmauth, E., 132
Banks, M. J., 90, 91
Bard, M., 36
Bellin, S. S., 294
Berelson, B., 16, 32
Berk, R. A., 36, 38, 98, 173, 174, 290
Berk, S. F., 35
Berry, S. H., 110, 115-117
Bertsche, L. A., 90, 91
Bevan, W., 272, 272
Biderman, A. D., 162, 170
Bieck, W., 61
Binner, P. R., 280
Bishop, Y.M.M., 164, 165, 167
Bissell, J. S., 18, 32
Black, D., 35
Blazer, D., 262
Bloom, H. S., 220, 222-225, 228, 234, 238
Bordua, D. J., 162
Boorstin, D. J., 185, 188
Borgatta, E. R., 109
Boruch, R. F., 105
Bradley, H., 165
Broskowski, A., 284
Brown, C., 39
Brunner, J. S., 295
Bureau of Justice Statistics, 162-164, 166

Burke, R. E., 186
Burnham, L. K. P., 165
Burstein, L., 17, 31, 44, 211-14, 270, 275, 292

Campbell, D. T., 16, 31, 52, 99, 226
Cannell, C. F., 132
Cantor, D., 170
Ceci, S. J., 275, 277, 291, 292
ChandraSekar, C., 132
Chelimsky, E., 265, 267
Chiu, G., 90, 91
Ciarlo, J. A., 268, 269, 280
Cohen, D. K., 265
Comstock, G. A., 76
Conner, R. F., 113
Cook, T. D., 68, 82, 99, 280
Cormack, R. M., 165
Crittenden, A., 185
Cronbach, L. J., 16, 17, 32, 290, 301
Cunningham, P. H., 294

Daughety, V., 90, 91
Davenport, B. A., 283
Deitchman, S., 265
Delandshere, G., 44, 270, 275, 292
Dellinger, D., 253
Deming, W. E., 132
Dickens, C., 89
Dickinson, A. M., 271
Dieckman, D., 39
Dinkel, N. R., 294
Doeringer, P. B., 239
Dornbusch, S. M., 274-276
Duffy, H. G., 265
Duke Center, 252

El-Khorazaty, M. N., 165
Ennis, P. A., 162
Ericksen, E. P., 165
Eron, L. D., 68, 76-78

Feshbach, S., 68
Fienberg, S. E., 164, 165, 167
Fillenbaum, G., 254, 256, 257, 260
Fishman, D. B., 268, 272, 275, 280, 281
Flaherty, E. W., 270
Fleiss, J. L., 61
Fleming, G. V., 90-93, 99
Form, W. H., 109
Fowler, F., 132
Frankel, C., 276
Frankel, M. R., 95
Frederiksen, L. W., 271
Freeman, H. E., 17, 31, 44, 270, 275, 292, 301
Fuebringer, J., 201
Fukumotu, J. S., 265

Garet, M. S., 265
Garfinkle, J. B., 110, 115, 117
Gaudet, H., 16, 32
George, L. R., 254, 256, 257, 260
Gergen, K. J., 275
Greenberg, B. G., 52
Greenwald, A. G., 292
Grove, J., 52
Groves, R. M., 169

Hacker, A., 192
Hadley, S. W., 268
Haug, M. R., 109
Hayes-Roth, B., 110, 116
Heckman, J. J., 38, 98, 156
Heinsohn, I., 253
Herbers, J., 195
Hess, R. D., 274-276
Hicks, J. D., 186
Hoaglin, D. C., 201
Holland, P. W., 164, 165, 167
Hollis, M., 17, 31, 44, 270, 275, 292
Hollister, R., 135
Hornik, R. C., 274-276
House, E. R., 268

Hoven, C., 268, 269
Huesmann, L. R., 68, 76-78

Imbrey, P. B., 165

Johnson, C. F., 202
Johnson, L. A., 162

Kadane, J. B., 165
Kahn, R. L., 169
Kahneman, D., 54
Kamin, L. J., 275
Kamis-Gould, E., 285, 286
Kanouse, D. E., 110, 116
Kasper, J., 95
Kassebaum, G., 308
Kater, P. B., 294
Keesling, J. W., 211-214
Kelling, G. L., 39
Kemper, P., 135
Kenny, D. A., 79, 80
Kenzierski, D. A., 68, 82
Kerachsky, S., 135, 157
Kessler, R. C., 68
Kirkhart, K., 268, 269
Kmenta, J., 242
Koch, G. G., 165
Kremer, B., 90, 92, 93, 98, 99
Kuznets, S., 201
Kuhn, T. S., 248, 261, 271

Landerman, L. R., 254, 257, 260
Landsberg, G., 268, 269
Langley, R., 36
Laurie, W., 253, 260
Lazarsfeld, P. F., 16, 32
Lawless, J. F., 42
Lefkowitz, M. M., 68, 76-78
Lenihan, K., 307
Lewis, S. Z., 90, 91
Levy, R. R., 36
Lewin, K., 16, 32
Light, E., 268, 269
Light, R. J., 201
Lindhoff, H., 294
Loevy, S. S., 90, 92, 93, 98, 99
Long, D., 135

Loseke, D. R., 35
Lyle, J., 71

MacMurray, V. D., 294
Maddox, G., 253, 256, 260, 261
Madow, W. G., 132
Mallar, C., 135, 157
Manning, W. G., 122, 123, 131
Manpower Demonstration Research Corporation, 235, 244
Margarita, M., 35
Marquis, K. H., 110, 116, 132
Marquis, M. S., 132
Mathison, S., 268
Maynard, R., 135
McIntyre, J., 162
McKay, M., 209
McLaughlin, M. A., 220, 222-225, 228, 234, 238
McPeek, B., 201
Melnick, D., 183, 184
Michie, J., 209
Milavsky, J. R., 68
Miller, S., 283
Morris, C. N., 123, 132
Mosteller, F., 201
Mowry, G. E., 186

NCJISS, 162, 163
Neigher, W. D., 266, 268, 269, 272, 275, 284, 287
Newhouse, J. P., 122, 123, 131, 132
Newman, F., 268, 269
Nicol, J. P., 202
Nye, F. I., 162

O'Brien, G., 284
O'Brien, R. M., 271
Ochberg, F. M., 294
Olander, F., 294
Olsen, K., 270
Otis, D., 165
Owens, M. E. B., 163

Parker, E. B., 71
Parnas, R. I., 35
Pate, T., 39

Penick, B. E. E., 163
Perez, A. M., 110
Peterson, O. L., 52
Phelps, C. E., 132
Phillips, D. C., 274-276
Phipps, D. W., 280, 282, 283
Piliavin, R., 139, 144
Piore, M. J., 239
Pollock, K. H., 165
Postman, E. L., 295
Prevost, J. A., 284

Ramsey, J. A., 115
Reiss, A. J. Jr., 52, 162, 170
Rensberger, B., 290
Rhodes, A. L., 162
Rogers, W. H., 110, 115-117, 132
Riecken, H. W., 105
Roos, L. L. Jr., 202
Roos, N. P., 202
Rosnow, M. P., 271
Rossi, P. H., 263, 291, 301, 307
Rubens, W. S., 68
Rubin, D. B., 98
Rubinstein, E. A., 76

Scanlon, J. W., 265
Schoeff, D. A., 111
Schore, J., 139, 144
Schorr, B., 182
Schramm, W., 71
Schulberg, H. C., 266, 284
Schwartz, R. D., 52
Seber, G. A. F., 165
Sechrest, L., 52
Shadish, W. R., 280
Sherman, L. W., 36, 37, 173, 174
Shiskin, J., 193
Shoemaker, J., 281
Short, J. F. Jr., 162
Singer, D. G., 83
Singer, J. L., 83
Singer, R. D., 68
Sirotnik, K. A., 17, 31, 44, 270, 275, 292
Skolnick, J. H., 52
Smith, M. S., 18, 32
Smyer, M., 254

Solomon, L. C., 265
Sorenson, J. E., 280, 282, 283
Spain, R. S., 52
Stanfield, R. L., 184
Stanley, J. C., 226
Stipp, H. H., 68, 69, 83
Stone, J., 284, 287
Stone, A. V., 283
Stoto, M. A., 201
Stouffer, S. A., 16, 32
Struening, E. L., 268, 269
Strupp, H. H., 268
Subcommittee on Census and Population, 187, 194, 195
Subcommittee on Legislation and National Security, 184, 186, 188
Swenson, N., 294

Thomas, S. V., 68, 82
Thornton, C., 135
Tupek, A. R., 110
Turner, J. L., 57
Tversky, A., 54

U. S. General Accounting Office, 196-200, 244, 290
U. S. Bureau of the Census, 166

Van Kirk, M. L., 52, 57
Vogt, L. M., 265

Waizer, J., 285, 286
Walder, L. O., 68, 76-78
Walker, D. F., 274-276
Walker, E., 275, 277, 292. 292
Wallman, K. K., 190
Ward, D., 308
Ware, J. E., 110, 116
Webb, E. D., 52
Wellford, C. F., 169
Wells, W. D., 68
Weick, K. E., 49
Weiner, S. S., 274-6
Weir, A., 162
Weiss, C. H., 109, 118, 265
Weiss, C. J., 301
Westat, Inc., 228
White, G. C., 165
Wholey, J. S., 265
Williams, L., 268, 269
Wilner, D., 308
Wilson, N., 283
Windle, C., 267-269, 273, 274, 290, 294
Winkler, J. D., 116
Woy, J. R., 268, 269

Yin, R., 253

Zelman, W. N., 283
Zinober, J. W., 294